W9-CXO-541

**PSYCHOLOGY:
PERSPECTIVES ON THE HYBRID SCIENCE**

PRENTICE-HALL, INC.
Englewood Cliffs, N.J.

Edited by

Frank B. McMahon

Southern Illinois University at Edwardsville

PSYCHOLOGY: PERSPECTIVES ON THE HYBRID SCIENCE

PSYCHOLOGY: PERSPECTIVES ON THE HYBRID SCIENCE
Frank B. Mcmahon

ISBN: 0–13–732859–1
Library of Congress Catalog Card Number 71–183117
Printed in the United States of America
10 9 8 7 6 5 4 3 2

Prentice-Hall International, Inc., London
Prentice-Hall of Australia, Pty. Ltd., Sydney
Prentice-Hall of Canada, Ltd., Toronto
Prentice-Hall of India Private Limited, New Delhi
Prentice-Hall of Japan, Inc., Tokyo

CONTENTS

chapter fifteen
PSYCHOLOGISTS
AND PSYCHIATRISTS

PREFACE

This anthology is designed to be used with the text, *Psychology, the Hybrid Science*. The readings are keyed to chapters in the textbook and assume that you understand the material in those chapters.

You will find a couple of journal articles in this collection, and you will notice that they make rather rugged reading. I wanted to include them in order to give you *some* acquaintance with the writing that appears in psychology and psychiatry journals.

Most of the material, however, comes from sources other than textbooks and journals, for the simple reason that such discussions are much easier to understand. These selected chapters represent the work of some of the finest—and, more important, the clearest—writers in the areas that include or border on the "hybrid science." The disadvantage is that you do sometimes "come in at the middle," when an author refers to a previous chapter. In these cases, however, you will have covered the material in the textbook, and you should not get lost.

The footnotes you will find throughout this book were inserted to explain some terms and ideas with which you may not be acquainted. I have added these notes that you will not have to stop and look things up before continuing to read.

F. B. M.

PSYCHOLOGY:
PERSPECTIVES ON THE HYBRID SCIENCE

THE QUEST FOR A SCIENCE OF MAN
Alexander B. Adams

chapter one

PSYCHOLOGY: FROM PHILOSOPHY TO SCIENCE

Getting a psychologist to speculate about anything, without making experiments to verify (or disprove) his ideas, involves extinguishing hundreds of years of accumulated reinforcements. Even though the science of psychology is pretty well developed, psychologists are still on guard against the accusation of "philosophizing."

Psychology moved from philosophizing to experimenting —from the armchair to the laboratory—just as science in general moved toward more concrete, verifiable methods of inquiry. Though rooted in church-dominated philosophy, psychology became a countermovement against armchair speculation. The impetus for this change of method came from the fields outside psychology—mainly medicine, biology, and physics. Psychologists hoped to create a science of man by imitating the other sciences. They hoped to make great discoveries in human realms, discoveries to equal those of Newton and Galileo in the physical sciences.

It is this transition from speculation to experimentation that Adams makes vivid in the following essay. Do not assume, however, that early Greek philosophy lost its influence. Aristotle, a psychologist of the armchair type, wielded immense intellectual power, as Adams' essay shows. His thought so dominated the world of science that his theory of the workings of the universe continued to be believed long after evidence had accumulated that showed it to be incorrect.

THE QUEST FOR A
SCIENCE OF MAN

The earth spun on its axis; the seasons, growing warmer as the glaciers withdrew into the north, came and went, and stretched out into years. The years turned into centuries; life was born, died, and was born again. The centuries became millennia. Some groups of men, unable to survive, faded out; some met other groups and exchanged ideas. In time they discovered they could capture animals, herd them, and raise them. Unlike the men in the Lascaux cave,[1] they no longer had to hunt whenever they were hungry; they merely slaughtered the animals they already controlled. They planted seeds in the ground, making holes with long sticks they learned to weight with stones, and grew their own crops. Now they were no longer nomads—an important change if civilization was to advance—because only relatively large numbers of people settled permanently in one place could accumulate quantities of knowledge.

Even with this advantage, civilization was like seed scattered over indifferent ground. In some locations, it failed to take root; in others, it grew slowly and feebly; in a few, it flourished; and nowhere was its emergence more splendid and dazzling than in Greece.

Out of the north came a group of men who took possession of the peninsula and then, in the course of time, moved to the Aegean Islands and to the shores of Asia Minor. They mingled and bred with the men and women already there and infused them with a new quality: curiosity. For the Greeks were not content merely to know that a certain thing could be done or could happen; they wanted to know, as far as possible, how and why. This unprecedented lust for knowledge drove them into study, observation, and contemplation and produced some of the finest thinkers in the ancient world, men who laid the foundations of European culture: Thales, the successful merchant, who helped start men on the

From THE ETERNAL QUEST: THE STORY OF THE GREAT NATURAL-ISTS, *by Alexander B. Adams (New York: Putnam's, 1969), pp. 17–21, 30–34, 41–44; copyright © 1969 by Alexander B. Adams; reprinted by permission of the publisher.*

[1]A cave in France used by Stone Age human beings.

5

search for general scientific laws; his pupil, Anaximander, who became an excellent geographer; Pythagoras, who worked at philosophy and mathematics; Democritus, who believed that all matter was composed of indivisible "atoms" and the space between them; Hippocrates, who studied medicine and encouraged a rational, questioning approach to scientific problems; and Socrates and Plato, who studied the interrelations of people, sought ideal standards, and attempted to develop a perfect form of government. The list of such men is a long one, but one of the greatest, especially in natural history, was Aristotle, who was always inquisitive about the world around him—from the stars over his head to the animals that inhabited the seas at his feet.

Although his thoughts have survived the centuries, not many details are known about Aristotle's personal life, and a considerable number of the stories surrounding him are more legend than fact. Yet few persons have ever exerted a more profound or prolonged effect on human thinking.

He was born in 384 B.C. at Stagira, a city in Macedonia, where his father served as physician to King Amyntas II. When he was still in his teens, he was sent to study at Athens and came under the influence of Plato. On the death of the philosopher, Aristotle decided not to follow in his father's footsteps as a court physician but instead moved to a city in Asia Minor near Troy. Here, with his intensely inquisitive mind, he apparently became interested in two diverse subjects, marine biology and international politics. The first he pursued by collecting specimens along the shore; the second he absorbed through listening to the local inhabitants. The community, being close to the edge of the Greek world and under constant threat from the Persians, was strongly nationalistic, and when, a few years later, Aristotle moved to Mytilene on the island of Lesbos, he had become indoctrinated with Pan-Hellenism,[2] the philosophy that also dominated the thinking of King Philip of Macedonia.

When Philip ascended the throne, Macedonia, which had remained for the most part outside the sphere of Greek politics, was besieged by enemies on every hand and had almost no means of defense. The new king, who was two years younger than Aristotle, quickly changed this. He strengthened the army, restored its discipline, and then embarked on a plan of conquest that was to make him the master of the Greek world.

At the same time, he searched for a tutor for his son, Alexander, and finally selected Aristotle. Exactly why he chose him is not certain, for Aristotle had not yet gained his later reputation as an intellectual. Prob-

[2]A belief in the possibility of political unity for all Greeks.

ably he was influenced by the long service of Aristotle's family at the Macedonian court, by his excellent training at Athens, and by his interest in Pan-Hellenism. Yet the situation was a curious one. Aristotle was a man of thoughts; Philip, a man of action. Aristotle was no warrior (he preferred contemplation to battle); Philip, on the other hand, saw in the glitter of swords and spears the answer to all political problems, and his mind was obsessed with dreams of conquest. Greece lay before him like an apple ready for the picking, a temptation that he could not resist. So he spent his days plotting the subjugation of the independent states, which, not realizing their danger, were slow to unite against him. But death brought his career to an abrupt end, when, during the wedding festivities held for his daughter, he was murdered by a young nobleman.

The new king, Alexander, had spent years studying under Aristotle; but he was a true son of his father, a warrior, not a philosopher, and once he took command of the Macedonian forces, he was determined to continue with Philip's plans. Whether he and Aristotle fell into disagreement or whether Aristotle wisely foresaw no future for himself as adviser to the aggressive young king is not clear, but in any case Aristotle returned to Athens and opened his famous Lyceum, the school where he taught his pupils while he walked up and down a favorite corner of his garden. This was a peaceable life, much better than following the warlike Alexander in his overseas adventures, but it was halted by the king's death. For once Alexander's restraining influence was removed, the Athenians vented their pent-up hatred by persecuting the Macedonians. Aristotle, who had remained a citizen of Stagira—he always retained some measure of patriotic provincialism—became one of the Athenians' intended victims. They charged him with impiety, but before the trial took place, he fled for his life to Chalcis, a city some thirty miles north of Athens on the island of Euboea, and died there the same year.

Outwardly his life had been so quiet and scholarly that the historians found little to record, but inwardly it had been one of constant searching. Alexander attempted the conquest of the known physical world; Aristotle attempted the conquest of all human thinking. His mind ranged over a broad range of subjects—moral and political philosophy, the writing of poetry, and many others—and much of his thinking is still valid.

He was also a scientist and talked to his students about astronomy, physics, and biology, impressing on them the need for direct observations and for drawing conclusions from ascertainable facts. He did not, however, have the proper instruments for astronomical observations, and so in this field he unwittingly allowed his own skepticism to lapse and accepted two assumptions of previous thinkers: one, that matter was continuous: two, that the heavens operated under laws that were dissimilar to those on earth. Building on this feeble base, he constructed a cosmos consisting of a spherical world in the center, surrounded by rings of matter. Although he so strongly urged men to question all scientific concepts, his theory of the universe ironically remained unquestioned and therefore dominant for almost 2,000 years, seriously impeding independent research and thinking. A curious set of circumstances accounted for this unfortunate situation. One was Aristotle's great reputation; he had one of the finest intellects of all time, and this led him to be considered the supreme authority on every subject. The other was the support that his ideas eventually gained from the Christian Church. His concept of an indestructible, but finite universe, suited the theologians so perfectly that they condemned any efforts to criticize him.

In the biological sciences, he was able to make direct observations, and given this opportuntiy, he used it to the utmost. He studied his specimens minutely, thrust aside the temptation to speculate, insisted on detailed proof of every thesis, and produced remarkably accurate work. Among his numerous accomplishments were descriptions of the lives and breeding habits of a large number of animal specimens. He studied chicken embryos and the growth of squid and octopuses. He did anatomical studies of the digestive systems of certain animals, and he recognized the importance of the heart and the circulatory system. Also, like the greatest of the naturalists that followed him, he attempted to draw general conclusions from what he had seen.

He was handicapped in doing this, for although he assembled more information than any biologist before him, he still did not have enough facts to arrive at any important basic truths. That would take centuries and centuries of study; one man could not accomplish it in a lifetime. So if Aristotle is studied today for his philosophy, but not for his science, that is only because his ideas, unusual as they were for his age, have since been outdated, a fate to which scientists are particularly prone.

Yet even with the restrictions imposed on him, Aristotle reached some outstanding conclusions. He never, of course, realized that one form of life could emerge from another—man would have to wait centuries to discover that truth—but he came surprisingly close to it, for he recognized that it was difficult to draw a sharp line of demarcation between certain forms. He saw, too, that all life could be arranged in order, with man at the top, followed by the mammals, and on down to the lower plants. This concept later became known as his ladder of life, and although his arrangement did not stand up under closer examination, it was still a considerable achievement for a scholar living in the ancient world. He also developed certain philosophic attitudes toward nature. For one, he decided that each part of the body was designed to fill a particular need, and therefore, the body as a whole had to fill a need. In this, he was a teleologist—a word derived from *tele*, meaning far off or end. Nature, he believed, did not have a purpose in the sense that men have purposes; nevertheless it was working toward ends. A chicken's egg, for example, was not to Aristotle simply an isolated combination of substances; it was the means of creating a chicken, and therefore it had an end. Later on, the theologians added the principle of design to Aristotle's teleology, arguing that everything in nature occurred according to a master plan established by God. The egg was then no longer limited to the purpose of creating a chicken; it was part of the complete plan. Aristotle, who failed to find direct evidence to support such a thesis, refused to admit any purpose in the workings of nature, but he laid the basis for an important aspect of Christian theology in the centuries to come.

During the Middle Ages his ideas, as interpreted by the church, represented the ultimate in authority. Particularly in astronomy, the sheer weight of his reputation and the church's endorsement prevented men from seeking better and more workable theories, and the few who had the courage to do so were reviled and criticized and sometimes imprisoned or put to death. Aristotle would have been horrified at the outcome of his work. He who desired truth above everything else eventually became one of the greatest obstacles to the search for truth.

When mankind finally broke free from his intellectual domination, his entire reputation as a scientist fell into disrepute. Men laughed at his conception of the universe, which they had been forced to accept so long, and in their laughter they included all his other scientific work. But when biology emerged as a distinct field and grew in importance, the naturalists again looked at the long neglected pages of Aristotle and were surprised by what they saw. Charles Darwin called him the greatest of them all.

. . .

. . . In the fifteenth and sixteenth centuries the light began to break again in Europe, and the Continent threw off the intellectual lethargy that had dominated it during the preceding years. Measured in terms of individual lifetimes, the period was long, but considered against the millennia of human history, it was remarkably brief. Suddenly man began to expand his knowledge of the physical world and to take renewed interest in physics, astronomy, and biology. The old traditions, firm but sterile, began to crack under onslaught after onslaught, as mankind began to gather both the information and the courage to throw them off. For it took courage to defy the accepted order. It meant flouting authority, particularly that of the church, an institution which could be deadly in its revenge. It meant destroying the tenets on which culture and faith had been built, leaving in their place only questions that seemed unanswerable. The foundations of life and living had to crumble to make way for the new, and for many, the resulting pressures and tensions were too much to bear. They went mad. For others, the conflict ended in intellectual triumph and physical defeat. They died in prison or at the stake. Others survived more happily, sometimes by couching their new findings in cautious words or by skirting the central issues on which tradition was most persistent. But together they moved learning ahead.

Inspired by a new alertness, men began taking another look at the world around them, and among the first to do so were the artists. As the pictures of plants in Botticelli's paintings demonstrate, some of the artists were remarkably accurate observers, but none more so than Leonardo da Vinci. With a mind that ranged far, he realized that when the "old moon is in the new moon's arms," the effect is caused by the reflection of light from the earth; he foresaw the development of airplanes and parachutes; he studied the flights of birds and drew plans for breech-loading guns; and he recognized that fossils were the remains of animals, not an entirely new idea, but one in opposition to the prevailing Aristotlelianism. Unfortunately, Leonardo did not publish his findings, merely recording them in his private notebooks, so he did not influence his contemporaries as he might have. In his own time, his principal scientific contribution was his interest in anatomy and his dislike of sterile classicism. To paint well, he had to discover how bodies operated, not only human bodies, but the bodies of other animals as well. The anatomical drawings that he consequently made for himself and his students stimulated many artists to do the same and laid a base for improved work in medicine.

Even some officials of the church were swept up by the new spirit of inquiry that was stirring Europe. Nicholas of Cusa, who was a cardinal and a philosopher, . . . struck a telling blow at the cosmos of Aristotle. If the universe was a sphere, as Aristotle had argued, then there must be something outside that sphere. Since that is impossible, the universe had to be infinite, in which case the world could not be at the center. Unfortunately, Nicholas did not have enough knowledge of astronomy to go beyond this point or any means of proving himself correct. Consequently, his ideas were not widely circulated—only scholars knew about them—but before he died in 1464, he had glimpsed the truth that would be discovered and proved by Copernicus, who was born some nine years later.

. . .

Nicolaus Koppernigk (Copernicus is the Latin version of the name) was a successful merchant who lived for a while at Cracow and then moved to Torun, where he married one of the wealthy Waczenrodes. She bore him four children, the youngest of whom he named after himself. When the boy, who had been born in 1473, was only ten years old, his father died, and he was adopted by his uncle, Lucas Waczenrode, a church dignitary who shortly became Bishop of Ermland, one of the four dioceses of Prussia. A highly intelligent man, Waczenrode was determined that his adopted son should have the best possible education and, as soon as Copernicus was ready, sent him to the university at Cracow, one of the leading intellectual centers of Europe. Waczenrode intended his nephew to follow in his own steps and enter the church, but Copernicus soon developed other ideas. Cracow at the time was famous for its school of astronomy, and Copernicus spent more time listening to its faculty than attending the classes offered by the theologians.

When the boy had finished his studies at Cracow, Waczenrode sent him to Bologna to study canon law, a useful tool for a future clergyman and, while he was there, appointed him canon of the cathedral at Frauenburg. Thus, Copernicus' future was ensured, for he had both an education and a position. But he was in no hurry to return home and, since his family could afford the expense, went to Rome for a year and on to Padua, where he again studied canon law and obtained his doctorate, as well as taking courses in medicine. By this time he could no longer postpone the assumption of his clerical duties, so he went back to his uncle, but because it was now clear that he was more a scientist than a theologian, he became his uncle's private physician and personal assistant and lived at the bishop's palace at Heilsberg.

Although nepotism[3] inspired his appointment, the post was no sinecure, for Ermland was endangered by the constant threat of invasion. The Teutonic Knights, who held lands surrounding it and much of the land within the state itself, wanted to gain complete control. Poland, on the other hand, was equally ambitious, and Ermland was an obvious target for its expansionist plans. Waczenrode, therefore, was constantly trying to play one enemy against the other as the only means of preserving his independence. Protracted and delicate diplomatic negotiations

---

[3]*Nepotism* is appointing a member of one's own family to political office.

took up a large part of the bishop's daily life, and he entrusted many of them to Copernicus, who seems to have handled them capably.

Although his duties were heavy, Copernicus still had time to pursue a question that had bothered him for many years: the inability of Aristotelianism to explain many observable phenomena in the universe. His research was temporarily interrupted by the death of Waczenrode. With the loss of his uncle's protection, he was forced to return to Frauenburg and take up his responsibilities as a canon. Much of his time and energy, therefore, was devoted to administering the civic and church affairs of two communities, Allenstein and Mehlsack, and to protecting Allenstein from invasion when open warfare broke out between the Teutonic Knights and Poland. But the lessons he had learned from his uncle served him well, and he fulfilled his duties successfully. Although he led the busy life of a practical administrator and man of affairs, he never neglected his hunt for a better theory of the universe and, whenever time permitted, continued his calculations.

As a direct observer, he was not especially competent; indeed, he was not as good as some of the astronomers of the ancient world. But he brought to the subject an inquisitive, imaginative mind, unhampered by traditional thinking. If Aristotle's theories could not account for the universe's action, something else must, and starting with that premise, he continued studying his own records of the movements of the heavenly bodies and the records of those who had preceded him, examining them and reexamining them in a painful and prolonged search for the truth. After years of deliberation he finally decided that the earth could not possibly be at the center of the universe. What he reasoned was this: the sun was at the center; the earth turned on its axis once each day, and the moon revolved around it; Mercury and Venus circled the sun inside the earth's orbit, the other planets outside it; and the "fixed" stars—he still believed in fixed stars—were farther away. In substance, it was not a complicated theory—indeed, it retained many of Aristotle's ideas—and the facts are now so obvious that their discovery does not seem startling. But in Copernicus' day they struck at the roots of man's scientific, philosophic, and religious tenets. More than that, they destroyed man's conception of his dignity and importance. If the earth was not at the center, neither was man. Such findings may have frightened even Copernicus as he worked alone in the night watching the stars against the sky. Somewhere out in the black heavens was the God whom he had learned to praise as a boy in his uncle's palace. But if God no longer sat where his uncle had placed Him, where was He?

Copernicus wrote an abbreviated account of his theory and passed copies among his friends without publishing it. In this way, his ideas became known to a number of people, but none of them took him seriously. The concept was too ridiculous. (Even Luther, who should have welcomed such an attack on Catholic tradition, dismissed Copernicus as a fool who was trying to turn astronomy upside down. It was silly, Luther said, to suppose that Joshua had ordered the earth to stand still when the Bible clearly stated that He had halted the sun!)

Gradually the men Copernicus had known when he was young died, and he led a more and more lonely life. Yet he kept revising and adding to the now bulky manuscript that contained his complete theory without having any thought of publishing it. It was a strange situation— the discoverer of one of the most startling truths uncovered in mankind's history suppressing his findings. Perhaps he was one of those perfectionists who will not release their life's work until it is exactly what they want it to be. Perhaps he feared exposing himself to ridicule or to the anger of the church. In any case, the manuscript remained in his possession and was read only by those who came to see him. One of his visitors was a professor of mathematics at the university of Wittenberg, whose Latin name was Rheticus. Although he was a Protestant, he was interested in the new astronomical theory developed in the Catholic center of Frauenburg. To show his respect for Copernicus, he had brought with him a number of presents, including a copy of Euclid, and he finally gained Copernicus' confidence and a chance to read the manuscript, which so impressed him that he sent a short summary of it to a friend of his in Nuremberg. This summary was subsequently published with Copernicus' permission, but the *First Account*, as it was called, contained only the information dealing with the various motions of the earth. Then, suddenly, Copernicus, reversing his former attitude, gave the complete manuscript to Tiedemann Giese, Bishop of Ermland, who promptly sent it to Rheticus, who in turn placed it with a printer in Nuremberg for publication. Rheticus had intended to serve as editor, but because he received an appointment at Leipzig, he had to surrender the responsibility to a minister named Andreas Osiander.

Copernicus was now an old man and approaching his end. In 1542 he suffered a severe hemorrhage and stroke, which paralyzed him almost completely and brought him to the verge of death. But he lingered on that winter, as the pages of his book slowly came from the press. Gradually the snows melted, the cold gave way to the first warm airs of spring, the flowers broke through the ground, and life flooded around him, while his own life ebbed and his mind failed. By May, 1543, little was left of one of the most vigorous intellects in history.

On the twenty-fourth of that month the first printed copy of his book arrived from Nuremberg. There it was at last, the great theory that would shake the foundations of Aristotelianism, printed and bound and available to any library that wanted it.

They handed him the book. He was so sick he could hardly have been conscious of what he was receiving. And that day he died.

. . .

He [Kepler] published findings in 1609 under the title of *New Astronomy*. (Nine years later, he worked out a mathematical relationship between the time it took a planet to revolve and its distance from the sun.) Unfortunately Kepler's *New Astronomy* was written in rather poor Latin, and he buried the main points in a mass of detail that described everything he had done, not just the investigations that eventually proved fruitful. As a result, his book was not read as widely as it should have been, but it struck a further devasting blow at Aristotelianism. Not only did Kepler prove that Copernicus' basic conception was correct, but he also demonstrated that the whole idea of circular orbits was false.

In the year Kepler published his historic book, Galileo Galilei, who was teaching mathematics at the university of Padua, learned about the construction of telescopes in Holland, and when a friend in France confirmed the existence of these new instruments, Galileo decided to make one for himself. He first prepared a tube of lead and fitted it with two lenses. Looking through it, he computed its magnification as nine times. He then built two more, each more powerful than the last, and turned the best of them on the heavens. What he saw he reported in a small pamphlet that he published in the following year. Although it was only forty-eight pages long, it shook the intellectual world. The Aristotelians had always held that the heavenly bodies were spheres, becoming more nearly perfect the farther they were removed from the earth. Galileo announced that the moon was ridged and pockmarked like the earth. He also wrote about the hundreds of new stars that he had discovered and the four satellites revolving around Jupiter. These he called the Medicean planets in the hope that this honor to the Medici family[4] would help him secure an appointment at Florence.

Kepler and Galileo had had only a slight correspondence, and Galileo had never commented on Kepler's books, but he now turned to Kepler for a favor. Would Kepler please write him a letter endorsing his new publication? It would be helpful in applying for the position at Florence. Kepler although he had no way of directly confirming what Galileo had

---

[4]An influential branch of the ruling family.

written, responded generously, thus contributing to Galileo's eventually leaving Padua.

The move was unfortunate. Earlier, as a result of some intrigue, he had been forced to resign a post at Pisa, and the Senate of Venice, under whose jurisdiction the university at Padua came, had taken him in. After he had presented the Senate with one of his telescopes, they had gratefully voted him a lifetime salary of 1,000 florins. This, combined with the income he earned by giving private instruction, made him comfortably off, but he resented the time required by his teaching. As he wrote to a friend, no one in a republic like Venice could exempt him from performing the duties for which he received wages. Only a despot could do that. This was true, but Galileo, for all his brilliance, overlooked an important point. The Senate of Venice was one of the most powerful and independent political forces in Italy, and it was the only one capable of defending a free-speaking scientist from the church. Galileo surrendered this protection when he moved to Florence.

At first his position seemed to have improved. True to his word, Cosimo de Medici, the Duke of Tuscany, gave Galileo the time he needed for his research, which included many aspects of physics, as well as astronomy. But as he spoke and wrote—he could be sharp and sarcastic in his writing, and he liked an argument—various groups began to join in opposition to him. In addition to his somewhat cantankerous personality, they objected to his espousing the works of Copernicus. Until then, few people had taken Copernicus seriously. His theory was too ridiculous, and besides, the second preface clearly stated that it was incorrect. But now Galileo, backed by the evidence he had discovered with his telescope, was proclaiming the validity of Copernicus' ideas.

The position of the church was clearly stated in a letter on the subject written by a cardinal. First, the cardinal said, there was no danger in stating the Copernican theory as a hypothesis and employing it as a device, but it should never be expressed as a positive fact. Second, the Bible cannot be interpreted according Copernicus but must be considered solely in the light of what the Holy Fathers had said. Third, and here the cardinal somewhat repeated himself, the assumption that the sun is central may explain certain phenomena, but it is simply not true. After all, Solomon, one of the wisest men of all time, had said that the "sun also ariseth, and the sun goeth down, and hasteth to the place where he arose." Who would dare argue with Solomon?

Kepler, too, was beginning to run into difficulties. Emperor Rudolf was displaced, and Kepler was forced to leave Prague and accept a lesser post at Linz. He still, however, had time to work and write and produced more publications, but misfortunes dogged his remaining years. His wife died; his mother was tried as a witch, and he had to undertake her defense (the proceedings dragged on for years); he was excommunicated by the Lutheran Church; he was frustrated in his attempts to publish the astronomical tables he had constructed from Tycho's records;[5] and he suffered during the two-month long siege of Linz, during which the printing shop where he was publishing his tables was set on fire. All the printed sheets were destroyed, but fortunately Kepler's manuscript was saved. He moved from Linz to supervise its printing in another town and, from then on, never had a permanent home. For a short time he served as mathematician to General Wallenstein, who had won military fame by checking the Danish invasion. But Wallenstein was not interested in the motions of the planets except as they provided the basis for astrology. Since Kepler hesitated to submit forecasts of political and military events, Wallenstein finally used him only to supply information on the planets to more cooperative and also more imaginative astrologers. The two unlikely associates soon separated, and Kepler, with the little money he still had left, went to Ratisbon, where the Diet[6] was sitting, in the hope that he could collect from the emperor the back salary owed him. This amounted to 12,000 florins. (The nag on which he rode to Ratisbon was worth only 2; it was the best horse he could afford.) While waiting for the financial relief that never arrived, he came down with a fever and died.

Galileo fared better, but not much. His quarrel with the church became more and more serious in spite of his efforts both to defend himself and to seek some sort of compromise. At last he secured permission from a friendly Pope to write his *Dialogues Concerning the Two Chief World Systems*. In this, it was agreed, he would discuss the traditional astronomy and also the Copernican theory, but he was to state categorically that Copernicus' ideas were merely hypothetical, following the line of thought expressed in Osiander's second preface.

To be fettered like this was humiliating, but Galileo had no choice except to accept the terms dictated by the Pope if he wished to write at all. As he worked on his new book, he tried to stay technically within the limits imposed on him, but when the book appeared in 1632, Galileo's enemies persuaded the Pope he had broken his word and had also ridiculed the Pope personally. The end of his freedom was drawing near.

He was ordered to Rome to appear before the stern judges of the

---

[5]Tycho was a brilliant mathematician whose calculations helped establish the transit of orbiting bodies.
[6]A legislative body.

Inquisition. No one in Italy was powerful enough to protect him, and the outcome of his trial was foreseeable. The church, unable to defend itself and its beliefs by logic, had resorted to the final argument of all—physical violence. Galileo was placed under perpetual arrest and forbidden ever to publish again. Silence or death. That was the Inquisition's response to the great revelations of Galileo's telescope.

But even the Inquisition could not check the wave of rising skepticism.

CONTROLLING THE EXPERIMENT
Paul de Kruif

chapter two

SCIENCE DEVELOPS A METHOD

If a scientist wanted to study the influence of LSD, he would have to control his subjects' intake of food and liquid before they took the drug. If one subject was drunk, for instance, and another sober, their reactions to LSD might differ in startling ways.

As science developed, one of the most important concepts to emerge was control—*keeping track of and eliminating the influence of unwanted factors, so that the scientist could examine just what he wanted to study.*

Control is basic to all science. In the LSD experiment, the scientist wanted to learn the effects of LSD alone, not of the drug combined with various amounts of alcohol; he had to control the experiment and make sure that all the subjects had eaten and drunk the same things in about the same quantities. This control made the procedure standard and prevented unwanted factors from influencing the results of the study. Once the experimenter had established the drug's effects, he might turn to a study of the effects of LSD and alcohol. Then he might use a control group that was sober and an experimental group that wasn't. Despite the change in the experiment, the scientist is still controlling *what he studies, and how.*

The Microbe Hunters *provides one of literature's most dramatic examples of control. Louis Pasteur went to remarkable lengths in trying to eliminate unwanted factors. Already certain that his idea was correct—that there is no such thing as spontaneous generation—he was trying valiantly to control his experiment so as to make an airtight case against such a notion, and thus to give his opponents no room to contradict him.*

CONTROLLING THE
EXPERIMENT

. . . Then Pasteur dropped philosophy and set to work. He believed that his yeasts and rods and little animals came from the air—he imagined an air full of these invisible things. Other microbe hunters had shown there were germs in the air, but Pasteur made elaborate machines to prove it all over again. He poked gun cotton into little glass tubes, put a suction pump on one end of them and stuck the other end out of the window, sucked half the air of the garden through the cotton—and then gravely tried to count the number of living beings in this cotton. He invented clumsy machines for getting these microbe-loaded bits of cotton into yeast soup, to see whether the microbes would grow. He did the good old experiment of Spallanzani[1] over; he got himself a round bottle and put some yeast soup in it, and sealed off the neck of the bottle in the stuttering blast lamp flame, then boiled the soup for a few minutes—and no microbes grew in the bottle.

"But you have heated the air in your flask when you boiled the yeast soup—what yeast soup needs to generate little animals is *natural* air—you can't put yeast soup together with natural unheated air without its giving rise to yeasts or molds or torulas or vibrions or animalcules!" cried the believers in spontaneous generation, the evolutionists, the doubting botanists, cried all Godless men from their libraries and their armchairs. They shouted, but made no experiments.

Pasteur, in a muddle, tried to invent ways of getting unheated air into a boiled yeast soup and yet keep it from swarming with living sub-visible creatures. He fumbled at getting a way to do this; he muddled—keeping all the time a brave face toward the princes and professors and publicists that were now beginning to swarm to watch his miracles. The authorities had promoted him from his rat-infested attic to a little building of four or five two-by-four rooms at the gate of the Normal

From MICROBE HUNTERS, *by Paul de Kruif (New York: Harcourt Brace Jovanovich, 1954), pp. 74–78, 79–81; copyright 1926, 1954 by Paul de Kruif; reprinted by permission of Harcourt Brace Jovanovich.*

[1]Another experimenter who had worked on the same problem.

School. It would not be considered good enough to house the guinea pigs of the great Institutes of today, but it was here that Pasteur set out on his famous adventure to prove that there was nothing to the notion that microbes could arise without parents. It was an adventure that was part good experiment, part unseemly scuffle—a scuffle that threatened at certain hilariously vulgar moments to be settled by a fist fight. He messed around, I say, and his apparatus kept getting more and more complicated, and his experiments kept getting easier to object to and less clear, he began to replace his customary easy experiments that convinced with sledgehammer force, by long drools of words. He was stuck.

Then one day old Professor Balard walked into his workroom. Balard had started life as a druggist; he had been an owlish original druggist who had amazed the scientific world by making the discovery of the element bromine, not in a fine laboratory, but on the prescription counter in the back room of a drugstore. This had got him fame and his job of professor of chemistry in Paris. Balard was not ambitious; he had no yearning to make all the discoveries in the world—discovering bromine was enough for one man's lifetime—but Balard did like to nose around to watch what went on in other laboratories.

"You say you're stuck, you say you do not see how to get air and boiled yeast soup together without getting living creatures into the yeast soup, my friend?" you can hear the lazy Balard asking the then confused Pasteur. "Look here, you and I both believe there is no such thing as microbes rising in a yeast soup by themselves—we both believe they fall in or creep in with the dust of the air, is it not so?"

"Yes," answered Pasteur, "but"—

"Wait a minute!" interrupted Balard. "Why don't you just try the trick of putting some yeast soup in a bottle, boiling it, then fixing the opening so the dust can't fall in.[2] At the same time the air can get in all it wants to.

"But how?" asked Pasteur.

"Easy," replied the now forgotten Balard. "Take one of your round flasks, put the yeast soup into it, then soften the glass of the flask neck in your blast lamp—and draw the neck out and downward into a thin little tube—turn this little tube down the way a swan bends his neck when he's picking something out of the water. Then just leave the end of the tube open. It's like this—" and Balard sketched a diagram.

Pasteur looked, then suddenly saw the magnificent ingeniousness of this little experiment. "Why, then microbes can't fall into the flask, be-

---

[2]He is thus *controlling* dust particles—that is, eliminating them as a possible causative agent in the formation of microbes.

cause the dust they stick to can't very well fall upward—marvelous! I see it now!"

"Exactly," smiled Balard. "Try it and find out if it works—see you later," and he left to continue his genial round of the laboratories.

Pasteur had bottle washers and assistants now, and he ordered them to hurry and prepare the flasks. In a moment the laboratory was buzzing with the stuttering ear-shattering b-r-r-r-r-r of the enamelers' lamps; he fell to work savagely. He took flasks and put yeast soup into them and then melted their necks and drew them out and curved them downward—into swans' necks and pigtails and Chinamen's queues and a half-dozen fantastic shapes. Next he boiled the soup in them—that drove out all the air—but as the flasks cooled down new air came in—unheated air, perfectly clean air.

The flasks ready, Pasteur crawled on his hands and knees, back and forth, with a comical dignity, on his hands and knees, carrying one flask at a time, through a low cubbyhole under the stairs to his incubating oven. Next morning he was first at the laboratory, and in a jiffy, battered notebook in his hand, if you had been there you would have seen his rear elevation disappearing underneath the stairway. Like a beagle to its rabbit, Pasteur was drawn to this oven with its swan-neck flasks. Family, love, breakfast, and the rest of a silly world no longer existed for him.

Had you still been there a half hour later, you would have seen him come crawling out, his eyes shining through his fogged glasses. He had a right to be happy, for every one of the long, twisty-necked bottles in which the yeast soup had been boiled was perfectly clear—there was not a living creature in them. The next day they remained the same and the next. There was no doubt now that Balard's scheme had worked. There was no doubt that spontaneous generation was nonsense. "What a fine experiment is this experiment of mine—this proves that you can leave any kind of soup, after you've boiled it, you can leave it open to the ordinary air, and nothing will grow in it—so long as the air gets into it through a narrow twisty tube."

Balard came back and smiled as Pasteur poured the news of the experiment over him. "I thought it would work—you see, when the air comes back in, as the flask cools, the dusts and their germs start in through the narrow neck—but they get caught on the moist walls of the little tube."

"Yes, but how can we prove that?" puzzled Pasteur.

"Just take one of those flasks that has been in your oven all these days, a flask where no living things have appeared, and shake that flask so that the soup sloshes over and back and forth into the swan's neck part of it. Put it back in the oven, and next morning the soup will be cloudy with thick swarms of little beasts—children of the ones that were caught in the neck.

Pasteur tried it, and it was so! A little later at a brilliant meeting where the brains and wit and art of Paris fought to get in, Pasteur told of his swan-neck flask experiment in rapturous words. "Never will the doctrine of Spontaneous Generation recover from the mortal blow that this simple experiment has dealt it," he shouted. If Balard was there you may be sure he applauded as enthusiastically as the rest. A rare soul was Balard. . . .

.   .   .

. . . He[3] gathered up the rest of the bottles and hurried to the train—it was the time of the summer vacation when other professors were resting—and he went to his old home in the Jura mountains and climbed the hill of Poupet and opened twenty bottles there. He went to Switzerland and perilously let the air hiss into twenty flasks on the slopes of Mont Blanc; and found, as he had hoped, that the higher he went, the fewer were the flasks of yeast soup that became cloudy with swarms of microbes. "That is as it ought to be," he cried, "the higher and clearer the air, the less dust—and the fewer the microbes that always stick to particles of the dust." He came back proudly to Paris and told the Academy—with proofs that would astonish everybody!—that it was now sure that air alone could never cause living things to rise in yeast soup. "Here are germs, right beside them there are none, a little further on there are different ones . . . and here where the air is perfectly calm there are none at all," he cried. Then once more he set a new stage for possible magnificent exploits: "I would have liked to have gone up in a balloon to open my bottles still higher up!" But he didn't go up in that balloon, for his hearers were already sufficiently astonished. Already they considered him to be more than a man of science; he became for them a composer of epic searchings, a Ulysses of microbe hunters—the first adventurer of that heroic age to which you will soon come in this story. . . .

. . . Nothing could convince these enemies of Pasteur that microscopic beasts did not come to life without parents. They were sure there was such a thing as life arising spontaneously; they decided to beat Pasteur on his own ground at his own game.

Like Pasteur they filled up some flasks, but unlike him they used a soup of hay instead of yeast, they made a vacuum in their bottles and hastened to high Maladetta in the Pyrenees, and they kept climbing until they had got up many feet higher than Pasteur had been on Mont Blanc. Here, beaten upon by nasty breezes that howled out of the

[3]Pasteur

caverns of the glaciers and sneaked through the thick linings of their coats, they opened their flasks—Mr. Joly almost slid off the edge of the ledge and was only saved from a scientific martyr's death when a guide grabbed him by the coat tail! Out of breath and chilled through and through they staggered back to a little tavern and put their flasks in an improvised incubating oven—and in a few days, to their joy, they found every one of their bottles swarming with little creatures. Pasteur was wrong!

Now the fight was on. Pasteur became publicly sarcastic about the experiments of Pouchet, Joly and Musset; he made criticisms that today we know are quibbles. Pouchet came back with the remark that Pasteur "had presented his own flasks as an ultimatum to science to astonish everybody." Pasteur was furious, denounced Pouchet as a liar and bawled for a public apology. It seemed, alas, as if the truth were going to be decided by the spilling of blood, instead of by calm experiment. Then Pouchet and Joly and Musset challenged Pasteur to a public experiment before the Academy of Sciences, and they said if one single flask would fail to grow microbes after it had been opened for an instant, they would admit they were wrong. The fatal day for the tests dawned at last—what an interesting day it would have been—but at the last moment Pasteur's enemies backed down. Pasteur did his experiments before the Commission—he did them confidently with ironical remarks —and a little while later the Commission announced: "The facts observed by Mr. Pasteur and contested by Messrs. Pouchet, Joly and Musset, are of the most perfect exactitude."

Luckily for Pasteur, but alas for Truth, both sides happened to be right. Pouchet and his friends had used hay instead of yeast soup, and a great Englishman, Tyndall, found out years later that hay holds wee stubborn seeds of microbes that will stand boiling for hours! It was really Tyndall that finally settled this great quarrel; it was Tyndall that proved Pasteur was right.

WALLACE SUPPORTERS AND ADHERENCE TO "LAW AND ORDER"

Lawrence S. Wrightsman

chapter three

SCIENCE TURNS TO HUMAN BEHAVIOR

Were the people who supported a "law-and-order" candidate—George Wallace—for president actually more law-abiding than those who favored other candidates? What, in fact, was the level of obedience to the law at the time of the 1968 presidential campaign?

Studying such questions might seem to be a rather simple task, one that could be performed with just a few controls. The following article very quickly shows that in fact the author had to control a large number of extraneous factors in order to get useful results—that is, results which really measured what the author wanted to measure, and nothing else.

Wrightsman was venturing into social psychology when he experimented with the behavior of human beings. No study is more difficult than this kind, because thousands of factors could conceivably influence the results, and as many as possible must be controlled.

This scientist's study is not as conclusive as Pasteur's, and not as influential, but then Wrightsman was studying something much more complex and much less clearcut than Pasteur's subject—human beings.

WALLACE SUPPORTERS
AND ADHERENCE TO
"LAW AND ORDER"

During the 1968 presidential election campaign, the issue of "law and order" was a salient one. Though it was often unclear as to just what surplus meanings were attached to this provocative phrase, it was more strongly advanced as a campaign issue by George Wallace than by the other two major candidates. The present study was generated by a curiosity as to whether supporters of Wallace were, in fact, more law abiding than were supporters of the other candidates. A second reason for doing the study was that locally, a convenient opportunity to measure obedience of law occurred just at the time of the election.

Obedience to the law is a variable, which if measured by a self-report questionnaire[1] or interviews, is clearly classifiable as a "reactive" one (Webb, Campbell, Schwartz, & Sechrest, 1966); that is, a respondent's response might well be colored or altered by his considerations of social desirability, his needs to appear law abiding, etc. Therefore, a behavioral "unobstructive measure" of law obedience was sought—one which could be assessed without having to ask the subject anything at all.

An excellent unobtrusive measure of obeying one law manifested itself in Nashville and Davidson County, Tennessee, during the pre-election period. Earlier in the fall of 1968 the Metropolitan Council of Nashville-Davidson County (a consolidated government) passed a law requiring all motor vehicles in Davidson County to display a new automobile tax sticker, effective November 1, 1968. The sticker (henceforth to be called "the Metro sticker") went on sale by mail and at the County Courthouse early in October, at a price of $15 per vehicle. It was announced early in October that failure to possess a Metro sticker after November 1 was illegal and subject to a $50 fine. (In actuality, on Thurs-

"Wallace Supporters and Adherence to 'Law and Order,'" by Lawrence S. Wrightsman, JOURNAL OF PERSONALITY AND SOCIAL PSYCHOLOGY, 13, no. 1 (1969), 17–22; reprinted by permission of the American Psychological Association.

[1]A questionnaire which asks the subject to give information about his own attitudes, behavior, etc.

day, October 31, it was announced that two days of grace—till midnight Saturday, November 2—would be given because of the long lines waiting to buy the sticker.) Abetted by an influential local newspaper, a great deal of public sentiment developed against the sticker, not only because it was an added tax, but also because the present municipal administration had campaigned against an earlier tax sticker established by the previous administration. Shortly after the present administration took office it terminated requirement of the then-current $10 sticker, only to institute its higher priced one in 1968 (6 years later). However, despite grumbling, many Davidson Countians bought the sticker and slapped it on their car's windshield.

Thus, presence of the Metro sticker on the car served as an operational definition of obeying the law.[2] (It is recognized that this refers to obeyance of only one specific law.) Support of a presidential candidate was assessed by observing the car's bumpers and back window to determine the presence of a political sticker. The following classification was used:

Sticker	Tabulated as:
"Nixon-Agnew," "Nixon," or "Vote Republican"	Nixon supporter
"Humphrey-Muskie," "Humphrey," or "Vote Democratic"	Humphrey supporter
"Wallace-LeMay," or "Wallace"	Wallace supporter

Cars bearing stickers for other political candidates (McCarthy, local congressional candidates, Snoopy, etc.) were *not* counted as political supporters *or* as controls. Cars with *no* political bumper stickers of any kind were used as controls. Many of the owners of these cars obviously had political preferences, too, but we feel it is defensible to assume their allegiance to and identification with a candidate was less strong than those displaying bumper stickers. There is a problem in the comparability of the strength of allegiance of Wallace supporters versus those of the other two candidates. During much of the campaign, Wallace stickers were not given away free in this area, but rather were sold for $.50 or $1; in the last week of the campaign they were given away. Humphrey and Nixon stickers were generally available for the asking, although donations were accepted. Thus it is probable that the average Wallace bumper-sticker car reflected its owner's stronger allegiance than did cars belonging to supporters of the other two candidates. The extent of difference, if any, is impossible to assess.

---

[2]In other words, the fact that they did or did not have the sticker by its very nature showed obedience or disobedience of *this* law.

METHOD

Cars were observed during the period from 1 P.M. Friday, November 1, through 6 P.M. Tuesday, November 5 (Election Day). Only cars parked in specified parking areas were used (shopping centers, church parking areas, college campus lots and parking areas for large companies). Observer-recorders were instructed to survey a parking lot until they found a car with a presidential bumper sticker. If the car bore a Davidson County tag (Tennessee license plates include the name of the county), the following was recorded: type of presidential sticker, license plate number, presence or absence of Metro sticker, and make and age of car. For the latter a crude designation of "new" (post-1964) or "old" (1964 or pre-1964) was used. Then the observer-recorders were instructed to go to the left of the presidential bumper-sticker car and find a "control car" without any bumper sticker. Usually the adjacent car qualified by being from Davidson County and possessing no political bumper sticker. The information about presence or absence of Metro sticker, license plate, and make and year were recorded for this car, also. Thus, after surveying a given area, the recorder would have a list of x number of cars with presidential stickers and the same number without. The recording of the controls was carried out in order to have a comparison on "nonsupporters"(or at least less committed supporters) *who came from the same socioeconomic backgrounds* as the political supporters. It was assumed that if two cars were adjacent in the same lot (church, shopping center, etc.) they came from relatively similar or homogeneous socioeconomic backgrounds.[3]

A total of 46 parking areas were surveyed; these included 14 shopping centers, 13 church and synagogue parking areas, 6 college campuses, 2 voting areas, and 11 lots for large factories and businesses.[4] Coverage of the different predominantly white areas of the county was good, ranging from upper class to lower class. Only one predominantly Negro area was surveyed—the parking lots in the Fisk University area.

Observer-recorders usually worked singly, although some, working in pairs, checked each other. It should be recognized that the possibility of recording errors motivated by experimenter expectation (Rosenthal, 1966) exist in this study; that is, after recording the presence of a

[3]I.e., roughly, middle class, upper class, lower class.
[4]An analysis by days indicated that fewer cars had Metro stickers on the first 3 days than on Monday and Tuesday, but this difference had no effect on the candidate differences (author's footnote).

particular bumper sticker a solitary observer could fail to see a Metro tax sticker that was actually there. Several precautions were taken, however. Observers were instructed to walk to the front of the car, observe the presence or absence of the Metro sticker, record, and observe again. The fact that there were supporters of all three major candidates among the 26 observers is also of relevance to possible recording bias. The tabulation of presidential preferences of the observer-recorders was as follows: Humphrey, 15; Nixon, 8; Wallace, 1; none, 2. An analysis of recording results by observers' presidential preferences will be reported in the Discussion section.

RESULTS

Table 1 presents the results of this study. It is estimated that approximately 180,000 cars are registered in Davidson County. A total number of 1,686 cars were observed and recorded in this study. Of these, 304 had Nixon (or Republican) bumper stickers, 178 had Humphrey (or Democratic) stickers, and 361 had Wallace stickers.[5] The remaining 843 cars, without presidential stickers, served as controls.

As Table 1 indicates, 86.5% of the cars of Nixon supporters displayed the Metro sticker, compared with 80.6% of their adjacent controls. The probability of this difference occurring by chance was $p < .05$ (two-tailed test). The percentage of Humphrey cars with the Metro sticker was 86.5%, the same as the Nixon percentage. As was the case with the Nixon cars, the percentage was significantly greater ($p < .02$) than the percentage for the controls (which for the Humphrey controls was 77.0%).

Of the 361 Wallace cars, 270 or 74.8% had the Metro sticker. This percentage is significantly lower ($p < .0001$) than the percentage (83.9%) for the Wallace controls, and is also significantly lower than the percentages for Nixon cars ($p < .0001$) and Humphrey cars ($p < .001$).

It thus appears clear that committed supporters of Wallace were less

[5]These percentages are as follows: Nixon, 36%; Humphrey, 21%; Wallace, 43%. The unofficial vote in Davidson County on November 5 was the following: Nixon, 44,228, or 32.4%; Humphrey, 44,739, or 32.79%; Wallace, 47,464, or 34.79%. However, these totals include the Negro votes (approximately 15%) and the Negro areas of the county were only mimimally included in our survey. The predominantly Negro precincts voted strongly for Humphrey (examples: Pearl High School precinct, Humphrey, 1,025; Nixon, 17; Wallace, 0; and Hadley Park precinct, Humphrey, 1,235; Nixon, 23; Wallace, 2). If the all-Negro and predominantly Negro boxes are removed from the voting total, the results are as follows: Nixon, 43,117, or 35.05%; Humphrey, 33,350, or 27.10%; Wallace, 46,562, or 37.84%. These latter percentages are closer to those of the bumper sticker sample (author's footnote).

Table 1

NUMBERS AND PERCENTAGES OF CARS BEARING METRO TAX STICKER

No. cars	Groups	With tax sticker		Without tax sticker	
		n	%	*n*	%
304	Nixon	263	86.51	41	13.49
304	Nixon controls	245	80.59	59	19.41
178	Humphrey	154	86.52	24	13.48
178	Humphrey controls	137	76.97	41	23.03
361	Wallace	270	74.79	91	25.21
361	Wallace controls	303	83.93	58	16.07
843	Political-sticker	687	81.49	156	18.51
843	Controls	685	81.26	158	18.74

Note.—Tests of statistical significance for the difference in two proportions (Walker & Lev, 1953, p. 76): Wallace versus Wallace controls: $z = -5.31$, $p < .0001$; Nixon versus Nixon controls: $z = 1.97$, $p < .05$ (two-tailed); Humphrey versus Humphrey controls: $z = 2.33$, $p < .02$ (two-tailed); Wallace versus Humphrey controls: $z = -3.12$, $p < .001$ (two-tailed); Wallace versus Nixon controls: $z = -3.77$, $p < .0001$ (two-tailed).

frequently law abiding than were other groups, including committed supporters of other candidates or others who were not demonstrably committed to any candidate. This difference is even more impressive when one considers that some of the control cars (no bumper stickers) were no doubt Wallace supporters, too; that is, the "control" group possesses some—albeit less committed—experimentals.

It is interesting to note that the percentages of political-supporters cars and control cars having the Metro stickers were almost exactly the same—81.49% and 81.26%, respectively. This is a difference of only 2 cars out of 843.

DISCUSSION

This section of the paper will deal with possible causes of the less frequent law obeyance by Wallace supporters. Several possible explanations, such as defiance of authority and a rejection of the actions of bureaucrats, are not testable by our data. It may be that Wallace supporters are more often characterized by these feelings, but the investigators did not interview any of the owners of cars in the sample and cannot say. Several car owners told the recorders that they had purchased Metro stickers but were carrying them on their person rather than placing them on their car's windshield. They were waiting for the police to stop them, they said, so that they could show the police they were law abiding. There were not enough cases of this interesting (possibly passive-aggressive) behavior, however, to relate it to presidential preference.

Another possible reason that fewer Wallace supporters displayed a Metro sticker is that they are poorer and are less able to pay the $15. Perhaps Wallace supporters are law abiding except when it costs money. The Gallup Poll (1968) and other polls have shown that a relatively greater percentage of Wallace supporters came from the lower socioeconomic class. Therefore it is important to determine whether a social class difference existed between Wallace supporters and their controls. To determine this, the age distribution of Wallace cars was compared with that of the Wallace controls. A total of 208 of the 361 Wallace cars were classified as "new" or "recent" (1964 or later), compared with 231 of the Wallace controls. These percentages—57.6% versus 64.0% —are not significantly different ($z = 1.83$, $p < .10$) although in the direction of a greater number of Wallace supporters having older cars. The Wallace supporters do less often have newer cars than do the Nixon supporters (74.3%) or the Humphrey supporters (74.7%). (These percentages are amplified in Table 2.)

Of more direct relevance to the issue of age of car (as a measure of socioeconomic status) and presence of a Metro sticker is the fact that the percentage of *old* Wallace cars with the Metro sticker—74.5%, or 114 of 153 cars—is almost identical with the percentage of *new* Wallace cars with the sticker—75.0% or 156 of 208. Apparently lower socioeconomic-level does not serve as an explanation of the candidate-supporter differences in law obeyance.

Could the differences in sticker percentages be a function of observer-recorder bias? Might observers who are pro-Humphrey, for example, fail to "see" the Metro tax sticker when it was on a pro-Nixon or pro-Wallace car? Table 3 presents data relevant to this question, as it shows the number and percentage of each type of car bearing the Metro tax sticker, separated by presidential preference of the obeserver-recorder. For example, when tabulating Nixon cars, the 15 pro-Humphrey observers reported that 88.39% of the Nixon cars had the Metro sticker, compared to a report by the 8 pro-Nixon observers of 82.79% of *their* Nixon cars possessing the Metro sticker. Table 3 reports these percentages for each of six types of cars (Nixon, Humphrey, and Wallace cars and controls for each); chi-squares were computed and in none of the six sets were the observed frequencies different from the expected.[6] It may be concluded that in observing cars allied with a particular can-

[6]A statistical measure which supports the author's conclusions in this particular study.

Table 2

PRESENCE OF METRO STICKER IN NEW AND OLD CARS

Group	Sticker present	%	Sticker absent	%	Total	%
Nixon supporters						
New	195	86.28	31	13.72	226	74.34
Old	68	87.18	10	12.82	78	25.66
Total	263	86.51	41	13.49	304	100.00
Nixon controls						
New	181	80.08	45	19.91	226	74.34
Old	64	82.05	14	17.95	78	25.66
Total	245	80.59	59	19.41	304	100.00
Humphrey supporters						
New	119	89.47	14	10.53	133	74.72
Old	35	77.78	10	22.22	45	25.28
Total	154	86.52	24	13.48	178	100.00
Humphrey controls						
New	98	83.05	20	16.95	118	66.29
Old	39	65.00	21	35.00	60	33.71
Total	137	76.97	41	23.03	178	100.00
Wallace supporters						
New	156	75.00	52	25.00	208	57.62
Old	114	74.50	39	25.49	153	42.38
Total	270	74.79	91	25.21	361	100.00
Wallace controls						
New	200	86.58	31	13.42	231	63.99
Old	103	79.23	27	20.77	130	36.01
Total	303	83.93	58	16.07	361	100.00

didate, the observer's presidential preference was unrelated to the percentage of cars he reported bearing the Metro tax sticker.

The data in Table 3 may be studied in another way. One may ask: Do Humphrey supporters report a greater percentage of law-abiding cars for their candidate? Table 3 indicates that pro-Humphrey observers reported that 88.18% of the Humphrey cars had a Metro sticker, 88.39% of the Nixon cars did, and 77.84% of the Wallace cars did. Pro-Nixon observers reported that 82.79% of the Nixon cars, 85.19% of Humphrey cars, and 70.63% of the Wallace cars had a Metro sticker. Thus both pro-Humphrey and pro-Nixon observers reported a slightly higher percentage for another candidate than for their own. The lone observer who was pro-Wallace reported higher percentages of Nixon and Humphrey cars having the tax sticker (100%) than the Wallace cars (75%, or 3 of 4).

Although the data of Table 3 are not a conclusive test of the possible effects of observer bias, there is nothing in the table which indicates that the observer's presidential preference influenced his recording.

Table 3

NUMBERS AND PERCENTAGES OF CARS BEARING METRO TAX STICKER,
SEPARATED BY PRESIDENTIAL PREFERENCE OF OBSERVER-RECORDER

Possess Metro tax sticker?

No. observers	Observers' preference	Nixon cars				Control cars (Nixon)			
		Yes	%	No	%	Yes	%	No	%
15	Humphrey	137	88.39	18	11.61	133	85.81	22	14.19
8	Nixon	101	82.79	21	17.21	90	73.77	32	26.23
1	Wallace	14	100.00	0	0.00	11	78.57	3	21.43
2	None	11	84.62	2	15.38	11	84.62	2	15.38
Total		263	86.51	41	13.49	245	80.59	59	19.41

		Humphrey cars				*Control cars (Humphrey)*			
15	Humphrey	97	88.18	13	11.82	88	80.00	22	20.00
8	Nixon	46	85.19	8	14.81	40	74.07	14	25.92
1	Wallace	5	100.00	0	0.00	3	60.00	2	40.00
2	None	6	66.67	3	33.33	6	66.67	3	33.33
Total		154	86.52	24	13.48	137	76.97	41	23.03

		Wallace cars				*Control cars (Wallace)*			
15	Humphrey	144	77.84	41	22.16	162	87.57	23	12.43
8	Nixon	101	70.63	42	29.37	112	78.32	31	21.68
1	Wallace	3	75.00	1	25.00	3	75.00	1	25.00
2	None	22	75.86	7	24.14	26	89.66	3	10.34
Total		270	74.74	91	25.21	303	83.93	58	16.07

Note.—Chi-square for the differences; Nixon cars: $x^2 = 4.11$, $p < .25$; Nixon controls: $x^2 = 6.47$, $p < .10$; Humphrey cars: $x^2 = 5.27$, $p < .25$; Humphrey controls: $x^2 = 2.18$, $p > .50$; Wallace cars: $x^2 = 2.24$, $p < .50$; Wallace controls: $x^2 = 6.08$, $p < .25$.

Further evidence for candidate-supporter differences emerges from an independent study by John McCarthy[7] of law-breaking also done in Nashville in the fall of 1968. He stationed observers at a Nashville intersection with a stop sign and recorded the percentage and types of cars failing to stop. A significantly higher percentage of cars with Wallace bumper stickers failed to stop.

It seems that while Wallace has advocated "law and order," his supporters, in their own behavior, subscribe to it to a less frequent degree than do other citizens.

REFERENCES

Gallup, G. Voting profile in 1968. *Nashville Tennessean*, December 8, 1968, 5B.

[7]J. McCarthy. Personal communication, December 2, 1968 (author's footnote).

Rosenthal, R. *Experimenter effects in behavioral research.* New York: Appleton-Century-Crofts, 1966.

Walker, H., & Lev, J. *Statistical inference.* New York: Holt, Rinehart & Winston, 1953.

Webb, E. J., Campbell, D. T., Schwartz, R. D. & Sechrest, L. *Unobtrusive measures: Nonreactive research in the social sciences.* Chicago: Rand McNally, 1966.

PERMANENTLY WIRED-IN BEHAVIOR PATTERNS OF LOWER ANIMALS

D. E. Wooldridge

chapter four

RELATING ANIMAL AND HUMAN BEHAVIOR

The brain of a cat looks remarkably like that of a human being—so much like it, in fact, that the experimenter can confidently transfer what he has learned about animal behavior to the realm of human behavior.

This transfer process is probably not a new idea to you. What about the opposite process? Can what the scientist knows of the human brain conceivably shed light on some pretty highly organized, sophisticated behavior in lower animals? Can your behavior illuminate the actions of cats, or ants, or spiders?

Wooldridge's exploration of this question and others having to do with human and animal brain mechanisms is clearly written and most intriguing. It ought to broaden your perspective on nerve and brain operations. As a side benefit, it provides a good discussion of the mechanisms of inheritance.

PERMANENTLY WIRED-IN
BEHAVIOR PATTERNS
OF LOWER ANIMALS

This is a book about the human brain. Nevertheless we have already devoted considerable attention to the nervous systems of other animals, and we shall continue to do so. The basis for the expectation that animal studies will prove pertinent to understanding of the human nervous system is the time-honored principle, so often verified by the biologist, that similarity in structure and similarity in function usually go hand in hand. And the fact is that the nervous tissue of the lower animals is remarkably similar to our own. We find the same neuronal building blocks with similar arrangements of dendrites and axons, and similar operating characteristics. We find the same tendency for groupings of richly interconnected neurons to occur at crossroads between the incoming streams of sensory data provided by the afferent nerves and the outgoing systems of orders sent over the efferent nerves to the muscles and other effector mechanisms. In some instances, the aggregations of neurons that appear to perform the data-processing tasks in lower animals have the semblance of a full-blown brain, although usually of modest size and complexity by comparison with the human organ. In other instances, a small animal might employ one or more groupings of neurons, or "ganglia," appearing, from their construction and from the general understanding of these matters that we have been developing, to be the sites of special-purpose neuronal reflex or control centers.

Because of these anatomical similarities the neurologist rather confidently expects to be able to transfer much of the knowledge acquired from experiments with the simpler species to man and the other higher animals. Soundness of the extrapolation is usually confirmed when an opportunity arises to observe directly the corresponding human neural phenomenon.

But if such reasoning by analogy is sound, it ought to work both ways. What is learned about the properties of neuronal aggregates

From THE MACHINERY OF THE BRAIN, *by D. E. Wooldridge (New York: McGraw-Hill, 1963), pp. 74–96; copyright © 1963 by McGraw-Hill, Inc.; reprinted by permission of the publisher.*

through studies on the higher animals should also sometimes be capable of application to the lower ones. We have seen that the neural equipment of humans and other higher vertebrates includes a large number of reflex circuits whereby stereotyped patterns of muscular response are automatically triggered into existence by the occurrence of specific sensory stimuli. This suggests an interesting possibility: Could we have here the basis for an explanation of an aspect of animal life that has always been a mystery to scientist and philosopher alike—the ability of some of nature's lowliest and simplest creatures to engage in highly organized and seemingly purposeful behavior that frequently appears to involve an improbably high content of intelligence? Could their apparently reasoned acts instead be only the results of the triggering of patterns of automatic reflexes, built into the animal at birth, not involving conscious intelligence at all? To be sure, such a question does not bear directly upon the operation of the human brain, but it is believed to be a justifiable digression in view of its general interest. Therefore this chapter will be devoted to an explicit attempt to test how far we can go in explaining the puzzling behavior of the lower forms of animal life by invoking the operating properties of the same kinds of permanently wired-in reflex circuits that we have found to be so important in the central nervous system of man.

REFLEXES AND TROPISMS

Upon the approach of a possible enemy, a barnacle abruptly closes its shell, a tube worm snaps its exposed feeding tentacles back into its protective tunnel of sand, a sea squirt contracts into a gelatinous blob, burrowing bivalves withdraw their soft protruding siphons into the sand. A sea urchin turns its pointed needles in the direction of approaching danger, and the pincerlike jaws that inhabit the spiny jungle at the base of the needles stand up, ready to seize any enemy that comes too close.

These have indeed been found to be simple reflex actions. The barnacle, tube worm, sea squirt, and bivalve possess tiny photocells among their sensory neurons. The shadow cast by an approaching enemy causes these photoreceptors to generate their standardized trains of voltage impulses that stimulate the muscles employed in the resulting avoidance reaction. Even the more complex reaction of the sea urchin is of the same nature, although the receptor neurons in this case appear to be, not photoelectric, but chemical; they "taste" the surrounding salt water for signs of the characteristic flavor of an enemy. The completely automatic and local nature of the response is demonstrated by the fact that a tiny chip broken away from a living sea urchin's shell, with only a single spine or a single stalked beak attached to it, will show the same alarm and preparation.

In addition to reflexes, nature makes extensive use of tropisms in regulating the behavior of its simpler creatures. A *tropism* is an automatic response differing from other reflexes only in that it affects the movement of the complete organism. When an earthworm digs down and finds the moist decaying vegetation on which it thrives and at the same time avoids the surface where it might furnish a meal for a passing sparrow, it is not the intelligent, planned procedure that it appears to be. The muscles that turn the front end of the worm and thereby determine its direction of locomotion are constructed so as to receive their electric control signals from photo-sensitive receptors on either side of the head. As a result, the earthworm automatically heads away from the light in such a direction as to equalize the amount of illumination received by the left- and right-hand photoreceptors. This causes the worm to travel toward the darker regions, where it finds food and safety. The completely machinelike, unreasoning nature of this performance has been nicely demonstrated by exposing a worm simultaneously to two separate sources of light of controllable intensity and observing that the path followed is always one that orients the worm, in accordance with the positions and relative intensities of the lights, to equalize the amount of illumination of its two photoreceptors; and this occurs even though it may impel the worm along a course opposite to the one in which the proper conditions for food and safety are to be found.

The machinelike nature of the reflexes and tropisms that so extensively regulate the behavior of the lower animals was not appreciated as soon as it might have been by workers in the field. This was probably because these animal responses do not have the precision and detailed reproducibility that is usually observed in the commoner reflexes of higher animals. The spines of the sea urchin are likely to display a certain restless motion, even when no stimulus is present, and the orientation toward a potential enemy may involve a certain hesitation or lack of precision, together with a persistence of some of the original restless motion, even after the enemy has been sensed. In similar fashion, an earthworm, when exposed to light, does not instantly snap into an opposite heading and pursue a precisely straight course steadily away from the source of illumination. Instead, the trajectory pursued is modulated by wormlike twistings and turnings; these deviations may become particularly severe if, for example, it is necessary for the worm to avoid an obstacle that lies in its path. The reason for such unprecise response is that most tropisms do not provide such an overriding source of control voltage to the organism's effector mechanisms as to overshadow completely the effects of other sources of command signals. While the earthworm possesses neuronal connections that provide a steady bias to its muscles so that they tend to turn it away from a source of illumination, it also possesses a behavior pattern that provides for detouring around obstacles. Its actual muscular response at any given instant is a combination of these and several other reinforcing or competing built-in reflex or tropism mechanisms.

The restlessness of the spines of the sea urchin also results from a competing control signal, but one of a different kind. The nerve cells of these lower animals, like many of those in the human body, do not always wait to receive a specific stimulus before "closing the switch" and sending a voltage pulse out over the axon. Instead, there is a certain amount of random firing of the neurons. In the large and complex nervous systems of the larger animals, so many neurons must act cooperatively to produce significant movement of principal organs that the occasional random firing of a few neurons cannot produce a conspicuous result (although an occasional flicker of an eyelid or twitch of a muscle may be due to this cause). In some of the small and primitive animals that we are now dealing with, however, there may be only a few interconnected neurons in the circuit that controls a major element of the body. Under such circumstances, the random firing of one or two neurons can easily produce observable restless movement of the affected part.

COMPLEX TROPISMS

Tropisms that are themselves turned on or off by the presence or absence of other stimulating factors, or combinations of tropisms, can increase immeasurably the apparent "purposefulness" of the behavior of a simple organism. For example, the larvae of barnacles appear to decide whether they want to swim toward the surface or away from the surface of the sea. This apparent exercise of free will has been traced to a prosaic temperature-reversible tropism that causes the barnacle larvae to seek light in the cold and avoid it in warmth; similarly, many aquatic crustaceans, such as the water flea *Daphnia*, tend to swim downward in a bright light and upward in darkness.

An interesting tropistic mechanism causes the caterpillars of the gold-tail moth (*Porthesia chrysorrhoea*) to leave their hibernating nests in early spring and crawl to the only portions of the shrubs where their leafy food is to be found at that time of the year. The tropism involved is one whereby an adequate amount of warmth automatically causes the caterpillar to leave its nest and start crawling toward the light; it can be induced at any time by an experimenter simply by applying heat. This tropism results in the caterpillar climbing as high as it can go, which is to the top of the shrub where the new growth of green leaves first emerges early in the spring. However, if other effects than this simple tropism were not operating, the caterpillar would be in difficulty as soon as it had eaten the green leaves at the top of the shrub, for its food from then on would have to be found at lower levels; reaching such levels would be in conflict with a tropism that continuously impels it upward. This problem has been handled by nature by causing the upward-climbing tropism to operate only when the caterpillar is hungry. Therefore, having eaten, the caterpillar is free to creep in any direction and will eventually make its way down and find the new leaves as they commence to open.

As with all tropisms, the behavior of the goldtail moth is completely unreasoning. For example, if caterpillars are taken as they are leaving the nest and put into a glass tube lying near a window, they will all collect in the end of the tube nearest the light and stay there. If a few young leaves from their food shrub are put at the other end of the tube, farthest from the light, the hungry, unfed caterpillars will remain held captive near the lighted end of the tube, and there they will stay until they starve.

Tropisms, like the reflexes of higher animals, appear to be a direct consequence of the way the nerves and muscles have been put together. Usually they contribute to the health and well-being of the organism. The latter result, of course, would be an inevitable consequence of evolutionary selection; creatures with tropisms that lessen their chances of survival would presumably not have won out in the struggle for species existence. It is only when the creature is placed in historically abnormal or unusual circumstances that tropisms can work against survival, as in the instance of the caterpillars and the lighted tube. Similarly, the prawns that accumulate around the positive pole of a pair of electrodes placed in their tank do so because of a normally unimportant feature of their construction that weakens the effectiveness of their muscles when electricity passes through them in one direction and strengthens their effectiveness when the current is in the other direction. Moths and other phototropic insects that are irresistibly impelled to seek their own destruction in a flame are accidentally constructed so that superimposed upon the random motions characteristic of their flight is a steady "downhill" pull toward the light. If electric currents in the ocean or open flames in the forests had been important features of nature in the past, it is likely that prawns and moths would not have survived the evolutionary processes.

Although combinations of tropisms and simple reflexes seem to account for a surprising portion of the behavioral responses that the lower animals need to survive, such simple "wired-in" nerve circuits do not by any means constitute the extent of nature's provision for unthinking, unlearned, but constructive and complex behavior. Let us now pass to the evidence for the existence of stored programs not dissimilar to those we found in the human brain, whereby elaborate sequences of interrelated actions may be called forth by the receipt of suitable stimuli.

"STORED PROGRAMS" OF BEHAVIOR

As these words are being dictated from a shady spot just off Waikiki Beach, several birds are moving about in the grass a few feet away, occasionally stopping to peck at whatever it is that birds peck at in such grassy areas. Two species of birds are represented; they differ greatly in size and coloring, but they also differ in another way. One species progresses across the grass by hopping on both feet; the other's gait is a walk, one step at a time. While the two species of birds are physically quite different, this difference in their method of locomotion is not a consequence of muscular requirements or any other special aspects of their construction that we ordinarily consider to be physical. The birds that hop could just as well have been designed to walk, and the birds that walk could just as practicably have been designed to hop. What is involved is a difference in behavior. Birds of the one species inevitably become hoppers, and birds of the other species inevitably become walkers. They have no capability of changing their behavior patterns; the hoppers could no more walk than they could change their size and coloring, and the walkers will go through life taking their steps one at a time.

Birds provide many instances of species-connected peculiarities of behavior. Thus, while there is a similarity among the cries of alarm of all gulls, the number, pitch, and frequency of the staccato cries that constitute such a call vary between species. Then there are the four groups of birds that constitute the conventionally recognized family of titmice (Paridae). There are no physical features to differentiate these four groups, but their nest-building habits are quite different. One group always nests in hollow trees or other cavities; a second group builds an oval nest with lateral entrance in bushes and trees; a third group builds a peculiar retort-shaped nest of plant down worked into feltlike consistency; the fourth group builds a stick nest with a lateral entrance. While these birds are apparently physically identical, their innate, unlearned, nest-building habits serve to identify them as different species as clearly as though the four groups were marked with red, yellow, blue, and green feathers. In fact, it is not unusual for behavorial characteristics to provide important clues to the proper classification of animal species. For a long time, the group of desert birds called sand grouse (Pteroclididae), which has downy young greatly resembling young grouse (Tetraonidae), was considered to be a member of a closely related family. Later, more careful analysis of physical characteristics led to the suspicion that sand grouse were more closely allied with pigeons. This suspicion was finally confirmed and the classification corrected by employment of a behavior characteristic. While nearly all birds scoop water up with their bills and then let it run down into their stomachs by lifting head and neck, pigeons have a very different drinking behavior; they stick their bills into the water and simply pump it up through the esophagus. The fact that sand grouse are the only other birds with this behavior strongly reinforced the anatomical findings which placed them next to pigeons.

Inherited behavior patterns are by no means confined to birds. Separate family classification has been assigned to different groups of grasshoppers largely because of differences in their habits of cleaning their antennae. Thus, the Acrididae place a leg on one antenna and clean the antenna by pulling it through between the leg and the ground. Physically similar, the Tetrigidae family differ in that they clean their antennae by stroking them with the legs, which in turn are cleaned by being pulled through the mouth. And in the sea there are hermit crabs with the instinct to find castoff shells as houses for their unprotected abdomens, and other crabs that protect themselves by holding stinging sea anemones in their claws. There is the elaborate flight instinct of the squid, with its ejection of ink and a right-angle turn at the crucial moment. There are the octopuses, which have the instinct to build little walls of stones behind which they can lurk unseen.

Since the ability to learn is a characteristic that is possessed, to some extent at least, by a surprisingly large proportion of animals, including some that we consider to be quite inferior, it is necessary always to be alert to the possibility that behavior patterns such as those described may be the consequence of indoctrination of the young by their parents. For many years it was in fact assumed that learning processes were responsible for most of the adaptive behavior exhibited by animals. Only with the advent of experiments in which the animals were carefully reared, from birth or from the egg, without access to others of their kind, was it determined that much of what had been assumed to have been learned existed in the organism at the time of birth as a finished and complete pattern of behavior. Certain newly hatched birds, for example, will automatically crouch down in the nest when a hawk passes overhead. This is not simply a response to a dark object in the sky. The shape must be hawklike; a robin can pass overhead without evoking the slightest reaction. Then there is the so-called thermometer bird, or bush turkey, of the Solomon Islands. It lays its eggs in a heap of mixed plant material and sand, with all the eggs arranged to lie with the blunt end upward. Each chick, on breaking out of the blunt top of its egg, wriggles and struggles in such a way that its stiff feathers, which point backward, gradually cause it to work its way up to the top of the heap. On reaching the surface, the chick dashes cross country into the shade of the nearest undergrowth. Certainly, no learning is involved in this response pattern of the newly hatched chick. Similarly, a female canary that has been isolated from birth builds a nest competently the first time suitable material is presented and the occasion arises. And a caterpillar, when it is about to pupate, spins a cocoon. It has never seen its parents or a cocoon and yet automatically sets about to construct an edifice that, when analyzed, is a masterpiece of engineering.

Although observations such as those just described show conclusively that learning from experience is not occurring, the inheritance at birth of such detailed and purposeful behavior patterns is so different from anything we humans experience that it is necessary for us to fight against the tendency to imagine that reasoning intelligence is involved. We must therefore not ignore the evidence on this point. Consider again the thermometer bird, which on emerging from the egg executes exactly the kind of wriggling motion needed to bring it to the surface of the heap and then changes to a new mode of motion to bring it to the protection of shade. If the chick, after having emerged, is once more dug into the heap, it is quite incapable of coming out again but stays there struggling ineffectively until it dies. Its movements are now of the type adapted to running to shade, and not of the type that will bring it to the surface. And the caterpillar that builds such a wonderful cocoon displays the completely automatic nature of its performance if it is interrupted in the middle of its task and the half-finished cocoon removed; it does not start again from the beginning, but spins only what remained for it to do, in spite of the fact that the resulting half cocoon is completely useless for protection. The octopus that so "intelligently" builds a stone wall behind which it can hide unseen will with equal vigor construct the wall out of transparent pieces of glass, if this is the material that happens to be handy.

In the light of present knowledge, we can only conclude that these specific and detailed behavior patterns are built into the organisms at birth. The same kind of kinetic embryonic forces that determine the configuration of the animal, its coloring of skin or feathers, and all the millions of details that constitute the blueprint for its physical construction also act to determine the detailed pattern of interconnection of the neurons in its brain; and the patterns of behavior thus produced are as unique to the species as such obviously physical characteristics as size, shape, and coloration.

"INTELLIGENCE" OF INSECTS: TRIGGERING OF SUCCESSIVE STORED SUBROUTINES

A special challenge to our hypotheses is provided by the unusually elaborate patterns of conduct exhibited by some insects, such as ants, termites, bees, and wasps. For years, man has been fascinated by the complex behavior patterns of these insects. He has read into their organized behavior strong elements of similarity to the reasoning processes of humankind. Let us see if this interpretation survives close analysis, or if our concept of permanently wired-in neuronal circuits again appeared to fit the facts

Consider, for example, the solitary wasps. When the time comes for egg laying, the wasp *Sphex* builds a burrow for the purpose and seeks out a cricket which she stings in such a way as to paralyze but not kill it. She drags the cricket into the burrow, lays her eggs alongside, closes the burrow, then flies away, never to return. In due course, the eggs hatch and the wasp grubs feed off the paralyzed cricket, which has not decayed, having been kept in the wasp equivalent of deep freeze. To the human mind, such an elaborately organized and seemingly purposeful routine conveys a convincing flavor of logic and thoughtfulness—until more details are examined. For example, the wasp's routine is to bring the paralyzed cricket to the burrow, leave it on the threshold, go inside to see that all is well, emerge, and then drag the cricket in. If, while the wasp is inside making her preliminary inspection, the cricket is moved a few inches away, the wasp, on emerging from the burrow, will bring the cricket back to the threshold, but not inside, and will then repeat the preparatory procedure of entering the burrow to see that everything is all right. If again the cricket is removed a few inches while the wasp is inside, once again the wasp will move the cricket up to the threshold and reenter the burrow for a final check. The wasp never thinks of pulling the cricket straight in. On one occasion, this procedure was repeated forty times, always with the same result.

To the computer scientist, there must be a sense of familiarity to this type of behavior. It has the earmarks of a set of subroutines recorded in the permanent memory system of a computer and called into play by the appearance of certain conditions of the input data. In the instance of the solitary wasp, some triggering mechanism, perhaps the physiological state of the female, sets into motion the series of subroutines associated with the preparing of a nest and the laying of eggs. The first subroutine called forth is the preparation of the burrow. The completion of this subroutine is the trigger for the next, which consists in the searching down of a particular species of cricket and paralyzing it. This in turn is the trigger for the next act in the drama, bringing the cricket to the threshold of the burrow. The presence of the cricket at the threshold of the burrow is the signal for the wasp to go inside for a last check around. Emergence from the burrow and finding the paralyzed cricket at the threshold is the signal for pulling the cricket into the burrow, and so on. Just as in the design of complex programs for electronic digital computers, subroutines appear to be stored and triggered into operation by the particular combinations of stimuli called for by the stored control program of the mechanism.

This concept of stored subroutines that are triggered by specific stimuli goes a long way toward accounting for the surprising variety of detailed inherited behavior patterns exhibited by insects. A bee that has found food will, on its return to its hive, execute a characteristic wagging dance by means of which the direction, distance, amount, and quality of the food source are communicated to the other bees. But a worker that has found food will perform her dance as artistically in the absence of other bees as in the presence of an audience. All that is necessary to trigger the performance is stimulation of her antennae.

The social insects—ants, termites, and bees—all appear to be patriotic, in the sense that they will drive out and frequently sting to death individuals from other hives. But the trigger is odor. All is changed if the interloper is protected long enough to acquire the scent of the new hive. In fact, suitably odor-conditioned insects of entirely different species will frequently be allowed to live indefinitely in a colony of ants or termites.

The senses of odor and taste are used as triggers in many ways by the insects. The great devotion to their queen of termite workers, hundreds of whom are generally seen to be in attendance upon her, appears to be a simple consequence of the fact that she exudes an especially rich and fatty secretion; their apparent attentions consist in licking her to get something for themselves, sometimes so violently that they rasp holes in the royal side. Superficially similar, but for an entirely different purpose, is the phenomenon displayed by certain species of spiders, whereby the male is stimulated to suitable attentions toward the female by a doubtless agreeable substance that she exudes over her body.

Because of the specificity of the trigger mechanisms, these innate response patterns are, by human standards, ridiculously rigid and inflexible. Thus, a male nocturnal moth may fly unerringly to his mate for a distance of more than a mile; yet, if the feathery antennae that serve the male as sense organs are cut off, not only is he incapable of finding the female but, if placed alongside her, is incapable of mating. The trigger for this act apparently is the smell stimulus normally supplied by his sensory antennae. The odor that so stimulates the male moth is generated by two little scent organs located near the tip of the female's abdomen. These organs can be cut out without particularly inconveniencing the female. If they and the operated female are then put in a cage with a normal male not deprived of his antennae, his built-in pattern of mating actions will be triggered, but will be entirely directed toward the source of the stimulus; he will make vain attempts to mate with the two little scent glands but will entirely ignore the female.

An invertebrate animal may starve to death in the midst of plenty if the particular plant or animal material that serves as food for its species happens to be missing. Or an insect may doom its race (or at least its local colony) to extinction because of the absence of the particular stimulus that is required to set off its pattern of nest building or egg laying. While a *Sphex* wasp provides its grubs with crickets, the *Ammophila* must find and paralyze a caterpillar before it can continue with its nest-building and egg-depositing routine; the *Sceliphron* wasp recognizes only spiders as suitable larva food, and the *Podium* uses roaches. The *Pronuba* moth can lay its eggs only in a yucca plant, and a species of Trinidad mosquito can be triggered to deposit its eggs only by the presence of the leaves of a bromeliad plant floating in a pool of stagnant water.

So there is, indeed, abundant evidence of the employment by nature in the insects and lower animals of "permanently wired-in" inherited patterns of behavior. Ranging from simple reflexes and tropisms up through complex patterns of multistage behavior triggered into performance by the occurrence of specific stimuli, these automatic, machine-like responses have many of the earmarks of the library of subroutines that can be stored in the memory of an electronic computer and triggered into operation by the occurrence of a prescribed set of relationships among the data supplied to the computer by its input devices.

When a single organism possesses a number of reflexes, tropisms, and stored subroutines, each triggered by its own prescribed input stimuli, all of which can occur concurrently and sometimes in competing fashion, the complexity of the behavior of the animal is much increased and the machinelike nature of its responses is thus obscured. The superposition on these responses of a certain degree of randomness, arising from the spontaneous firing of the neurons, also enhances the "lifelike" character of the behavior. Furthermore, it must be admitted that the kinds of automatic mechanisms discussed in this chapter do not constitute the complete story of the behavior of insects and lower animals. Like electronic computers that modify their behavior in accordance with experience, these simple natural computers have a limited ability to learn. Although this does not have nearly so large an influence upon over-all behavior as in the case of higher animals, it is nevertheless a real and complicating factor that contributes materially to the appearance of detailed unpredictability in the behavior of even some surprisingly low forms of living creatures. But this need not detract from the sense of familiarity that the computer scientist should feel for the behavior of the lower animals. The detailed performance of some of his machines can also be unpredictable.

NATURE'S COMPUTER
FABRICATION TECHNIQUES

It is the existence in the nervous systems of the lower animals of permanently wired-in patterns of response to specific situations that constitutes the subject matter of this chapter; techniques employed by nature for accomplishing the construction of these computer/control circuits are essentially outside our scope. Nevertheless, in spite of the convincing nature of the evidence that we have examined, it would be disturbing if what were known about nature's methods of constructing living creatures were to be found in conflict with the requirements of a hypothesis that ascribes a major role to inherited automatic patterns of behavior. Therefore, we must conclude our present considerations by a glance at the pertinent features of the existing state of knowledge concerning the transmission of inherited characteristics in living organisms.

To be sure the immediate problem is clearly defined, let us recall that our present position, as computer scientists, is that we believe we have a sort of understanding of the automatic behavior we have been studying. By using electronic circuit elements and techniques presently available to us, we feel that we know how to build computer/control systems with permanently wired-in reflexes, tropisms, and behavior subroutines triggered by specific input stimuli; and such systems would in general exhibit the kinds of performances we have been studying. To be sure, we are a little worried about synthesis of animal responses to specific visual patterns, for our theory and laboratory experimentation has carried us only a small way toward a complete understanding of these matters, but we have made a start and have confidence that we shall one day be much less awkward in our handling of such problems than we are now. It is also true that the 250 neurons in the brain of an ant and the 900 neurons in the brain of a bee appear to us to be impressively small numbers of computer building blocks for the storage and control of the complex behavior patterns of these social insects; we are sure that we would have to use many times this number of electronic switches to accomplish the same task. A somewhat unsatisfactory rationalization for this difficulty is to say that, when we understand better than we do now the tricks that nature has worked out to control the behavior of these social insects, we shall discover the existence of a large number of short cuts like examples that have already been given—the employment of odor or taste in specific circumstances as an attraction device that directly results in the performance of acts that otherwise might require complex control machinery. A more satisfactory basis for an explanation is provided by our knowledge that a neuron is a much more complex component than a simple on/off switch—that in some circumstances, at least, a single neuron may possess a number of modes of operation which cause it all by itself to constitute a simple computer. Of course, this further emphasizes the disparity in size between the circuit elements the computer scientist has learned to build and those that nature employs. But this disparity, impressive though it is, offers no logical difficulty to the computer scientist; he too will be able to accomplish great miniaturization of his components once he has developed a technique for fabrication of devices on a molecular level.

It is, in fact, nature's techniques of miniaturized construction that we now wish to inquire about.

The molecular mechanisms of genetics

One of the most important and fascinating fields of modern science is genetics. In the last several decades, geneticists have learned a great deal about how nature prepares the blueprint and detailed plans for construction of each of its creatures. This blueprint exists in the nucleus of every cell in the body of each animal. The design information is organized into tiny specks called chromosomes, visible under a high-power optical microscope. Every human cell contains 23 pairs of chromosomes. Each cell of the fruit fly contains 4 pairs, of the mouse 20 pairs, of garden peas 7 pairs. Under the much greater magnifying power of the electron microscope, a structure is observed in each chromosome that is consistent with its division into a large number of still smaller parts. These smaller subdivisions of the chromosomes are called genes. The gene is the basic unit of heredity. It has been established that the principal working part of the gene is a gigantic molecule of *deoxyribonucleic acid*—DNA, for short. Each DNA molecule carries a coded message, written in a four-letter alphabet. Each of the four letters is represented by one of four different types of standard molecular fragments, or "nucleotides." These letters are arranged in a linear array along the "backbone" of the DNA molecule. The resulting message, conveyed by the several thousand genes that comprise the chromosomes of each cell, has a length of about ten billion letters—a few more for a man, a few less for a mosquito! This is the equivalent of one thousand large volumes of ordinary printed material. The original copy of the set of manufacturing instructions with which each animal starts its life comes to it in the fertilized egg—half from its mother, half from its father. As this original cell divides, and the resulting cells divide again and again to form the final adult organism, the one-thousand-volume library of manufacturing instructions is faithfully duplicated at each cell division until, in a human, about one hundred million million copies have been made. And it is this library of instructions, and this alone, that determines whether the resulting animal is to be a flea, an earthworm, or a man.

Of course, a set of specifications is of little value unless arrangements are provided for actual fabrication of the desired structure in accordance with these specifications. Some of nature's fabrication arrangements are now known. For example, the DNA molecules, which are exclusively confined to the nucleus of the cell, act as templates for the formation of molecules of *ribonucleic acid*, or RNA. Each RNA molecule is very similar to the DNA molecule that supervises its synthesis out of the raw materials floating around in the nucleus. In fact, the RNA molecule is believed to carry an exact duplicate of the coded message arranged along the backbone of the parent DNA. RNA differs slightly from DNA in the atomic composition of the nucleotides that make up the four-letter alphabet of its message, and in the chemical composition of its long backbone, but the accuracy of the resulting set of specifications is not diminished by these differences. The chemical differences between RNA and DNA do have an important result, however. They permit RNA to leave the nucleus and travel to the surrounding cytoplasm of the cell, where the real business of fabrication of the materials for constructing the organism is carried on.

Once in the cytoplasm, the RNA molecules guide the formation of specific kinds of protein material, the enzymes. Apparently the particular arrangement of "alphabet" nucleotides along the backbone of the RNA molecule operates in some sort of lock-and-key fashion, through the employment of chemical forces, to assemble out of the material of the surrounding cell the right kinds of ingredients and arrange them in the proper order for the fabrication of the types of enzyme molecules required by the embryonic growth processes. The enzymes accomplish their effects, in turn, by highly specific catalytic properties whereby they govern just what chemical reactions take place in the cell fluids to build the kinds of organic material that, finally, constitute the tissue, bones, and blood of the completed organism.

This brief description of how the genetic material controls the embryonic growth processes is, of course, far from complete. One obvious deficiency of the discussion, for example, is that it provides no explanation for the vital phenomenon of cell differentiation. If every nucleus of every cell contains the same, complete genetic specification for the entire organism, why do not the processes described always cause all enzymes, specified in the DNA/RNA code to be indiscriminately produced, thereby resulting in a mass of homogeneous, undifferentiated cells? Obviously, mechanisms must exist that selectively activate parts of the gene-directed enzyme formation. A start has been made toward an understanding of these mechanisms by James Bonner and his associates at the California Institute of Technology.

The Caltech group has established that histone, a protein constituent of the chromosomes, inhibits the DNA-directed synthesis of RNA in the nucleus. In laboratory experiments, it was found possible to control the rate of RNA generation at will by adding or withholding this ingredient. It is also known that changes in the histone content of cells are sometimes associated with important metabolic phenomena. In some instances, at least, tumor cells have been found to possess an abnormally low concentration of the growth-inhibiting histone (Cruft et al., 1954). And there is also evidence that the transition of a plant from the vegetative to the flowering state is preceded by a massive loss of histone from the cells that participate in flower formation (Gifford, 1963). These observations, together with the determination that histone produces its effects through inhibition of the DNA-controlled synthesis of RNA in the cell nuclei, have led Bonner to put forth some very interesting speculation. He suggests that histone may possess a variety of different structures, each form of which is a specific inhibitor of the RNA-generation effectiveness of a particular DNA molecule. If so, some kind of programming mechanism, yet to be identified, could control the abundance of the different types of histone and thereby selectively turn on and off the effects of different portions of the DNA material in the genes. This, in turn, would regulate the generation of the different kinds of RNA molecules and, through them, the various types of enzyme proteins manufactured in the cytoplasm. In this way, cells could be caused to develop differently in accordance with their positions in the organism and the timing of their growth processes.

It is still too early to be sure that we have, in the results obtained in the Caltech laboratories, the basis for a complete explanation of the most important phenomenon of cell differentiation. However, new discoveries, such as those of Bonner and associates, are flowing out of research laboratories at a rapid rate. Their cumulative effect is not to upset the DNA/RNA theory of genetics, but rather to extend it and to fill in its gaps. There seems little doubt of the essential validity of these modern molecular concepts of the genetic processes.

General features of
modern genetic theory

An extensive treatment of the theory of genetics is beyond the scope of this book and certainly well beyond the competence of the author. For our present purposes, we need concern ourselves with only two or three of the features of the theory. To begin with, the blueprint, or better, the library of specifications, contained in coded form in the genes, extensive though it is, is still not complete enough to describe in detail how every cell is to be fabricated and connected with the other cells of the body. Fortunately, this degree of detail is not necessary. We have already seen an example of the kinds of short cuts nature has learned to use in its technique for ensuring proper interconnection of peripheral neurons with their corresponding components in the brain. The genetic message need not include such detail as "the neuron in the retina of the eye that is 1,048 from the left and 579 up from the bottom must make connection with the neuron in the left occipital lobe of the brain that is exactly 104,954 cells left of the center line and 3,045 cells up from the mid-line of the calcarine fissure." If this were required, the one thousand volumes of specifications to which the genetic content of the human being is equivalent would not begin to stretch far enough to permit the desired machinery to be defined. But instead we saw in Chapter 2 that the instruction coded into the genes for this part of the job order is simply that each retinal neuron must establish contact with a cortical neuron of the same relative content of two specified chemicals and that, further, such simplified instructions are coupled with a method of design of the nerves and associated structures that permits the searching axons to wander about more or less at random during the course of the embryonic development, thus providing opportunity for close approach to any given target neuron. Hence the required end result is achieved with a great reduction in the length of the genetic message that otherwise would be needed. It is likely that nature employs many such ingenious simplifying devices to minimize the communication problem and make it possible for the necessary specifications of the individual to be transmitted by the no more than approximately ten billion nucleotides in each cell that appear to be devoted to that purpose.

Although it is these genetic specifications coming to the new individual from its parents by means of the sperm and egg cells that determine whether it will be an amoeba or a chimpanzee, the inherited specifications are not identical for all amoebae or for all chimpanzees. The inherited characteristics that differentiate individuals, as well as those that differentiate members of different species, are a consequence of the fact that the genetic library of specifications differs in some details from one individual to another. These various libraries of specifications corresponding to individuals of different characteristics within a species seem to possess remarkable stability and permanence. Not only are the genetic specifications replicated without error thousands of billions of times as a single multicelled individual grows from the original sperm and egg cell, but also apparently they can be propagated successively through many generations without substantial modification. It is likely that those of us in the twentieth century who have light eyes or hemophilia come by this characteristic through an unbroken chain of successive reproduction and transmission of the same complex coded pattern of thousands of precisely arranged genetic molecules through generation after generation, extending back into prehistoric times.

Although genetic libraries of specifications are remarkably stable, they are not completely changeless. A breed of cattle characterized by long legs will sometimes produce a short-legged offspring. Cats and dogs are occasionally born without tails. These spontaneous changes in content of the genetic instructions propagated from parent to offspring are known as *mutations* and appear to be a form of cosmic accident. Many, perhaps most, such mutations are produced by radiation. A high-energy charged particle arising from the cosmic radiation that contiunally permeates space or from natural radioactive minerals of the earth occasionally passes through the sexual equipment of a prospective parent in such a way as to disarrange the pattern of molecules in the genes of one of its cells—to produce a "typographical error" in its library of specifications. This error or change is then reproduced in the sperm cell or ovum that ultimately participates in the formation of a new individual, and a modified library of specifications is then propagated by that new individual to its offspring. Mutations, however caused, result in new genetic specifications that are as stable and reproducible as the original genetic instructions and can therefore be passed along for generation after generation. When, by X-ray-induced mutation, fruit flies are produced with white eyes, it is found that after seventy-five generations flies with the mutant gene possess eyes as white as those first produced! And the breeders of race horses, beef cattle, and new varieties of dogs all make use of the permanence and continuity of the genetic design information handed along from parent to offspring. They know that, if once developed and then kept uncontaminated, a new genetic strain producing the characteristics they desire in their animals will henceforth breed true.

Of course, mutations provide the raw material for evolution. If the new characteristics resulting from the mutation have survival value, the individual is apt to live longer and have more offspring than its nonmutated contemporaries. Many of these offspring, in turn, will be more successful than their contemporaries in surviving until they reproduce offspring; thus the next generation will have a still higher proportion of individuals whose cells contain the new genetic specifications. Individuals with the new characteristic with higher survival value may ultimately displace completely the unfortunate inheritors of the old-fashioned set of genes.

Genetic control of behavioral characteristics; evolutionary hypothesis

Interesting and important though all this may be, what is its pertinence to our present subject of the "permanently wired-in" computer/control functions of the brain? Simply this: these behavioral characteristics are also a consequence of the physical construction of the organism—in this case, of the specific way in which the neurons are interconnected. The specifications for these interconnections, like those for the more obviously physical characteristics of the organism, are carried by the genes. The same built-in mechanism by means of which the genetic blueprints, in their interaction with the surrounding chemical materials, compel precise adherence to their design specifications in the embryonic growth of the muscles or visceral organs, automatically and accurately "wires" the neurons into the precise computing/control circuits required by heredity. And the same processes must control the evolutionary development of inherited behavior characteristics. Presumably, changes in the inherited behavior patterns of individuals are produced by mutations in the genes that specify the wiring of the neurons. If the change in behavior results in increased survivability for the individual affected, the descendants of the individual will grow more numerous from generation to generation, and the new behavioral characteristic will ultimately become typical of the species.

At least in the case of simple reflexes and tropisms, it is easy to visualize the workings of evolutionary principles upon behavior as upon the more obviously physical characteristics of the species. A mutation in the neuronal scheme of the nocturnal moth resulting in a more effective interconnection between the sensory neurons responsive to the scent of the female and the effector neurons controlling the flight muscles could easily result in a new strain of moths of enhanced mating effectiveness. If individuals of this new strain produced on the average 20 per cent more progeny than the nonmutated individuals, only four generations would be needed for a colony of moths of the new strain to attain twice the population of a colony of old-style moths of initially the same size. Of course, in an actual situation in which the new strain starts out as a tiny minority element in an unmodified population, with no artificial forces at work to speed the process by controlled interbreeding of the individuals having the desired characteristics, much longer periods of time are required by the evolutionary processes to produce noticeable changes. On the other hand, we must remember that the population in any one generation of insects and some of the other lower animals may run into many billions and also that the life span of an individual in these lower forms is so short that a complete generation may be compressed into a few weeks or months. Therefore it is easy to imagine that nature, in the millions of years it has had for working its evolutionary wonders, should have found its random statistical methods adequate for refinement to today's state of the reflexes and tropisms that form so much of the basis of behavior of some of the simpler forms of life.

But simple reflexes and tropisms are one thing—the inherited behavior pattern of a solitary wasp or of a social insect appears to be quite another. Consider the complex, precise pattern of interneuronal wiring needed in the memory and control system of a wasp to provide the set of subroutines and triggering arrangements involved in its nest-building activities. Is it really logical to assume that this pattern could have been arrived at by evolutionary selection from among the literally millions of different ways in which the dendrites and axons of only a few hundred neurons can conceivably be interconnected? This question, of course, was raised more generally a few decades back about all evolutionary processes, including those responsible for properties that appeared to be simpler than those that concern us here. The question lost much of its cogency as improved methods for determining the age of the earth revealed that nature's evolutionary processes have been going on much longer than had originally been thought. However, in the nineteenth century, prior to these geophysical developments, the Lamarckian evolutionists had a way of reconciling the apparent shortness of the time that had been available for evolution with the extensiveness of the resulting accomplishments. They believed that acquired characteristics could be inherited. If, with the passage of time, the individuals of successive generations of a species made more and more use of their legs in running down their prey, the increased musculature in the legs thus acquired by an individual would somehow be passed on to his offspring who would, as a result, start out in life with stronger legs than the parent and evolve from there. It is easy to see that such a hypothesis would be particularly effective for explaining the evolutionary development of inherited behavior. With such an approach, we could reason as follows. If, for whatever cause, a female wasp while under the influence of the biological urge to make a nest and lay eggs comes across a certain species of caterpillar, stings it, and brings it to its burrow just before the urge to lay eggs becomes controlling, the no doubt pleasurable associations in the brain of the wasp between the egg laying and the caterpillar episode could in some way produce changes in the genetic material passed on to the next generation of wasps and result in some probability that they, too, would associate the two kinds of behavior. By such a hypothesis, given many generations to work with, we could probably develop a fairly comfortable feeling about the adequacy of evolutionary processes to account for the remarkably detailed inherited behavior patterns of some of the lower animals.

Unfortunately for the Lamarckian hypothesis, all the modern science of genetics conspires against it. No one has ever succeeded in showing the slightest effects on subsequent generations of any kind of physical or behavioristic experience of previous individuals (with the exception of the special experiment of exposing the parents to radiation and thereby inducing mutations to occur at a rate higher than normal). Numerous investigators have tried every device they could think of to modify by special conditioning of the parent the genetic information transmitted to an offspring. In the course of this work, "animals and plants were drugged, poisoned, intoxicated, illuminated, kept in darkness, half smothered, painted inside and out, whirled around and around, shaken violently, vaccinated, mutilated, educated, and treated with everything except affection from generation to generation."[1]

One investigator even cut off the tails of generation after generation of mice, only to find the tails of the final progeny as long as those of the first. Not only such experimental evidence, but also the increasingly well-established basic theory of genetics, leads to the conclusion that there is nothing in the experience of the parents that can have any effect whatever on the "library of specifications" contributed by them to their offspring. The genetic instructions that will one day be passed along to subsequent generations are precisely determined at the instant the sperm and egg cells meet and initiate the processes of embryonic cell division that finally result in the adult parent. Only unpredictable, random mutations, probably for the most part produced by radiation, but never the result of intervening activity or experience of the parent, can make changes in the "literary content" of the genetic package.

The fruitlessness of any attempt to find an accelerating factor in the evolution of inherited behavior leaves us in the position of having to rest

[1]A quotation from H. J. Muller, the American geneticist who received the Nobel prize in 1946 for his discovery of the production of mutations by means of X-ray irradiation.

our confidence in the validity of the existing hypothesis on the statistical effectiveness of the large numbers of individuals and generations involved. Perhaps we can be adequately comfortable in contemplation of this situation if we again recall the propensity of natural processes toward ingenious simplifying techniques. It is likely that throughout the ages the evolutionary processes of nature have automatically developed certain packaging concepts for the specification of neuronal wiring diagrams. A mutation in a gene that is involved in the specification of the nervous system probably results, not simply in the reconnection of individual neurons, but instead in a change of the method of deployment or in the weight factor associated with an aggregation of interconnected neurons, without thereby upsetting the operational integrity of this more or less self-sufficient package. If this hypothesis is correct, the number of random mutations required to carry the inherited behavior of a developing species through a wide range of variations could easily become mere hundreds instead of millions. When the science of genetics has developed to the point where the library of specifications passed on from parent to offspring can be decoded, we shall probably discover a large number of simplifying factors such as this. These simplifying factors, coupled with the tremendous capacity for change inherent in the basic principle of evolution when applied to billions of individuals over millions of generations, will presumably be found adequate to explain what appears today to be the remarkable specificity and sophistication of the inherited patterns of behavior of some of the insects and lower animals.

Genetic control of behavioral characteristics; direct evidence

Evolutionary hypotheses are by their very nature difficult to confirm by factual observations. However, no such uncertainty need extend to the interpretation of the experimental evidence for the genetic specification of behavioral characteristics. In experiments with rats, for example, strains have been isolated that exhibit marked differences in their behavior toward strangers. In one genetic strain, extreme aggressiveness and hostility is displayed; in another strain of rats that in other respects appear identical, the behavior is docile. These behavioral characteristics breed true, just as do the physical characteristics determined by the genes. In another animal experiment, a particular gene of a fruit fly has been identified that controls one of the details of behavior during the act of mating. Specifically, a modification in this gene decreases the strength and duration of the vibrations of the wings and antennae with which the male fly caresses the female at a certain stage in the courtship procedure!

Evidence for the hereditary control of the properties of the neurological circuits is also supplied by human victims of genetic defects. *Phenylketonuria*, a defect that often causes mental retardation, has been determined to be hereditary in nature. So is *juvenile amaurotic idiocy*. The obscure *Kuru disease*, which regularly kills nearly half of the members of a particular remote tribe in New Guinea, is another case in point. This disease, which causes progressive degeneration of the nervous system, has been traced to a single defective gene. And several other mysterious diseases of the nervous system are suspected to be genetic in nature. These include, for example, two different types of muscular tremor, each highly specific to local population groups in New Guinea, a progressive dementia found in certain islands of the Western Pacific, and so on.

With the growing understanding by physicians of the possible genetic significance of the symptoms of their patients, clues to the existence of hitherto unrecognized hereditary defects are being discovered at a rapid rate. Because so many more humans than animals come under medical scrutiny, it is from such sources, rather than from animal experiments, that most new evidence is coming for neurological genetic defects.

In summary, the inextricably intertwined modern concepts of evolution and genetics appear to provide an explanation of the development and propagation of permanently wired-in computer/control networks of the type required to account for the inherited patterns of behavior of many of the lower animals. The same evolutionary/genetic mechanisms, of course, would also appear to be responsible for the development of the many reflex mechanisms in the higher animals, which we have seen are so similar to the inherited behavior patterns of lower forms and which contribute so much to survival capability. None of this is to say that there exists today anything like a complete understanding of these complex matters. But in view of the evidence that has been secured so far, it would be difficult to question the validity of the basic concept of a library of specifications transmitted by the genes in coded form from one generation to the next. In the ensuing years, it is to be expected that great progress will be made in deciphering the genetic code. When more is known about the physical and chemical laws by means of which the structural pattern of a gene controls the molecule-building processes in the surrounding protoplasm, we may be able to work out a detailed translation of the messages conveyed by the genes of a specific individual. It is not inconceivable that eventually the designers of computer/ control devices will learn to synthesize the types of genes that control the formation of the nervous system in animals. If so, they may be able to fabricate computer components from organic materials on a molecular scale, as nature does, to substitute for the current electronic devices that in future terms of reference may appear fantastically naïve, large, and inefficient.

REFERENCES

Asimov, I., *The Intelligent Man's Guide to Science* (Basic Books, Inc., Publishers, New York, 1960), "The Cell," pp. 497–551.

Bastock, M., "A Gene Mutation Which Changes a Behavior Pattern," *Evolution*, vol. 10 (1956), pp. 421–439.

Bonner, J., R. C. Huang, and N. Maheshwari, "The Control of Chromosomal RNA Synthesis," in press.

Cruft, H., C. Mauritzen, and E. Stedman, "Abnormal Properties of Histones from Malignant Cells," *Nature*, vol. 174 (1954), pp. 580–585.

Dobzhansky, T., "Eugenics in New Guinea," *Science*, vol. 132 (1960), p. 77.

Eibel-Eibesfeldt, I., "The Interactions of Unlearned Behaviour Patterns and Learning in Mammals," in *Brain Mechanisms and Learning*, ed. by Fessard, Gerard, Konorski, and Delafresnaye (Charles C Thomas, Publisher, Springfield, Ill., 1961), pp. 53–74.

Emerson, A. E., "The Evolution of Behavior among Social Insects," in *Behavior and Evolution*, ed. by Roe and Simpson (Yale University Press, New Haven, Conn., 1958), pp. 311–335.

Gajdusek, D. C., "Kuru: An Appraisal of Five Years of Investigation," *Eugenics Quarterly*, vol. 9 (1962), pp. 69–74.

Gifford, E. M., Jr., "Variations in Histone, DNA and RNA Content During Flower Induction," in press.

Horowitz, N. H., "The Gene," *Scientific American*, October, 1956, pp. 79–90.

Huang, R. C., and J. Bonner, "Histone, A Suppressor of Chromosomal RNA Synthesis," *Proceedings of the National Academy of Sciences*, vol. 48 (1962), pp. 1216–1222.

Mayr, E., "Behavior and Systematics," in *Behavior and Evolution*, ed. by Roe and Simpson (Yale University Press, New Haven, Conn., 1958), pp. 341–362.

Muller, H. J., "The Darwinian and Modern Conceptions of Natural Selection," *Proceedings of the American Philosophical Society*, vol. XCIII (1949), pp. 459–470.

Pittendrigh, C. S., "Adaptation, Natural Selection, and Behavior," in *Behavior and Evolution*, ed. by Roe and Simpson (Yale University Press, New Haven, Conn., 1958), pp. 390–416.

Taylor, J. H., "The Duplication of Chromosomes," *Scientific American*, June, 1958, pp. 37–42.

Thompson, W. R., "Social Behavior," in *Behavior and Evolution*, ed. by Roe and Simpson (Yale University Press, New Haven, Conn., 1958), pp. 291–310.

Thorpe, W. H., "Some Characteristics of the Early Learning Period in Birds," in *Brain Mechanisms and Learning*, ed. by Fessard, Gerard, Konorski, and Delafresnaye (Charles C Thomas, Publisher, Springfield, Ill., 1961), pp. 75–94.

Wells, H. G., J. S. Huxley, and G. P. Wells, *The Science of Life* (Doubleday & Company, Inc., Garden City, N.Y., 1938), book eight, chap. I, "Rudiments of Behavior"; chap. II, "How Insects and Other Invertebrates Behave"; chap. III, "The Evolution of Behavior in Vertebrates."

PROGRAMMED LEARNING

John Annett

chapter five

TEACHING MACHINES AND LEARNING

Imagine a classroom teacher who can respond to each student's every mistake with remedial material, know exactly what progress each child is making, where more work is needed, where the child can skip ahead of his classmates, where he has unusual talents and capacities. Imagine, too, that this teacher can provide pictures, stories, sounds, algebraic equations, and other kinds of instruction and entertainment whenever asked for them.

Imagine, in other words, a teaching machine. The idea may turn you off—but you should consider just how personal and individualized teaching can be when a child's whole history* of learning can be stored and called out instantly.

The following essay is a careful exploration of various aspects of teaching machines. The author, a Britisher whose style may be a little difficult at first, goes into this topic, which currently enjoys a lot of attention, in much more detail than I had time to do in the textbook.

*Or yours—which may make the idea less appealing.

PROGRAMMED LEARNING

Programmed learning has been one of the most striking and significant developments in applied psychology in the last decade. In 1954 B. F. Skinner of Harvard in an article entitled 'The Science of Learning and the Art of Teaching' (1954) proposed ways in which principles derived from learning experiments on rats and pigeons could be applied to the education of children and adults. He went even further by suggesting that these principles could be applied more effectively by an automatic 'teaching machine' than by a human teacher. Coming at a time when education was becoming increasingly a matter of public concern these radical proposals caused something of a stir. Parents and teachers, prompted perhaps by magazine articles, began to ask 'Can children be taught like pigeons?' and 'Can a robot replace the human teacher?' Skinner soon backed up his claims with evidence that a properly programmed teaching machine *can* teach effectively, often more effectively than normal class instruction conducted by a human teacher. Ten years later programmed learning, the term now used to cover various kinds of automatic teaching, is being used successfully throughout the world and a preliminary assessment of this new development can be made. The rather emotional talk of pigeons and robots has been replaced by more serious consideration of the translation of laboratory results on learning into rules for practical teaching and attempts to analyse the possible role of automation in educational systems.

The two central ideas are the 'teaching machine' and the 'program'. In its currently most popular form the teaching machine is a box which holds a program of instruction. The program is a text in question and answer form, usually printed on sheets or rolls of paper. Instructional items or 'frames' can be seen, one at a time, through a small window in the box and answers are written, through another window, on a paper tape. The machine is designed so that the student sees and answers items

"Programmed Learning," by John Annett, in NEW HORIZONS IN PSYCHOLOGY, *edited by Brian M. Foss (London: Penguin Books); reprinted by permission of Penguin Books Ltd.*

in a prescribed order, is shown the correct answer immediately after completing each question and is prevented from changing what he has written, should it have been wrong. The student is active since the questions are frequent and require him to do something, and he works at his own pace, only going on to the next step when he has mastered preceding steps. Each correct response he makes is immediately and automatically confirmed and he is made aware of any error at once. The learning situation is very close to individual tuition in most respects.

Information is presented to students individually, the pace is determined by the rate at which the student can 'take in' the material and he is actively involved. The major difference, apart from the fact that the student is involved with a machine rather than another human being, is that the sequence of instruction is prearranged. The interplay between a student and a real tutor can often be more flexible. Because a single sequence is followed this type of programmed learning is called 'linear.'

In this form the machine is primarily a piece of ancillary equipment designed to facilitate the use of the programmed text and indeed, a co-operative student can work with the text alone quite as effectively. In other systems the teaching machine may have more elaborate functions and, as an intermediary between the student and the task to be learned, may either wholly or in part determine the course of the lesson. In these systems, which can take a variety of physical forms, the sequence of instruction is determined as we shall see by the design of the machine and the program is therefore said to be 'intrinsic.' The linear programmed text and 'intrinsic' techniques are the most common current examples of programmed learning. As well as sharing some, but not all aspects of the tutorial situation they have in common the essential feature that the instructional items have been carefully selected and ordered into a sequence or program. In the 'linear' type the sequence is prearranged; in the 'intrinsic' type the student's actual behaviour partly determines the sequence, thus if an error is made the machine interposes some extra remedial material—a 'branch'—before allowing the student to proceed on the main stream of the lesson.

Since, by historical accident, the term 'teaching machine' is better known than the term 'program' we shall first take a look at several types of educational hardware so that we can see how these two concepts are related.

VISUAL AND AUDITORY AIDS

Slide projectors, tape-recorders, closed-circuit television and working models take advantage of machinery of one kind or another to enrich the presentation of information. They imply the presence of a teacher who uses them as an extension of his own voice and hands. The teacher retains responsibility for the organization of lessons, assessment of students and so on. These are teacher *amplifiers* rather than teacher *substitutes* and are not generally classed as teaching machines.

LANGUAGE LABORATORIES
AND SIMULATORS

In these superficially dissimilar cases the dimension of direct student participation is added. In the language laboratory the student not only hears a canned lesson but also attempts to reproduce words and phrases, and his efforts are recorded so that both he and the teacher can compare these with some standard and assessments of progress are possible.

Simulators are now widely used in flight training. A more or less accurate mock-up of, say, an aircraft cockpit provides not only the relevant display (sometimes even including such features as 'stiffness' of the joystick) but also the opportunity to practise a variety of manoeuvres in safety and without using expensive operational equipment. Again practice can be monitored and evaluated by both student and teacher.

In both these cases the lessons may be carefully arranged and sequenced by the teacher, but this is not intrinsic to the machinery used.

AUTOMATIC SELF-SCORING
AND TESTING DEVICES

A whole class of devices which does not necessarily simulate inputs to the student provides for automatic and immediate evaluation of performance and thus relieves the teacher of a fairly considerable burden of testing and marking. The devices designed by S. Pressey (1950) during the 1920s are both typical of this group and are historically important in the development of teaching machines. The 'Tester-Rater' is an effective if unglamorous example. The student has a printed sheet of test questions in multiple-choice form. In a matrix of holes on the face of the 'punch-board' rows represent question numbers and columns answer choices. The student tries to push a metal stylus through the hole representing his chosen answer to a given question. If he is right a template allows the stylus to pass through making a hole in a piece of paper and if he is wrong the stylus stops halfway, in each case leaving a distinctive mark which cannot be altered and later can be scored either by hand or by a special machine (modern versions often use standard punched cards for this purpose). The student is encouraged to go on trying if his first answer was wrong, and in this way the student not only receives confirmation of his correct answers but is also able to discover or rediscover the right answers to all items on the test, and in this way the device not only tests but teaches.

Test items can, of course, be in random or sequential order, and there may or may not be an accompanying text. When there *is* the system approaches a complete self-instructional device, although again, apart from the provision of knowledge of results, the teaching function is not intrinsic to the device but depends on the lesson plan or program.

PRE-PROGRAMMED TEACHING MACHINES

The important advance which Skinner made on the pioneering work of Pressey was to concentrate on the form of the lesson presented on an automatic self-scoring device. As will be seen later in this chapter and in the chapter by Stretch (Chapter 15), Skinner had in his studies of animal learning paid considerable attention to the scheduling of training trials. Learning takes place when an act (technically an 'operant') is followed immediately by some reward which is said to reinforce the learned behaviour. To build up complex behaviour it is necessary to arrange a schedule in which individual components are reinforced singly and in proper sequence. Typically in the early stages approximately correct responses are reinforced and later only more and more precise versions of the desired response are rewarded.

By analogy, therefore, a typical Skinnerian teaching machine presents a carefully arranged sequence of items each providing the stimulus for an appropriate response and providing reinforcement for correct responses. The pigeon or rat is rewarded with food or water, but the human student is rewarded by the knowledge that he is right. In the typical Skinner teaching machine, the stimulus (information and question) appears in the left-hand window and the student makes his response by writing the answer in the window on the right. He pulls the level which moves his answer under a perspex cover, reveals the correct answer and the next item. An example of the linear type of program used in these machines is illustrated in Figure 1. On such a machine the lesson is self-administered so that the teacher is not required and the student can work at his own pace in his own time and never misses a point due to inattention.

An important modification of this type of device is to get rid of the hardware altogether. The function of the box is simply to guide the student's attention to the relevant stimuli in a prescribed sequence and to get him to make an active response before being able to see the correct

THE CONDUCTION OF
THE NERVOUS IMPULSE

FRONT OF CARD	BACK
1. The basic unit of which the nervous system is composed is the NERVE CELL or NEURONE. Hence we say that the brain and nervous system are made up of large numbers of_____ .	Nerve cells *or* Neurones
2. Now make a copy of *Picture 1*, and put it on one side where you can see it.	
3. 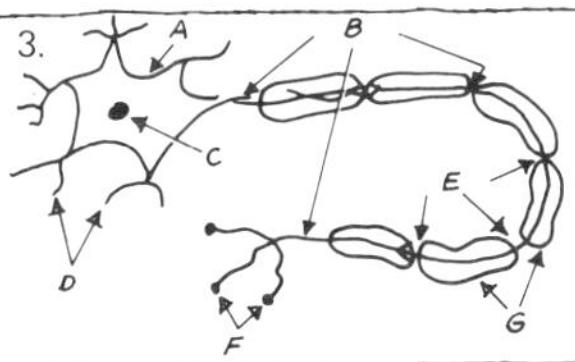 A. CELL BODY B. AXON C. NUCLEUS D. DENDRITES E. NODES OF RANVIER F. TERMINAL BOUTONS OF SYNAPTIC KNOBS G. MYELIN SHEATH	
4. The body of the cell contains the_____ .	Nucleus
5. From the body of the cell several processes stick out. 1. The single long one is called an_____ . 2. The short ones are called_____ .	Axon Dendrites
6. The axon, which is the_____ -est of the processes which leave the cell body, is covered by the _____ sheath.	Longest Myelin
7. The myelin_____ is made of fatty material, and is interrupted every few milli- metres by the_____ of_____	Sheath Nodes of Ranvier
8. The axon finished by dividing into fine fibres which end in_____ or synaptic knobs.	Terminal boutons

Figure 1

SAMPLE OF A LINEAR PROGRAM USED EXPERIMENTALLY AT THE UNI-
VERSITY OF SHEFFIELD

answer. A moderately cooperative student can follow these instructions, especially when he finds it does not help to skip ahead or to cheat and that it is easy to follow the prescribed program. Without the box the system simply becomes a *programmed textbook* and this is, in most cases, as effective as the machine plus text and, of course, rather cheaper.

A different kind of pre-programmed device is due to N. A. Crowder (in Lumsdaine and Glaser, 1960) and also exists in both machine and textbook form. Crowder, uncommitted to Skinner's views on learning, was struck by the fact that an important function of the teacher is to diagnose the student's strengths and weaknesses and to take appropriate steps to remedy incipient fallacies, to provide missing items of information and, when appropriate, to send the student on to more advanced material. Crowder devised a system in which this interplay between student and teacher was intrinsic to the design of the machine. In the AutoTutor Mark II a filmed program is shown on a rear-projection screen. Each frame gives a paragraph or two of information (rather more than appears on one frame of a Skinner program) and asks a question in multiple-choice form. The student answers by pressing the appropriately labelled button and the film is rapidly moved on to another frame, the next step in the lesson, if the answer was correct, or a remedial 'branch' if the student made a mistake. The questions are intended to be diagnostic so that by answering the student automatically presents himself with an appropriate 'cure' for his error. The lesson goes on somewhat like a game of snakes and ladders, but with learning rather than chance as the criterion of progress. As in the Skinner devices learning is individual and self-paced.

In its 'software' form the program is presented as a 'scrambled' book (see Figure 2). Instead of reading the pages in order the student starts on page 1 and has to answer a multiple-choice question in order to find out which page to go to next. The difference between this and the AutoTutor is simply that the student turns the pages himself rather than having the machine do it for him. The scrambled book, like the programmed text, is a little more clumsy and more open to abuse by uncooperative students than the machine counterpart, but considerably less expensive.

It could be said that the Crowderian 'intrinsic' programming adds a further dimension to the Pressey-Skinner concept of a teaching machine in so far as it makes provision for the individual characteristics of the learner. While the lesson is pre-programmed, even the remedial branches, the selection of branches depends on the individual students unlike the invariant or linear sequence of a Skinner program.

ADAPTIVE TEACHING MACHINES

The final stage in the hierarchy of teaching machinery is reached with machines designed to play an even more important role in the selection and ordering of instructional items. While visual aids mechanize the presentation of information, the Pressey, Skinner and Crowder machines mechanize practice and marking, the adaptive machine mechanizes the decisions taken by the teacher. It takes over to a large extent the task of programming, and to do this it must itself be capable of learning. A good teacher does not simply reproduce his lessons like a gramophone but is sensitive to the varying needs of his students. He has available to him a variety of teaching strategies which he can use as appropriate, and which he can test and develop in the course of practising the art of teaching.

One of the most sophisticated examples of an adaptive teaching machine is described by Smallwood (1962). In this experimental system lessons are controlled by a digital computer which can be programmed to function in much the same way as a tutor, that is, presenting information, testing and providing new or remedial items. Unlike the prearranged branching of the AutoTutor the computer could vary its tactics so that in the course of teaching a number of students it could learn which sequences typically led to error, and which sequences were most effective in a given situation. The built-in decisions about the course of instruction are modifiable according to the experience of the 'teacher'. The details of this system, although of considerable interest, need not concern us here since computer-based teaching is still a long way from being a practical proposition for normal use. Smallwood's system and others like it (Coulson, 1962) are of value in providing a first approximation to a fully automated teaching system which simulates most of the distinctive features of the teaching process. We should not be deceived by the lack of resemblance to a human teacher. The limitations—and there are many—are principally in the varieties of student behaviour and subtleties of mood which the system can detect and the range of pedagogical gambits from which it can select to meet the demands of a teaching situation. The fully adaptive system provides a heuristic model for research rather than an immediately practical tool for teaching.

SUMMARY

This brief outline of the main types of teaching mechanization illustrates the central concept of programming. Only those systems which pay special attention to the lesson plan and in particular make use of measures of student performance to modify the lesson plan can strictly be termed *programmed learning*. This may or may not involve the use of machinery, although Skinner saw clearly that the human teacher is limited in the extent to which he can perform important teaching functions

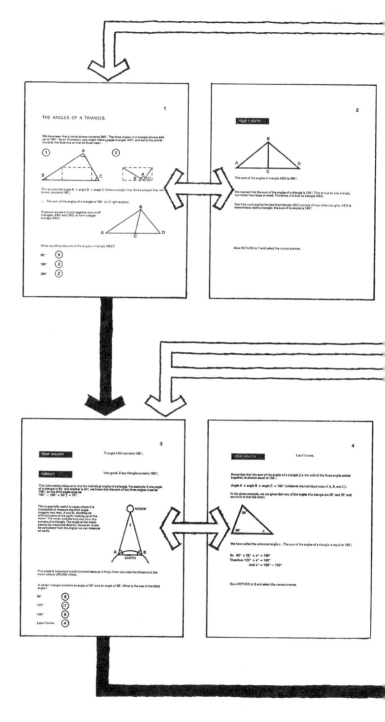

Figure 2
A TYPICAL BRANCHING SEQUENCE FROM AN AUTOTUTOR PROGRAM

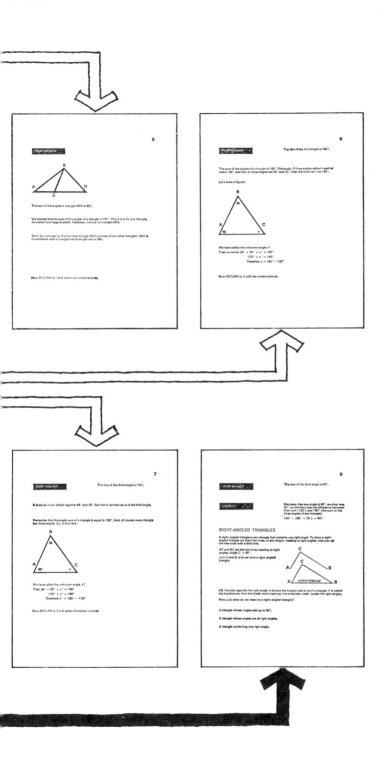

5

YOUR ANSWER

The sum of the angles in triangle ABD is 90°.

We learned that the sum of the angles of a triangle is 180°. This is true for any triangle, no matter how large or small. Therefore, it is true for triangle ABD.

Don't be confused by the fact that triangle ABD consists of two other triangles. ABD is nevertheless itself a triangle and its angle sum is 180°.

Now RETURN to 1 and select the correct answer.

6

YOUR ANSWER

The size of the third angle is 180°.

The sum of the angles of a triangle is 180°. Obviously, if three angles added together make 180°, and two of those angles are 85° and 35°, then the third can't be 180°.

Let's draw a figure:

We have called the unknown angle x°.
Then we know $35° + 85° + x° = 180°$
$120° + x° = 180°$
Therefore $x = 180° - 120°$

Now RETURN to 3 with the correct answer.

7

YOUR ANSWER

The size of the third angle is 120°.

It looks as if you added together 85° and 35°, but that is not the value of the third angle.

Remember that the angle-sum of a triangle is equal to 180°. And, of course, every triangle has three angles. So, in this case:

We have called the unknown angle, x°.
Then $35° + 85° + x° = 180°$
$120° + x° = 180°$
Therefore $x° = 180° - 120°$

Now RETURN to 3 and select the correct answer.

8

YOUR ANSWER

The size of the third angle is 60°.

CORRECT

We know that one angle is 85°, another was 35°, so the third was the difference between their sum (120°) and 180° (the sum of the three angles of any triangle).
$180° - (85° + 35°) = 60°$

RIGHT-ANGLED TRIANGLES

A right-angled triangle is any triangle that contains one right angle. To draw a right-angled triangle we draw two lines, of any length, meeting at right angles, then join up the two ends with a third line.

AC and BC are the two lines meeting at right angles. Angle C = 90°.

Join A and B, and we have a right-angled triangle.

AB, the side opposite the right angle, is always the longest side in such a triangle. It is called the hypotenuse, from the Greek word meaning 'line stretched under' (under the right angle).

Now, just what do we mean by a right-angled triangle?

A triangle whose angles add up to 90°.

A triangle whose angles are all right angles.

A triangle containing one right angle.

when faced with a large class. In particular, a teacher cannot score and reward students with the desirable speed under classroom conditions. Even though he is capable of detecting a wider range of student behaviour than any existing machine he is not in a position to do so often enough nor can he always take the appropriate action.

At the present time the devices I have termed 'pre-programmed' are most popular. They are cheaper and easier to maintain than highly automatic systems, and the printed text is more familiar and therefore more acceptable than a complex device. The rest of this chapter will therefore be devoted to showing how these methods came to be developed.

THE PSYCHOLOGICAL BASIS
OF SKINNER'S
PROGRAMMING TECHNIQUES

The typical Skinner machine with its printed program in question and answer form proceeding in a carefully programmed sequence of small steps has already been described.

From his animal studies Skinner has concluded that the process of reinforcement in which an act is followed immediately by a reward, is crucial to all learning. He starts from the point of view that learning must be discussed only in terms of behaviour and changes in behaviour. We teach people and animals in order that they should be able to do things in appropriate circumstances and their behaviour is at once the goal of instruction and the measure of its effectiveness. The Skinnerian programming technique therefore emphasizes a constructed response (rather than simply button-pressing) and the response must be immediately reinforced. But behaviour cannot be reinforced until it occurs, so that instructional items must be written such that a correct (reinforceable) response is likely to occur. This means that items must be carefully graded in difficulty, according to the actual abilities of students, that increments of new knowledge must be small and that hints and prompts of various kinds should be used, at least initially, to make correct responses highly probable.

Developing from this notion of eliciting and rewarding correct behaviour is Skinner's concept of *shaping*. If the aim is to teach complex forms of behaviour one does not have to wait until it occurs spontaneously. The simple technique is to begin by reinforcing gross approximations to the behaviour desired. For example, a pigeon can be quickly taught to walk in a figure-of-eight if we begin by rewarding it for any turning movement. By gradual stages the reward is provided only for better and better approximations to the correct sequence of right and left turns. In a similar way an animal can be taught to make a given response only in the presence of more and more precisely defined stimulus patterns. A pigeon can be rewarded first for pecking at a disc, then only when it is illuminated from behind, and finally, only when it is illuminated by light of a particular colour. So precise is this method that it has become possible to carry out quite precise experiments on the biochemistry of colour vision in these birds.

Despite the impressive results in animal-training most experimental psychologists are inclined to be more cautious in extending these principles to all aspects of human learning. The points at issue are complex and involve primarily matters of research strategy and technique rather than matters of fact. However, the analogy between 'reinforcement' in the pigeon experiments and 'knowledge of results' in programming is a central theme and is worth examination.

Skinner has always stressed the necessity for frequent responses followed immediately by confirmation—reinforcement—and he has consistently criticized Pressey and Crowder for their use of the more convenient multiple-choice technique on the grounds that choosing an answer is not the same as producing the response to be learned and that inevitably students are often wrong and are therefore not reinforced. As it turns out, research has not confirmed that multiple choice is inferior nor has it been shown decisively that it is necessary for the student to overtly construct his response. Indeed, reading the program with the answers already supplied is usually no less effective than having the student provide the answers. But linear programs are written in a heavily redundant style and frequently revised until correct responses are highly probable. So it should not surprise us that the student who reads conscientiously has little more to learn by writing down the obvious right answers and being told that they are right. Pigeons, reinforced with food, will stop working after a while if the food is withheld, but the human student does not always need frequent reinforcement by an external agent.

It has been suggested that the student is covertly reinforcing himself when reinforcement is not provided by an external agent. To say this, however, is not very helpful because it puts reinforcement into the category of internal variables which cannot be controlled by the experimenter and (even more important in this case) by the teacher. There have been many demonstrations of operant conditioning in humans. Sometimes social reinforcement (a smile from the experimenter) can be used to condition certain responses, for example, some gesture or use of words which can be made to appear more and more frequently. The technique is not, however, infallible and subjects who catch on to what is happening tend to withdraw abruptly. Small children can be reinforced by sweets or trinkets, but they, too, are much less prone to control than a hungry pigeon.

Both human and animal subjects clearly do learn from the consequences of their actions—by knowledge of results—and this fact is often used to support the assertion that knowledge of results or reinforcement is necessary to learning. However, there would seem to be a difference between an expected and an unexpected result following a response. When an unexpected result occurs as, for instance, when a chosen answer turns out to be wrong, new information is gained. When, however, the result is as expected, confirmation provides little, if any, new information—the result is redundant. In the former case knowledge of results is essential to learning and in the latter case it is not, and this supposition is confirmed by the experimental results. In the linear program knowledge of results is made highly redundant by making each answer dependent on a very small increment of knowledge, heavily supported by cues and hints and it is not surprising that knowledge of results is largely unnecessary. To postulate a process of reinforcement occurring covertly or occurring as the result of an unspecified reinforcing agent (social approval, the desire to do well, etc.) is to infringe the law of parsimony,[1] but Skinner has been led into this position by his attempt to preserve a weak analogy between different types of learning situations. To account for all learning by the same process would seem to be parsimonious indeed, but, unfortunately, it conflicts with the facts.

The theoretical debate on the nature and role of reinforcement will continue, but the practical outcome is that it always pays to provide a learner with knowledge of results as an insurance against the perpetuation of mistakes, but the preparation of the program in a logical order and an intelligible form would seem to be the key to effective programming in view of the present state of our knowledge about the mechanisms of human learning. In this sense Skinner's concept of shaping has been extremely helpful and the overt constructed response has been of even greater value to the program writer than to the student. Shaping implies a gradual progression of learning with the student managing to 'get the hang of it' virtually all the time. The requirement to produce an overt response or answer at frequent intervals is the means by which the program writer can discover, by trying the material out on students, if he is writing at this level. If the students fail to answer correctly the programmer has failed in his task of communicating.

---

[1]The *law of parsimony* states that explanations for behavior should be stated in the simplest, most mechanistic terms.

We turn now from theoretical debate to the programming techniques which have been developed, originally on the Skinnerian model, during recent years.

HOW PROGRAMS ARE WRITTEN

The program writer begins, not at the beginning but at the end by attempting to define the object of the course of instruction. In many traditional educational systems the goals of teaching are often ill-defined and it is not unknown for practices to continue so long after the original goal has changed that new reasons for doing the same things have to be found. Thus Latin was once taught with the modest object of enabling students to read the language in which most important documents were then written. When this was patently no longer true objectives such as 'training the mind' were produced to justify the continuation of the syllabus. While this is an extreme case it is true that precise educational objectives have received less attention than they deserve. The value of a clear statement of the objective is simply that it enables one to measure the efficiency of teaching, the discrepancy between the achievement and the desired result. Such discrepancies enable the programmer to evaluate and revise his program.

Skinner's behaviouristic viewpoint is highly consistent with this requirement that educational objectives are best stated in terms of the kinds of behaviour we want to teach. A modest goal might be to teach students to be able to read the colour code of a resistor, or to be able to manipulate trigonometric ratios, or to be able to detect and discriminate between a variety of faults in samples of paper and so on.

Programmers are inclined to fight shy of some of the grander objectives of education, such as 'character building,' but investigators are looking seriously at such important questions as defining 'creativity' and 'problem-solving capacity'. While it is, as yet, not possible to provide anything approaching complete behavioural definition of creativity this is the first and necessary step towards tackling the problem of being able to teach the special kinds of skills which lead to the development of new attitudes and concepts. But this is a field which we must for the present pass over to return to the programming of more mundane objectives.

Given that one or more objectives have been defined in measurable behavioural terms a formal analysis of the subject-matter must be undertaken. It is necessary to specify in some meaningful way the components of the knowledge or skill to detect any logical hierarchy among these components and to trace out relationships between sub-skills.

A useful technique known as the Ruleg System, has been devised by Evans, Glaser and Homme (1960). It is supposed that instructional material can be classified into rules and examples, the rules being general statements and examples being specific instances of one or more rules. Instruction often begins with a general statement followed by the presentation of a number of more specific exemplars, but it is also quite common to begin with examples and later to present or ask the student to deduce the rule. Tests of achievement typically require the person tested to produce or to complete general statements or to categorize specific examples under the appropriate rules or to construct or complete specific examples given a general rule. At an early stage in programming it is useful to list all the relevant rules and to assemble as large as possible a selection of specific examples. These will be the basic materials from which the text is constructed.

The next stage is to reach some decision about the ordering of these rules and examples. An expert on the subject matter is, almost by definition, one who can recognize the internal constraints which determine the logical order or presentation, but it can be that there is more than one possible order and that the traditional order is not necessarily the best. The wind of change currently blowing through traditional mathematics curricula is evidence of such a possibility even in a highly organized subject matter.

To help in the process of deciding on the ordering of subject-matter Evans *et al.* suggested that rules should be arranged in the margins of a series of matrices, the cells being used to trace any relationship between a given rule and any other. One can then compare rules, systematically, according to any chosen type of relationship, logical inclusion/exclusion, priority and so on. A similar system is worked out thoroughly in a book by Thomas *et al.* (1963). At this stage rigorous systems for subject-matter analysis do not exist and the programmer may well decide to devise his own system, but the point is to have a system, however crude, as an explicit basis for program development.

When some means of ordering the lesson content has been devised the writing of individual items can begin using the lists of rules and examples as the basic material. Although it was shown earlier in this chapter that overt responses add little to learning efficiency it is necessary at this stage to get student responses in some detail in order to test the effectiveness of the items. Often the choice of examples will depend on which of these are found, empirically, to be helpful to the student. Whether he needs more or fewer examples before the rule is introduced is also an empirical matter to be decided on the basis of actual use of the program.[2]

Skinner has made some fairly precise recommendations about the form of individual frames. For example, in introducing new material the correct response should be supported by prompts and cues which in later items are gradually withdrawn. To give a simple example in teaching the spelling of a word the first response may simply be to copy it out. Later one or more letters are withdrawn, and finally, the student is required to construct the entire word without any support or prompting. There are several variations on this basic technique. Context frequently is used to provide support as are analogies and sometimes even rhymes. On the whole it is best for the programmer not to copy the kinds of cueing methods he sees in other programs until he is convinced that they are appropriate. Rhyming prompts may appeal to nine-year-olds in some contexts, but cause hilarity or disgust if used with management trainees.

Programmers have found it convenient to try out the draft program on a few students before it has reached too advanced a stage. The programmer sitting with a student can quickly see where his exposition is lacking in clarity or interest. Failure of a program can show up in several ways. Although a student who has made a wrong response, perhaps through insufficient care in reading, can learn by being shown the correct response, one cannot, with a linear program guarantee this. A student error is often symptomatic of some confusion in the presentation of the material and a simple statement of the correct answer is not adequate. The programmer must trace the source of the error and may often have to include additional frames in his revised version to eliminate the error.

This process of eliminating errors during the writing of a program is known as *internal evaluation*. However, a further stage of *external evaluation* in which the efficiency of the program in teaching students up to an agreed criterion of performance is highly desirable.

The claims, some perhaps extravagant, which have been made for programmed learning do require some substantiation, but more than this a principle is involved. An automatic teaching system, either a machine or programmed text, is designed to exert a high degree of control over the student's behaviour in the learning situation. Whereas an ordinary textbook can be used quite successfully, in a variety of ways a program not only provides information but also prescribes the manner in which the student should work. The prescription is often very precise and neither demands nor permits attempts on the part of the student to teach himself.

---

[2]The *empirical matter* to be decided is whether the examples work in actual practice.

In this way the programmer shoulders a heavier responsibility than the author of an ordinary textbook. To fully discharge this responsibility the programmer should show that the detailed study procedures are actually justified in terms of results.

External evaluation. Three things are especially to be borne in mind: the target or criterion behaviour, the target population and the antici- pated conditions of use. Any criterion that should adequately sample the behaviour is specified in the original objectives. For limited objectives this is relatively easy. A student can either remember the values of a resistor colour code or he cannot. With more extended subject-matters the ques- tion becomes more complex for criterion tests can only sample the desired behaviour. Further complexity is introduced by asking when, or for how long it is desired that the student be capable of criterion performance and sometimes we are interested in how much the learning of one subject or skill can facilitate the learning of some other subject-matter or skill. Such criteria are as difficult to satisfy as they are to specify and even in the modern educational setting there is considerable resistance to 're- ducing' the outcome of teaching to test score results.

The problems of sampling the student population are, compared with those of sampling behaviour, much simpler. A random sample of students is desirable for the evaluation trials, but it seems that linear programs at least are capable of being used effectively by a fairly wide range of stu- dents although there may be some loss of time (and perhaps temper) among the brighter ones. Sampling the conditions of use is quite another matter. For the time being at least many programs will be used in a class- room situation with various kinds of interventions on the part of the teacher. For complete self-tuition (say, for example, on correspondence courses) very comprehensive programs are desirable. Clearly there is a danger that programs developed in one context may turn out to be in- adequate in another.

Both the American Psychological Association and the British Psycho- logical Society have sub-committees working on the possibility of setting some minimal standards of program evaluation. Whatever these turn out to be it does seem desirable that publishers should present data on the effectiveness of their programs. Such data are normally collected in the proper development of a program.

The points which have been made about the linear program apply in general to the construction of a branching program. The definition of objectives must be made and a subject-matter analysis carried out. Crow- der's rules of frame construction are, however, simpler to state. Straight- forward and unambiguous prose is recommended, but the programmer has to master the art of setting multiple-choice questions in such a way that guessing is to a large degree eliminated and the choices, especially the wrong ones, represent fully the range of possible ways of misunderstanding the material.

RESEARCH IN PROGRAMMED LEARNING

A useful bonus from the development of programmed learning has been the stimulus to research. Some, at least, of the psychologists engaged in laboratory research on learning have turned to programmed learning and teaching machines as a way of bringing rigorous controlled conditions into the classroom where real students learn real subjects. Many of the early studies were concerned with the apparently simple question of whether programmed learning works and teaching machines teach. The general procedure has been to compare learning gains of students taught by traditional or 'normal' methods and students using machines or programs. In some cases retention at a later date has also been compared and most studies compare the amount of student time required to teach a given criterion under the two methods. The results of an unselected group of such experiments are summarized in Table 1.

In general, programmed learning gives better results, often with a considerable saving in time and subsequent retention is as good or better. This is encouraging, but there are some difficulties. 'Normal' teaching is not a standard procedure but can be anything which is not programmed learning, and the 'normal' teacher may vary from a highly experienced person with a small class to an inexperienced teacher with a large class. In fact, most of the comparisons have been fair, the best teacher available has been put up against the machine, but in several cases where the

Table 1

Measure taken	Number of Studies	Program Group		
		Better	Equal	Worse
Immediate retention	54	35	17	2
Long-term retention	10	5	4	1
Learning time	26	24	1	1

Source: Hartley, *Some Guides for Evaluating Programs* (Association for Programmed Learning, 1963). The table refers to fifty-six studies, not all of which used all three measures, involving over 5,000 students of all kinds.

programmer himself has been the control teacher it has been found that he did as well as or even better than his own program.

A more sophisticated approach is to ask under what circumstances is programmed learning more efficient and/or cheaper than the existing techniques. For example, a sophisticated and very expensive simulator is more efficient, cheaper and safer than using a real aircraft, but a computerized typewriter trainer may not compare so favourably in terms of cost and efficiency with much simpler methods. A programmed textbook on mathematics may be the only feasible way of bringing reasonable math teaching to an understaffed girls' grammar school while still being less effective than class teaching carried out by a dedicated expert at another school.

On the general question of comparisons the argument should not be overlooked that programming is essentially a self-adjusting process which, by the use of feedback, 'homes' on to the desired target. The question that then remains is to find the most effective means of writing successful programs.

A great deal of research has recently been carried out to compare different aspects of programmed learning: such as the comparison of multiple-choice and constructed response modes, the optimal size of step, the usefulness of branching, machines versus programmed texts, various ways of providing or not providing knowledge of results and so on.

Most of these comparisons, recently surveyed by Schramm (1964), have failed to show significant differences between these variables, and studies which do find differences in one direction are not infrequently contradicted by other studies showing a significant result in the opposite direction. It is an axiom of statistical inference that failure to reject the null (no difference) hypothesis is not proof that no difference exists. Sampling error and lack of discrimination in measuring the dependent variable can obscure differences which really do exist. Once again one might criticize the over-general nature of the questions which have been asked. A series of multiple-choice questions may be an appropriate technique for establishing a fine discrimination, but in learning to play golf a complete response would, at some stage, appear to be necessary. Some variables, such as how much information per step, are difficult to define or rather admit of a whole series of definitions ranging from the number of words to a frame to the frequency of questions. Here again a more detailed analysis of specific teaching and learning problems seems, with the aid of hindsight, to be more appropriate.

The most generally valid conclusion which can be drawn from the first ten years of research into programmed learning is that careful analysis linked with empirical evaluation can be relied on to reap its reward.

There remain many important questions not simply to do with possible underlying learning processes. Should programmed learning come to be generally adopted, as indeed it may, some fundamental features of our educational system will have to be thought out afresh. A large number of students proceeding at their own pace alone could require a fresh outlook on school timetables, streaming, examinations and even the physical arrangement of classrooms. The question of setting up the appropriate machinery for the production and evaluation of programs has barely been considered. It is clearly not a task for the individual teacher working in his spare time. Above all, programmed learning has raised a wealth of new possibilities and problems which, in a world still starved of education and training can hardly be ignored. Some of the theories and some of the superficial characteristics of programmed learning are, no doubt, ephemeral, but a scientific approach to the analysis and synthesis of the teaching process can be regarded as a genuine and lasting development in recent psychology.

AN EXPERIMENTAL APPROACH TO DREAMS AND TELEPATHY

Montague Ullman and Stanley Krippner

chapter six

DREAMS
AND
TELEPATHY

A person sitting in a distant room and looking at a post-card of a famous painting can influence somebody else's dreams.

Does this notion seem incredible? The following study seems to show that exactly this phenomenon did occur, on several occasions, in a controlled experiment.

Ullman and Krippner's study is one of several fascinating experiments that support the existence of extrasensory phenomena. Their study was very carefully performed, and it measures up to the criteria suggested in the text as necessary to produce credible results. Here's the bind: the results, taken at face value, indicate that telepathy does work. Given these results, the authors must struggle to explain how it works. On the other hand, rejecting the conclusions requires that we provide a satisfactory explanation of how the authors got their results.

By now you know enough about probability to deal easily with the statistics that appear in this article. If you have any trouble, try writing down the items the authors are comparing. Keep in mind that the difference between pairs of items could occur by chance alone only very rarely, if at all, when the authors report a high P level.

AN EXPERIMENTAL
APPROACH TO DREAMS
AND TELEPATHY

Interest in the possible occurrence of telepathy in dreams moved from an anecdotal level (spontaneous reports of dreams purporting to depict actual events simultaneously occurring unknown to and at a distance from the dreamer) to a clinical level when reports of presumptively telepathic dreams of patients occurring in the context of the therapeutic situation began to appear in the psychiatric literature. This began in Freud's own writings and has clustered in publications appearing in the past two decades(3).

With the development of electro-physiological techniques for monitoring of dreaming during the total period of sleep it became possible for the first time to engage in a dream study in a way that freed the experimenter from a precarious reliance upon spontaneous recall. In its application to the study of the telepathic dream it became possible for the first time to transcend the limitations of the clinical approach and to introduce into the experimental design a number of factors. These included quantification—i.e., having a designated number of subjects spend a certain number of nights in the laboratory; control of variables relating to the type of target material one is trying to "send"; specification of the conditions under which the "sending" occurs—i.e., isolating the "sender" or agent from the subject; and random selection of the target picture. It was also possible to have independent judging—i.e., having outside judges who know nothing about the order in which the target pictures are chosen for a series of experimental nights attempt to both rank and rate their judgments as to which target comes closest to the material described in the transcribed record of the subject's dreams for a given night. Finally, appropriate statistical techniques for evaluating the results of the judging process were developed.

Following an earlier report(3) describing exploratory studies utilizing the application of the REM monitoring technique to the study of the tele-

Rapid eye movement
"An Experimental Approach to Dreams and Telepathy: II, Report of Three Studies," by Montague Ullman and Stanley Krippner, AMERICAN JOURNAL OF PSYCHIATRY, 126, no 9 (March 1970), 1282–1289; reprinted by permission of the authors and the publisher.

pathic dream, our laboratory has engaged in a number of follow-up studies involving repeated nights with a selected subject. Three of these studies will be summarized.

FIRST STUDY

The first experimental series to utilize a single subject was completed in 1964. The subject, a New York psychologist selected on the basis of his performance in a preliminary screening study, was paired with a staff psychologist working in the laboratory. The main hypothetical formulation stated that telepathic transfer of information from an "agent" (or sender) to a sleeping subject could be experimentally demonstrated.

Method

Seven postcard-size prints of famous paintings served as potential targets. The contents of this "pool" were unknown to the subject, but he was told that the agent would attempt to transmit an art print to him on each experimental night. This study was originally intended as a 12-night series; due to the illness of the subject, however, only seven nights were completed and the data were analyzed on that basis. The targets, randomly selected from the pool for the seven experimental nights, included "Bedtime" by Keane, "The Yellow Rabbi" by Chagall, "The Sacrament of the Last Supper" by Dali (figure 1), "School of the Dance" by Degas, "Paris From a Window" by Chagall, "Persistence of Memory" by Dali, and "Apples and Oranges" by Cezanne. An eighth target, "Boats on the Beach" by Van Gogh, was used in a preliminary screening session with the subject.

An eight-channel Model D Medcraft EEG was used to monitor spontaneous electrical brain activity and periods of rapid eye movement. All verbal communication between the subject and the experimenter at the EEG controls was mediated through an intercom system and was recorded on tape. The agent was in a room 40 feet distant, eliminating the possibility of verbal communication between agent and subject once the experiment had commenced. The agent selected an art print randomly once the subject was in bed. All target pictures had been placed in sealed envelopes so that their identity would be unknown until the agent reached his private room and opened the container.

The experimenter awakened the subject each time his EEG activity indicated that he had been dreaming and asked the subject to report his dream. As soon as the subject was awakened in the morning, a post-sleep interview was held over the intercom by the experimenter. The purpose of this interview was to obtain additional information and associative material relating to each dream. The tape was transcribed, and copies were sent to three outside judges.

Copies of the target pictures were sent to the judges, and a process of blind matching produced statistical data that could be used to evaluate the telepathy hypothesis. The instructions to the judges read, in part:

Familiarize yourself with all seven of the targets. Familiarize yourself with the first dream protocol. Rank the targets against the dream protocol, giving the rank of #1 to that target which comes closest to the dream content and the rank of #2 to that which comes next closest, etc. When you are finished, you will have seven separate rankings, one for each target. Go on to the second dream protocol. Again rank the targets, giving the rank of #1 to that target which comes closest to the dream content, etc. Repeat the procedure until all seven targets have been ranked against all seven dream protocols.

Figure 1
SACRAMENT OF THE LAST SUPPER

Salvador Dali, THE SACRAMENT OF THE LAST SUPPER (National Gallery of Art, Chester Dale Collection, Washington, D.C.).

Results

The ranks were initially evaluated by means of the Kolmogorov-Smirnov one-sample test; the rankings of one judge were not significant (Judge A: D =0.428, p <0.15) and those of two judges were statistically significant (Judge B: D =0.571, p <0.02; Judge C: D =0.571, p <0.02).

The means of the ranks of Judges A, B, and C were then subjected to two-way analysis of variance according to the Scheffé technique(2). These results were statistically significant (F =18.14, p<0.001, 1 and 34 df).

Example #1. The following excerpts illustrate the correspondences between the target and dreams when Dali's "The Sacrament of the Last Supper" was randomly selected:

FROM SUBJECT'S DREAM REPORTS: I haven't any reason to say this but somehow boats come to mind. Fishing boats. Small size fishing boats. . . . A dozen or so men pulling a fishing boat ashore right after having returned from a catch. . . . I was looking at a . . . Christmas catalog. Christmas season. . . . The picture . . . that I'm thinking about now is the doctor sitting beside a child that is ill. . . . It's one of those classical ones. . . . It's called "The Physician."

FROM SUBJECT'S ASSOCIATIONAL MATERIAL: The fisherman dream makes me think of the Mediterranean area, perhaps even some sort of Biblical time. Right now my associations are fish and the loaf, or even the feeding of the multitudes. . . . Once again I think of Christmas.

SUBJECT'S GUESS AS TO THE TARGET: "Having to do with . . . fishermen. . . . The picture of the physician."

SECOND STUDY

Two years following the completion of the first study with a single subject, a replication was attempted using the same subject-agent combination and the same judges. An eight-night series was completed in which a number of additional precautions were taken to ensure against sensory leakage. In addition, special efforts were made to involve the agent more deeply with the target material.

Method

A pool of ten postcard-size prints of famous paintings was created; each potential target picture was enclosed in an opaque envelope, which was sealed. Each envelope had a small letter in its upper corner matching a letter on a sealed box of multisensory material relating to the art print. During the first study, the nightly log of the agent indicated that he had spontaneously dramatized or acted out some of the scenes depicted in the target picture. In order to facilitate this dramatization as well as to more deeply involve the agent in the theme and mood of the target, an assistant prepared a series of the objects relating to each art print. These objects, taken in conjunction with the picture, were designed to create a multisensory involvement of the agent with the target picture. For example, Daumier's "The Barrel Organ" was accompanied by a Protestant hymnal. The other targets included "Downpour at Shono" by Hiroshige (figure 2), accompanied by a small Japanese umbrella and instructions to "take a shower" (figure 3), "Portrait of Jahangir as a Young Prince" by Bichitr (accompanied by Indian heads), "Both Members of the Club" by Bellows (accompanied by a boxing glove), the Major Pelham exhibit from the Civil War Centennial display in Richmond, Va. (accompanied by several toy soldiers), "The Descent from the Cross" by Beckmann (accompanied by a crucifix), "Interior of the Synagogue" by Katz (accompanied by candles and matches), and "Advice to a Young Artist" by Daumier (accompanied by water colors, a brush, and canvas).

Figure 2
DOWNPOUR AT SHONO

Hiroshige, DOWNPOUR AT SHONO (Tudor Publishing Company, New York, N.Y.)

During each experimental night the subject was sleeping in a darkened sleep room; the agent was situated in a suite 96 feet distant. Upon arriving in his suite, the agent opened the randomly selected envelope and the box containing the multisensory materials. He acted out the instructions in the box and utilized the multisensory materials in conjunction with the target picture, attempting to influence the subject's dreams.

After the protocols for all eight experimental nights had been collected and transcribed, three outside judges rated each of the 64 possible target-protocol pairs. These 64 pairs were presented to each judge in a different random order; eight judgings were presented at a time so that the "sitting" effect could be evaluated as well as the target effect, the experimental night effect, and the telepathy effect. A Latin-square analysis of variance was utilized to evaluate the data. The judging sheet for each target-protocol pair contained a 100-unit scale and read, in part, "Color the space that represents, in your judgment, the correspondence between target material and protocol content".

Results

Means of the three judges' ratings were entered in the analysis of variance matrix:[1] the eight actual target-protocol combinations were compared with the 56 incorrect target-protocol pairs. The resulting data were statistically significant (F $=6.43$, p <0.001, 7 and 21 df).[2] Therefore the telepathy hypothesis was confirmed and the results of the previous study were replicated.

Example #2. When Hiroshige's "Downpour at Shono" was randomly selected, the agent stood in a shower (located in his suite) under a small Japanese umbrella. The following excerpts demonstrate the type of target-protocol correspondences obtained.

FROM SUBJECT'S DREAM REPORTS: It's as though I was doing some drawing. . . . I had the feeling as though it were in a down position, like a low table. Down on the floor. Seems that's what I meant by "down" Something about an Oriental man. . . . Walking with someone on the street. Raining. . . .

FROM SUBJECT'S ASSOCIATIONAL MATERIAL: The fountain makes me think of pictures and scenes I've seen of Rome. . . . They have so many fountains. . . . I remember talking about fountains being renewing of life. . . . I was walking on the street. It seemed it was raining a little bit. . . . Of course, it was raining. . . .

SUBJECT'S GUESS AS TO THE TARGET: In terms of just standing

---

[1] An analysis of variance matrix is very complicated. For your purposes all you need to understand is the P level.

[2] Ignore F and df.

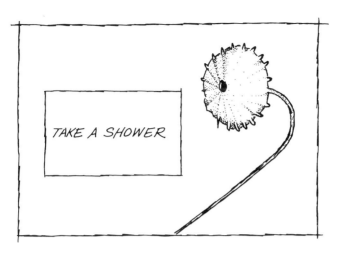

Figure 3
MULTISENSORY MATERIALS FOR TARGET 2

out, I would say the fountain. . . . For some reason I'm going to say that it had something to do with . . . fountains or something. . . . Fountain. Maybe water.

Supplementary Analysis. A frequent criticism of the first study centered around the allegation that dreams are so ambiguous that virtually any picture would correspond in some way to a dream transcript. This argument can be effectively countered by pointing out that the judges worked blind and that they matched each of the eight targets against each of the eight transcripts. Nevertheless, critics of the first study claimed that a "control judging" should have been attempted in which pictures that were not in the target pool were matched against the dream transcripts.

For the second study, a thorough check of this allegation was made. A fourth judge (Judge D) was given copies of the eight transcripts for the second study as well as the eight targets used for that study, the seven targets used for the first study, and a target used for a screening session. The 16 targets were paired with all eight protocols, producing 128 target-protocol combinations. These were judged by means of the 100-unit rating scale described previously.

Before Judge D attempted the 128 ratings, eight target-protocol combinations were randomly assigned by a consulting statistician using the eight "control" targets. "The Yellow Rabbi" became the control target for night one, "Persistence of Memory" for night two, "Apples and Oranges" for night three, "Bedtime" for night four, "Boats on the Beach" for night five, "The Sacrament of the Last Supper" for night six, "School of the Dance" for night seven, and "Paris From a Window" for night eight.

Upon completion of this judging process, ratings for the "correct" and the control target-protocol combinations were placed in separate analysis of variance matrices and were evaluated using the Scheffé technique(2). The "correct" target-protocol combinations received higher ratings from Judge D than did all other combinations in the matrix. These data were statistically significant (F =8.11, p <0.01, 8 and 64 df). The control combinations did not yield significant data (F =0.71).[3] Therefore, the allegation that significant data can be obtained from chance target-protocol combinations was not demonstrated.

In addition to the supplementary analysis, a number of special precautions were taken in this study to ensure that no sensory clues relating to the target could reach the subject:

1. The two rooms used to house the subject and agent were at opposite ends of the building and were 96 feet apart, separated by two bends in a corridor and three doors.

2. The agent remained in his suite for the entire night. The subject remained in his room for the entire night, with the exception of occasional visits to the nearby washroom. Thus, communication from the agent to the subject was impossible due to their physical location.

3. The range of target material was unknown to any of the individuals present at the experiments. The targets and the multisensory material had been prepared by staff members who were never present on any of the experimental nights.

THIRD STUDY

Method

For this eight-night series, the procedure outlined for the second study was followed with certain modifications. The subject, a psychologist on the staff of an out-of-state university, was selected on the basis of successful performances in a telepathy experiment at another dream laboratory. He was allowed to select his own agent from the Maimonides staff, having been introduced to several staff members during a day's visit. Over the course of the eight-night study, two female agents and one male agent were utilized.

A total of several dozen target pictures was prepared. Eight were randomly chosen on each experimental night by the agent, who then selected at random one of the eight as his target picture. The target pictures actually utilized included "The Discovery of America by Christopher

[3]He is saying that *P* would not be significant.

Figure 4
GANGSTER FUNERAL

Jack Levine, GANGSTER FUNERAL (Collection Whitney Museum of American Art, New York, N.Y.)

Columbus" by Dali, "The Wine Taster" by Vermeer, "The Repast of the Lion" by Rousseau, "Kathak Dancing Girls" by an unknown Indian artist, "The Enigma of Fate" by De Chirico, "Trees and Houses" by Cezanne, "Gangster Funeral" by Levine (figure 4), and "Man with Arrows and Companions" by Bichitr.

The introduction into the experimental design of a different target pool for each session enabled the subject, a psychologist, to do his own judging each morning. He followed the ranking procedure previously described.

It was decided in advance to consider as "hits" all correct target pictures that had been ranked as #1, #2, #3, or #4, and to regard as "misses" all pictures that had been ranked as #5, #6, #7, or #8. Additional judging, utilizing the ranking technique, was accomplished by Judge D.

Following the subject's judging, he was told the correct target by the agent. The subject was then interviewed by a staff psychiatrist. This interview centered around the dreams and associational material of the subject as well as around the agent's written associations to the target picture.

Results

The results of the subject's rankings were assessed by the binomial method. When the ranks were inspected, there were eight "hits" and no "misses." This distribution is significant at the 0.004 level.

The rankings of Judge D were assessed by the binomial method. Five direct correspondences (i.e., ranks of #1) were obtained; this is significant at the 0.001 level.

An analysis of the motivational factors that came into focus during the psychiatric interview suggested that the telepathic effect was linked to sexual and aggressive content. In the example that follows the subject revealed guilt about sexual fantasies concerning the agent—an attractive female social worker. The guilt involved the psychiatric interviewer (Dr. Ullman) as a superego figure who appeared in the dream's reference to "security police."

Example #3. Levine's "Gangster Funeral" was used on a night when the following material was collected:

FROM SUBJECT'S DREAM REPORTS: There was a conversation going on at a table between myself and two other male characters. . . . One of them was Fred. . . . I was sort of joshing or kidding him about the clothing that he was wearing. He had on a rather garish suit. . . . It seems as if he had on a vest which was not exactly matching the suit. . . . And it seems as if I had to talk to the police, the security police. . . . It seemed like there were maybe six people there . . . and this one guy who seemed to be lying down on the bed was saying something about, "this means he has a dirty mouth."

FROM SUBJECT'S ASSOCIATIONAL MATERIAL: . . . He had on this loud, garish, woolen suit with a vest that didn't quite match. . . . It seems I had to report into the security police or something . . . but for some reason I had to check in with the security police. I think the association very clearly is Monte[4] as security police. . . . Lying over on the couch

[4]Dr. Ullman.

fairly close to me there was some guy who said, "Let's play the dirty record. . . . Something about inpatient service . . . and that they were running it much more like a jail or a prison . . . but he was pleased about it. Almost seemed to be boasting about it—the tough methods that they were using in the prison.

SUBJECT'S GUESS AS TO THE TARGET: My guess would be that . . . the target picture had a great deal of rich textual quality to it . . . I would say people have to be in it because this was a very people-dominated night from beginning to end. There was never any episode that did not involve people. . . . Also, it *seemed* as if there was a lot of emphasis on sitting postures. . . .

DISCUSSION

If our findings are interpreted as supporting the idea that extrasensory effects can be made to appear in dreams on a greater than chance basis— and we see no other interpretation at the present time—they raise many questions and provide few answers. The demonstration either that information transfer can occur through as yet unidentified sensory channels or that a resonance effect can be induced linking, in remarkably congruent ways, the brain activity of two individuals in sensory isolation from each other would give some credence to at least a proportion of the many spontaneous and anecdotal accounts of such happenings. More important, however, would be the open question of just how much communication of this kind does gain access to dream consciousness under normal conditions.

It is obvious that the phenomenon we are tracking remains very elusive. Our studies suggest that it is a focused effect, i.e., that it occurs between a designated agent and percipient rather than capriciously. This is by no means exclusively so, and the full range of adventitious or capricious effects is an unknown quantity. Two other leads have emerged. One is that not everyone has the same power acting as agent; the other that not everyone has the same power acting as subject. The idea of a field effect in which the key variables are linked to the subject-agent interaction suggests itself. We have taken a few beginning steps in the direction of exploring this possibility. In the last series completed the subject-agent relationship was structured on the basis of personal selection and rapport, while the emotional climate in which the experiment took place was explored between subject and agent in a dynamically oriented interview situation on the morning following the experimental night. Approaching it in this fashion, we highlight certain immediate here-and-now emotional linkages. We are also interested in the possible influence of constitutional and developmental linkages as these might occur if the pairing of subject and agent were to take place on the basis of kinship. In this connection, working with identical twins might be helpful.

Can further psychological manipulation of either subject or agent or both further enhance the effect? Our present design is limited to generating a spontaneous altered state of consciousness in the subject. What would happen if we also generated an altered state in the agent through hypnosis or by somehow linking the target to the dreaming consciousness of the agent? We are beginning to test out some of these ideas in a pilot fashion.

In an effort to further define subject-agent interaction it might be fruitful to explore the possible relevance of differing or congruent perceptual styles. Along the dimension of field dependency, for example, what might be the best combination of subject and agent?

The importance of the target material itself and the degree of involvement of the agent in the target has received emphasis in the successful results obtained by Moss and Gengerelli(1) when target material was selected with a view to eliciting sharp and dramatic affective responses in the agent. We have begun to make more use of multisensory stimuli. The visual impact of the target picture is reinforced by presenting the agent with an array of objects and tasks, all of which are related to the theme of the picture but which invoke the use of other sensory modalities.

Further studies are needed to assess the relative facilitating influence of dream consciousness compared with the kind of cognitive recall that can be obtained from other stages of sleep. We have some data to suggest that hypnagogic and hypnopompic states are as favorable to the occurrence of paranormal effects as the dream state itself.

At this point in time we find ourselves in a kind of parapsychological "Catch 22." In order to test out some of the above ideas we must continue to get an identifiable yield of paranormal data. In order to get a continuing yield of paranormal data we must be able to identify and control the significant variables. This dilemma is not new to parapsychology. What makes for some optimism in connection with our own approach is the hope that, with the vast amount of dream research being carried out currently, replication of our results may be forthcoming from other laboratories.

REFERENCES

1. Moss, T., and Gengerelli, J. A.: Telepathy and Emotional Stimuli: A Controlled Experiment, J. Abnorm. Psychol. 72:341–348, 1967.

2. Scheffé, H.: The Analysis of Variance. New York: John Wiley & Sons, 1955, chap. 10.
3. Ullman, M.: An Experimental Approach to Dreams and Telepathy, Arch. Gen. Psychiat. 14:605–613, 1966.

METHODS OF STUDYING SLEEP
Ian Oswald

chapter seven

SLEEP

Few things are more personal than sleeping habits. Most people are accustomed to sleeping each night in the same bed, in the same room, with curtains and ventilation adjusted to their liking. It's easy to imagine the kinds of problems an experimenter encounters when he seeks to explore people's sleeping habits.

The next study does just that. Not only are the experimenter's conclusions about sleep intriguing in themselves; he also reveals a lot about experimental methods and about the physiological mechanisms of sleep. And last but not least, you get the benefit of both his knowledge and his clarity: a well-known experimenter in the area of sleep, Oswald is also an excellent writer.

METHODS OF
STUDYING SLEEP

Suppose a pharmaceutical firm produces a new drug which it thinks will have hypnotic (i.e., sleep promoting) properties. First, the drug will be given to animals in varying doses. If it looks promising the day will arrive when rigorous testing on humans must begin, and the smallest dose capable of inducing and maintaining sleep must be determined. A rough guide to the latter will be provided by the dose which had been found suitable for the animals, allowance being made for the difference in body weight. Then a carefully designed trial must be embarked upon. Let us call the new drug X, and suppose that it has been decided to try out the effectiveness of a 100-milligram dose, and to compare this with the effect of a standard dose of some well-tried drug, B.

Some tablets, probably sugar-coated and capable of being easily swallowed whole, must be prepared. They must all look alike and taste alike. One batch will contain the drug B, another batch will contain 100 milligrams each of X, and a further batch will contain nothing but milk-sugar. Then either volunteers or, perhaps, persons who suffer from insomnia must be collected and the detailed design of an experiment worked out in order to discover how each kind of tablet affects their sleep. Suppose each person came and slept in a laboratory where one could measure his sleep, and suppose each came on three nights only. If then he got the milk-sugar tablet on the first night, drug B on the second night, and drug X thereafter, the results, whatever they were, would probably be meaningless. He might have slept least well on the first night, not because the sugar tablets were less effective than, say, drug X, but because he got the sugar tablet on the first night in a strange bed when he was suffering from apprehension about the whole business. He might have slept more deeply the second night because he was exhausted after too little sleep the previous night. Another complication may arise because, if a drug alters the pattern of sleep one night, on the next night, even though that drug has left the body, sleep can be affected because of a swing towards a reverse pattern. A sort of compensation

From SLEEP, *by Ian Oswald (London: Penguin Books, 1966), pp. 15–40; reprinted by permission of Penguin Books Ltd.*

can arise. So that if drug X were always given the night after drug B, some spurious notions about the action of X might arise through after-effects attributable to B.

Certainly it is complicated. Even when you have got your results and there appears to be some difference between sleep after 100 mg of X and sleep after milk-sugar, you have got to carry out calculations to determine what are the chances of the differences you have observed being purely fortuitous. If your statistical calculations show that the difference might have arisen through chance alone less than once in a hundred times, then you can infer that the difference is probably a genuine one. But no matter how clever and impressive the statistical calculations, they can never compensate for poor design of the experiment itself. It is always worth taking trouble over the planning and design of an experiment. Generally it pays to make a small 'pilot' study first, the results of which are not used in the end; to gain a little practical experience of what you had planned can reveal all sorts of snags. Then one can try and eliminate the snags before starting one's more elaborate study.

An experimental method which is sometimes adopted is to use a design like that shown below, where $S =$ milk-sugar tablets; $B =$ well-tried drug B tablets; $X100 = 100$ mg of new drug X tablets.

A design of this kind would involve at least six persons, or some multiple of six. You will see, for example, that each variety of tablets would be handicapped equally by being used on the first night. Furthermore, drug B would follow milk-sugar just as often as sugar would follow B, and so on. One would hope that spurious components in the results of the study which were really attributable to the *order* of presentation of the different tablets would cancel one another out.

A trial of this kind can in fact always be executed according to a number of alternative designs or methods, each having some advantages and disadvantages. A disadvantage of the foregoing example is that probably the laboratory could not handle all six persons on the same night. It might only be possible to manage one per week. This might introduce at least one additional uncertain factor, the weather. If the first man came in the spring and the last in the summer, the summer testees might have difficulty in falling asleep because of heat and humidity, or more noisy road traffic, and this might affect the tablet order then in use more than

Volunteer		Nights	
Number	*1st*	*2nd*	*3rd*
1	S	B	X100
2	S	X100	B
3	B	X100	S
4	B	S	X100
5	X100	B	S
6	X100	S	B

some preceding tablet order—one could not assume that it would not. On the other hand, if one person came every week, he could at least use the same bed, wheras if all came on the same night, some beds might be softer than others. But then again the laundry might have changed its practice of starching the sheets over the months and this just might affect sleep—and so on. Perhaps no design can be perfect!

MEASURING SLEEP

Throughout the preceding part of this chapter, I have referred to a hypothetical investigation for comparing sleep under the influence of different factors, namely, different drugs. How should sleep be compared? One can rely simply upon a subjective estimate, by asking each individual at breakfast-time whether he thinks he slept well, slept badly, or slept indifferently. If each says he slept 'well' after one sort of tablet, and if each says he slept 'badly' after another, then clearly the pharmaceutical firm will be pleased or disappointed depending on which of the tablets was their new one. A simple study of this kind is the most necessary for many medical purposes. But if we want objective evidence about their sleep—how long they took to drop off, how long they slept, how often and when they awoke in the night, and what sort or quality of sleep it was—then we must find some criterion of the presence or absence of sleep and some method of measurement. This becomes even more important if we wish to conduct research into the fundamental nature of sleep.

One convenient measure that has often been used is provided by the number of times the individual moves in the night. Immobility is an obvious sign of sleep. A convenient method is to attach a sensitive microphone to the central bed springs. Any movement of the bed will be picked up by the microphone. A cable from it can be run to another room. The tiny electro-magnetic disturbances created can be amplified and then recorded by some form of moving pen writing on paper which is slowly, steadily and automatically moved beneath it. In the morning, the experimenter can come along and count the number of large movements or groups of movements which occurred between specified hours.

As an example of this, at Edinburgh we compared the sleep of six mentally-ill patients and six normal volunteers of the same age and sex. Between 1.30 a.m. and 5.30 a.m., the normal people moved on average forty times, whereas the patients moved on average sixty-nine times, confirming their own claim that they suffered from insomnia. When the nights on which they received a genuine sleeping pill were compared with nights on which only dummy pills were given, the patients were found to have made, on average, five times as many movements per hour under the latter circumstances.

An entirely different approach requires decisions at certain fixed intervals, say every thirty minutes, about whether the person is asleep or awake. This carries the assumption that the difference between the two states is a sharp one. Obviously, a group of persons suffering from insomnia would be expected to score highly on number-of-times-awake compared with number-of-times-asleep. But how shall we decide whether a person is awake or asleep? He might just be keeping still with his eyes closed. Unless he is snoring, simple observation is not good enough. One method that has been used to provide a criterion of being awake, or, in a modified form, a criterion of the depth of sleep, is that which involves some stimulus to which the sleeper has been asked to respond.

A small pebble dropped from a height of three feet on to the centre of a gong can serve as stimulus. If the individual responds to the noise, as requested earlier in the evening, by opening his eyes, then one may infer that he was either awake, or at least sleeping less deeply before the noise than if he remains undisturbed. In modern times more sophisticated techniques are available. A loudspeaker by the bed can easily provide a short musical note of fixed loudness and the experimenter can arrange an automatic device to provide the noise so that he himself can go off to bed. Instead of being there to watch the sleeper opening his eyes, the experimenter can arrange an automatic device to make a record every time a small switch is pressed by the unfortunate individual who is trying to sleep.

The study of sleep has leaped forward in the last fifteen years owing to the development of a new tool. If one looks back over the history of biology one can see again and again how the really major advances followed upon the development of some new technique, some new apparatus. In the last century, the development of first-rate optical microscopes had a profound influence upon our understanding of the function as well as the structure of living organisms, including, of course, bacteria. In this century the electron microscope is making possible revolutionary advances in the study of the chromosomes, those minute structures which carry the genetic blueprints of life. Equally, the development of reliable and highly sensitive electronic devices for telling us about the electrical activity of the brain has led to some quite new ideas about sleep and dreaming.

THE BRAIN WAVES

If you take a piece of wire and attach one end to one terminal of an electric battery, then lightly flick the other end of the wire across the other battery terminal, you will hear a little crackle and see a tiny spark which tell you electricity has flowed. It flowed because there was *difference of electrical potential* between the two battery terminals. This potential difference built into an ordinary torch battery is large by biological standards. It is present because of chemical interaction within the battery. Living cells contain interacting chemicals also and they too produce tiny differences of electrical potential.

The brain is composed of a countless number of individual cells. From the brain nervous messages can pass directly or indirectly to control the function of the entire body, and certain forms of variation in these nervous messages are reflected in our state of activity: whether that of wakefulness or sleep.

If an electrical connexion, usually involving a little damp, salty jelly, is made between the scalp and two small silver discs, or electrodes, placed thereon at some distance from one another, tiny moment-to-moment fluctuations of electrical potential difference between the two points on the scalp can be demonstrated. These tiny fluctuations of potential differences were first discovered by Richard Caton, a man of diverse gifts and sometime Lord Mayor of Liverpool. He used rabbits and monkeys, and in 1875 presented to a meeting of the British Medical Association in Edinburgh the results of his research, including the effect upon the brain's electrical activity of a bright light shining into the rabbit's eyes. Some fifty years later, the existence of similar electrical potentials over the human brain was established by an Austrian psychiatrist, Hans Berger of Jena.

The tiny fluctuations of potential difference between the electrodes on the scalp can be recorded on paper. If you were to take again your electric battery, and if you joined it by your wire to a galvanometer, and led a wire from the other galvanometer terminal to the opposite terminal of the battery, and if you touched that terminal with the wire, took it off again, on and off, on and off, on and off, then the needle of your galvanometer would swing to and fro, to and fro, to and fro. If you arranged to run a little ink out of the tip of the needle and made it write upon paper moving steadily beneath it, then you would get a wavy ink line which would form a record of the needle's excursions. It would also form a record of the fluctuations of potential difference between the two wires as you took one on and off its battery terminal. Similarly, a wavy ink line can serve as a record of brain electrical activity. A machine called an electroencephalograph is used. It is really just a highly sensitive galvanometer, a kind of electronic voltmeter with a needle or pen for writing out the brain waves or electroencephalogram (EEG for short). Generally, several pens are used side by side, and simultaneously, to write out the electrical activity from various parts of the scalp or from elsewhere on the body at the same time.

While the eyes are closed during relaxed wakefulness, the EEG from the back of the human head reveals rhythms at about 10 ripples (or cycles) per second. This is the so-called alpha rhythm (Figure 1). It disappears if the eyes are opened, or if the individual is suddenly shouted at, or given a difficult problem to work out. It also disappears if he becomes sleepy (Figure 1). The alpha rhythm is an indication that the brain is functioning at one particular level of efficiency, alertness or 'vigilance'. When the eyes are opened or a problem undertaken, the alpha rhythm vanishes because of a shift to a higher level of alertness on the part of the brain. When the alpha rhythm is lost in drowsiness, the brain is functioning at a lower level of effectiveness. As drowsiness passes into sleep, so the EEG waves become larger and slower, so that when they are very large and slow, with waves at 1–3 cycles per second, sleep is profound. Brief bursts of faster waves are generally mixed in with these slow waves, and, unlike the alpha rhythm, are especially prominent in recordings from the front of the head. They are an important and characteristic feature of the EEG of sleep and are known as sleep 'spindles' (Figure 1).

The EEG provides both the most sensitive index we have of the presence or absence of sleep, and one measure of the kind of sleep. By its use, one can, to within a minute or two, state how many minutes a man or woman slept, so gaining a delicate tool for use, for example, in comparing one hypnotic drug with another. It is a much more sensitive tool than that provided by measuring the number of body movements. In the comparison (see p. 107) of normal volunteers and patients troubled by insomnia, between 1.30 A.M. and 5.30 A.M., the former were awake on average twenty-three minutes, the latter seventy-six minutes. The difference was much more consistent among the different individuals than the difference in number-of-times-moved, and statistical calculations showed the EEG results to be significant in the sense that the likelihood of the observed difference being due to chance was less than one in a hundred.

BRAIN MECHANISMS

The brain is encased within the skull, a hard and unyielding container. If a tumour begins to grow, if bleeding occurs, or if a part of the brain becomes inflamed and swollen because of infection, there is little room to spare. In consequence, the brain will get squashed and pushed out of shape. The space inside the skull is divided up into compartments by tough, living, tent-like flaps which are also unyielding. This means that if, because of a tumour, the brain gets squashed, it will not be squashed to a uniform extent throughout. Particular zones of the brain will get more compressed than others, according to which compartment contains

ALPHA RHYTHM - AWAKE

IRREGULAR LITTLE SLOW WAVES - DROWSY

BIG SLOW WAVES AND SPINDLES - ASLEEP

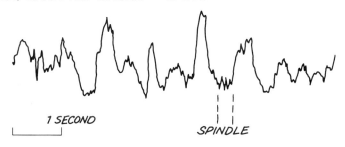

1 SECOND

SPINDLE

Figure 1
THE APPEARANCE OF THE ELECTROENCEPHALOGRAM (EEG). THE BRAIN
WAVES DURING WAKEFULNESS, DROWSINESS AND SLEEP.

the growing tumour. Obviously, if part of the brain is squashed, it cannot function properly.

It was noticed by brain surgeons that some parts of the brain, notably
the cerebral cortex or grey matter, could be badly damaged without
causing loss of consciousness. On the other hand, when quite small parts
lower down in the brain, within the 'brain-stem' (Figure 2), were slightly
squashed, the patients almost always were unconscious. Furthermore, in
an epidemic illness, caused by a virus and called *encephalitis lethargica*,
or sleeping sickness, which swept the world just after the First World
War, the victims were overwhelmed by persistent sleepiness and tended
to become wholly unrousable prior to death. Yet when the brains of those
who died were examined at post-mortem, it was not the grey matter or

cerebral cortex where inflammation was found. It was the brain-stem which was severely inflamed.

It, therefore, seemed that sleepiness and loss of consciousness resulted especially from impaired functioning of the brain-stem. A girl was admitted to a brain surgery hospital at Oxford in an unconscious state. Her EEG resembled that of deep sleep. It was discovered that within her upper brain-stem there was a cyst, a fluid-filled tumour. The surgeon inserted a hollow needle into the cyst and sucked out the fluid so that it collapsed (just as a grape would collapse if you sucked out its soft contents). The pressure on the surrounding normal brain tissues was thus relieved. The girl sat up and talked, apparently restored to health. Unfortunately, the fluid reformed and the cyst pressed again upon its surroundings. Again the fluid was withdrawn through a needle, again she revived, but final cure could not be achieved. The unhappy story nevertheless provides a dramatic illustration of how the welfare of a crucial part of the brain exerted a controlling influence upon consciousness. Does it mean that there is a master zone within the brain-stem for controlling sleep and consciousness?

While human diseases, 'nature's experiments', can teach a great deal to the doctor prepared to ponder upon the significance of what he sees in his patients, for a fuller understanding, deliberate, systematic experiments are necessary. Obviously, these cannot always be performed upon man and it is necessary to use animals.

There are, unfortunately, people who conduct hysterical campaigns bolstered by misleading, sentimental stories which evade the basic issues, in order to further the cause of 'antivivisection', as they call it. These people, who remain blind to millions suffering from disease, and who forget the other millions who are today alive and healthy, instead of dead or sick, thanks to the advances of medical knowledge in the last thirty years (penicillin and anti-diphtheria inoculation, for example), try to prevent all experiments, no matter how simple, which involve animals. They speak of 'torture' of animals by scientists even when referring, for instance, to small and harmless injections. Of course it hurts to have an injection. Most of us know that. But it is not 'torture'. I have carried out experiments for many years upon humans, often involving such things as moderate electric shocks. It was far easier to use human volunteers than face a shrieking charge of 'torture' from the sort of people who send protests to Russia and the U.S.A. when mice, dogs or monkeys are sent into space to find out if humans too could live there.

In fact, the 'poor, dumb animals' upon which developing medical science depends, often delight in the extra attention they receive through experiments. Unless they are happy, they are not healthy. Only healthy animals are of use for experiments.

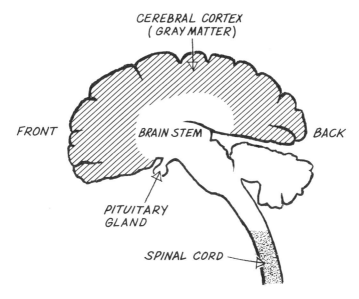

CEREBRAL CORTEX
(GRAY MATTER)

FRONT

BRAIN STEM

BACK

PITUITARY
GLAND

SPINAL CORD

Figure 2

THE CEREBRAL CORTEX
The diagram shows the cerebral cortex (which is actually present in the form of two large 'hemispheres,' left and right) and below it the 'brain stem,' which, at its lower end, is continuous with the spinal cord. The cerebral hemispheres and brain stem are located within the skull. The spinal cord extends down inside a bony canal within the vertebrae which make up the spinal column of the back.

Experiments into the brain mechanism of sleep have mainly involved cats. A Belgian physiologist, F. Bremer, in the 1930s, made a cut right through the upper brain-stem. The animal remained alive but quite inert, unreactive to smells and obviously unconscious. The pupils of the eyes were very small, as is the case during sleep, and the EEG resembled that of sleep. The brain in this condition he called the *cerveau isolé* or isolated fore-brain preparation (Figure 3). In other cats, the cut across the brain was made at its lower end, about where the spinal cord begins. This was the *encéphale isolé* (Figure 3) or whole-brain preparation. It proved very different from the *cerveau isolé*. In the *encéphale isolé*, periods of the kind of EEG normally associated with wakefulness, dilated pupils and other characteristics of what might be called 'front-end' wakefulness alternated with sleep-like periods.

What was the essential difference between these brain preparations? The fact that in one the cerebral cortex or grey matter was permanently cut off from nervous connexion with the greater part of the brain-stem,

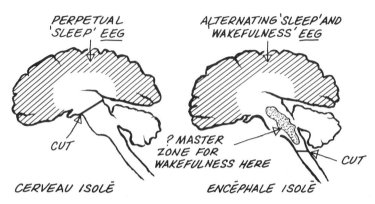

PERPETUAL 'SLEEP' EEG

ALTERNATING 'SLEEP' AND WAKEFULNESS' EEG

CUT

? MASTER ZONE FOR WAKEFULNESS HERE

CUT

CERVEAU ISOLÉ

ENCÉPHALE ISOLÉ

Figure 3
BREMER'S ENCÉPHALE ISOLÉ AND CERVEAU ISOLÉ.

If the connexion between cerebral cortex and brain-stem was cut, EEG signs of wakefulness were never seen in the cortex. Bremer supposd this was caused by reduction of input from sense organs. Later the view prevailed that the explanation lay in a master zone for controlling sleep and wakefulness located in the brain-stem.

wherein, we have already tentatively concluded, a master zone for the control of wakefulness and sleep could be presumed to lie. In the other preparation, the *encéphale isolé*, the cerebral cortex was not cut off from that master zone, and the alternating periods of sleep and wakefulness signs could be interpreted as attempts by that master zone to continue its customary regulation of the rhythm of life.

In the late 1940s an Italian physiologist, Guiseppe Moruzzi, was working in the U.S.A. with H. W. Magoun. They inserted fine wires into the central core of the brain-stem in *encéphale isolé* preparations. The wires were insulated except at their tips. When the *encéphale isolé* preparations were 'asleep', they passed small electrical pulses through the needle tips in an attempt to stimulate the near-by nervous tissue (a common experimental technique of physiologists). They succeeded. The preparations promptly 'woke up', the EEG rhythms changing abruptly from the big, slow waves of 'sleep' to the rapid waves of 'wakefulness'.

Subsequent experimenters, using monkeys as well as cats, have inserted similar fine wires into the otherwise normal brains of healthy animals. (I may add that such procedures are carried out under anaesthesia, involve no great discomfort, and now, having been shown to be safe by animal experiments, are sometimes done on human beings for treatment purposes.) The wires ended at terminals fixed to the scalp. A few days passed, giving time for the animals to recover fully from the operation. Then long, fine cables were attached to the terminals, leaving the animal still freely able to roam around its cage. When later the animal fell into a normal sleep, stimulating electrical pulses were passed into the brain-stem of the intact brain, just as Moruzzi and Magoun had passed them into the *encéphale isolé*. This time it was not a matter of apparent 'sleep' passing into apparent 'wakefulness' but of obvious natural sleep being superseded by very obvious natural wakefulness and activity on the part of the intact animal. Stimulating the central core of the brain-stem caused a transition from sleep to wakefulness.

Instead of stimulating the brain electrically through needles inserted into it, the experimenters could just as readily have caused awakening by more natural stimulants, such as a shout or a tug on the tail. Such procedures would have stimulated sense organs. Sense organs are known to pass information to the brain in the form of small electrical impulses passing along from the periphery. Could it be that those impulses travel to the central core of the brain-stem and by an action at that site provoke awakening?

It was known that, via relays, the impulses actually went to the cerebral cortex. Might they go to both destinations? The answer could not be found through the sort of philosophical speculation beloved by our forefathers: only systematic experiment could reveal the truth. The study of 'evoked potentials' provided the answer.

We have already seen how an electroencephalograph machine can pick up and amplify tiny electrical potentials from nervous tissue. A cathode ray oscillograph can do the same. If electrodes connected to either machine are placed upon a nerve travelling up the leg, and if then a sudden stimulus such as a bang on the big toe is given, a moment later there is a sudden, brief potential change at the recording point higher up the body. It is the 'evoked potential'. With further electrodes recording the activity of the cerebral cortex, an 'evoked potential' is found at the cortex too, a fraction of a second after it was present in the nerve lower down the body (Figure 4). Nerve messages travel fast. In practice, the big toe would get bruised, so that small, sharp electric shocks either to the skin or directly to the sensory nerve are generally used in both human and animal studies. On the other hand, the special sense organs can be stimulated in ways appropriate to them—a flash of bright light before the eyes, a loud click near the ear. Evoked potentials always follow in the nerves and brain.

Fine wires were therefore inserted into the central core of the brain-stem, into the *reticular formation*, as it is called on account of its appearance under a microscope. They were not for stimulating, but for recording evoked potentials. Others were inserted through the skull onto various zones of the cerebral cortex. An electric shock to the foot was followed by an evoked response in the cortex and in the brain-stem

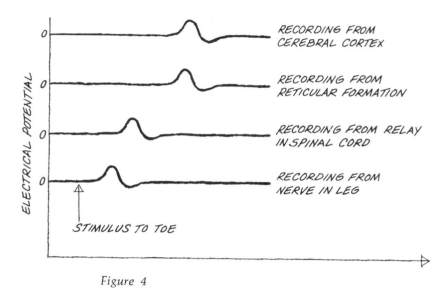

Figure 4

The electrical 'evoked potential' recorded at different points on its upward path to the brain. Notice that the nerve message from the peripheral sense organs reach both cortex and reticular formation.

reticular formation. A loud click by evoked responses in the part of the cortex which is specially concerned with hearing and in the reticular formation. A bright flash of light was followed by an evoked potential in the rear part of the brain, which subserves especially visual function, and, once more, in the reticular formation. So it gradually became established that all the main sensory paths from sense organs give off branches or 'collateral afferents' which turn off into the reticular formation while the main path continues, via relays, to the cortex. Once the impulses arrive in the reticular formation they probably lose any characteristics which distinguish their origin, they are all equally grist to the mill, fuel for the fires which keep the reticular formation excited. A flash of light and a shock to the foot applied at the same time do not give an extra large evoked potential in the reticular formation, the pair are submerged into a single potential which does not differ from that which would have been produced by either alone.

So here is a working hypothesis. All sense organs, when stimulated, send impulses to the brain, and always impulses branch off to excite the reticular formation, the master zone for the control of wakefulness, so that the sleeping animal becomes an awake animal. But how to confirm this? After all, the impulses go on to the cortex, could it not be these that cause awakening?

This question was answered by a group of research workers in Los Angeles. They took two groups of cats, anaesthetized them, and operated on their brains—it sounds easy, put like that, but actually involves great skill and patience. In one group, let us call it group *A*, they destroyed the upper reticular formation, taking great care not to damage the main sensory pathways from sense organs to cerebral cortex. In the other group, group *B*, they left the reticular formation intact but cut the main sensory pathways to the cortex *after* the collateral afferents to the reticular formation had branched off. The anaesthetic soon wore off and, as the days passed, there was revealed a striking difference between the two groups of cats. Group *A* cats lay in perpetual sleep, with the usual sleep EEG; the sense organs still sent impulses to the cortex but, without the benefit of a functioning reticular formation, the cats remained in oblivion. Group *B* cats, with the reticular formation intact and open to excitement via the collateral afferents, slept from time to time. A noise would awaken them; at other times they wakened spontaneously and roamed around, obviously fully awake even though a little unsure of the world.

The essential conclusions that have arisen out of all this work by men of diverse countries, are depicted in Figure 5. All the great sensory paths to the brain give off collateral afferents to the reticular formation, along which impulses pass to help keep the reticular formation in a state of, as it were, effervescent excitement in which it gives off 'non-specific' impulses—invigorating or vitalizing impulses—which pass not only upwards to the cortex but also downwards to the spinal cord. The cortex and the spinal cord are thereby pepped-up, are more able to respond efficiently—incoming information can be competently dealt with, so leading to perception and appropriate action. The muscles of the body are toned up, the mind is eagerly receptive.

The reticular formation is conceived of as a zone of nervous tissue, the excitement of which periodically undergoes both abrupt and gradual variations. In consequence, the upflow of non-specific impulses, which keep the grey matter pepped up, undergoes continual variations in intensity. It is the presence of an efficiently working cortex which makes possible 'clever' activity, learned activity, the weighing of past with present evidence, and a rational decision to embark upon, and the power to execute, skilled behaviour. Without the upflow from the reticular formation the cortex cannot serve these purposes. The intensity of the upflow can vary from very high levels, through moderate, to very low levels. A person can be in a state of efficient wide-awakeness, a state of inefficient drowsiness, or a slumbering state of total ineffectiveness. In the first, he may be capable of witty repartee, in the second of some mumbled indication of his latent powers, in the third of only oblivious snoring.

It soon became realized that quite a number of things help to keep the

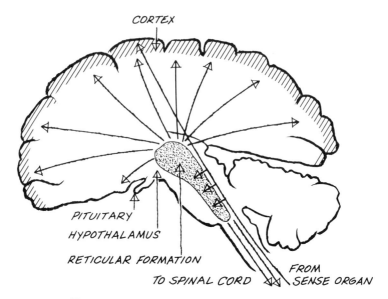

Figure 5

A diagram which represents the reticular formation being excited by impulses from sense organs via branches or 'collaterals' from the main traditional pathways to the brain. The excited reticular formation gives off streams of non-specific impulses which, for example, ascend to the cortex to increase its efficiency.

reticular formation excited. Whenever a sense organ is stimulated, nerve messages pass from it to the brain, some of them going to the reticular formation. If the stimulus is a particularly violent one, the reticular formation suddenly becomes very excited, and we may feel ourselves abruptly alerted. However, it does not need a loud bang to alert us, a quiet whisper can do so just as easily if the words are, for example, abusive, or in some other way specially significant for us, because the sense organs pass the messages also direct to the cortex where their significance can be assessed. The cortex can then send its own signals to the reticular formation to help excite the latter which, in turn, will then enable the cortex to deal competently with the *sequelae* to the whisper. Equally, most of us are aware how worry can keep us from sleep—the cortex sending signals to the reticular formation, so keep the latter active —or so one would suppose.

Can we prove the existence of this route—sense-organ to cortex, to reticular formation, and then up again? We cannot trace it in its entirety by any direct method. In monkeys, it has been shown that when parts of the cortex are suddenly and artificially stimulated by electric pulses during sleep, the animal will awaken, and one may infer that messages had been passed down to excite the reticular formation.

Using Oxford students a few years ago, we tried to investigate this role of the cortex, to discover whether it could cause awakening by sending messages down to excite the reticular formation in response, not to a loud bang, but to a specially significant word. A word is a natural stimulus, unlike the artificial electrical pulses applied directly to the cortex of the monkey. How to be sure that the cortex was involved in the circuit? By ensuring that the brain had to carry out complex discriminations between different words. We know from cases of injury or disease of the brain in humans and animals that unless a certain area of the cortex is working, one complex pattern of noise cannot be discriminated from another; more particularly, speech sounds cannot be understood or responded to. So, if the brain was discriminating between words, the cortex must be doing the job.

What sort of techniques must be employed in such experiments? Firstly, it is essential that if a person wakens from sleep the possibility that he may have done so spontaneously, and not as a consequence of your stimulus, must be borne in mind. One must therefore compare how often he appears to awaken after the deliberate stimulus, with how often he appears to waken spontaneously at comparable periods of the night. Secondly, one must bear in mind that novelty is a very potent awakener. People who have slept through continuous loud noise will often awaken if the noise stops—the silence is so different from what they have become accustomed to. Sudden awakening after calling out the sleeper's name, or even the tape-recorded voice of her child calling, *Mummy*, would not necessarily indicate responsiveness to speech. It might simply be that the quality of the noise was novel, quite different from the sounds of the preceding couple of hours (passing traffic, the sighing of the wind, the rattling of the door). The experimental stimulus must be no more novel than other noises which precede it.

We therefore made a very long tape-recording in which fifty-six names were called out one after another, over and over again in different orders, with several seconds between each name. Having persuaded a volunteer to come and sleep in the laboratory we would attach electrodes to his scalp and to his hands. He was told that if during sleep his own name, say, *Peter*, was called out, he should respond to it by clenching his hand, and that he should do the same if one other particular name, say, *David*, was called. He then fell asleep while the tape recording was played, drowsing off through an endless barrage of words, occasionally clenching his hand as one of the crucial names came. Eventually, he fell asleep and, sure enough, would very often suddenly rouse from sound sleep and clench his fist just after either of the crucial words.

Next we had to get a man called David to volunteer. He too was asked to pick out, during his sleep, the names *David* and *Peter* from all the others (the degree of novelty of either word being no greater than that of other names adjacent in time). And so on with name-paired volunteers.

It was necessary to use pairs of people like this for they served as 'controls' for each other, balanced each other out. It might have been that we could have recorded *Peter* more loudly than *David*, so that had we used only Peter, he might have picked out his own name in sleep more often than *David* just because it was louder. Or because it contained more disturbing, high-pitched sounds. If, on the other hand, Peter responded much more often to *Peter* than to *David* and David responded much more often to *David* than to *Peter*, it would seem that the reason for the name being picked out in sleep was that it was David's or Peter's own name.

The upshot of all this was that, whereas spontaneous awakenings and movements (which we counted during the period of each ten names that preceded each crucial one) were very rare, fist-clenching after 'own' name had been called was so frequent that the difference could not reasonably be attributed to chance. The same was true of the 'other' name— Peter responded best to *Peter* but was also able, though with less certitude, to pick out *David* during sleep. Furthermore, even if fist-clenching did not occur, the EEG of sound sleep, with slow waves and sleep spindles, was much more often disturbed by a person's own name than by any other name. The electrical response (called a K-complex) was an indication of a sudden increase in the upflow of exciting impulses from the reticular formation to the cortex. In some additional experiments, these electrical responses in the EEG occurred much more often after any meaningful name, such as a name played forwards by the tape recorder, than after the same name made meaningless by being played backwards.

Even in the sleeping brain, the cortex evidently was getting enough help from the reticular formation to enable it to maintain a sort of unconscious scrutiny of outside noises, for it was discriminating between the names. Only the cortex would be capable of that complex task. After certain discriminations had evidently been made, selective arousal occurred. Therefore, after discrimination by the cortex, messages must have left the cortex ('Hey, this is important, you'd better help me wake up!'), travelled down to and excited the reticular formation, and then led to an increase of the invigorating upflow from it.

Incidentally, some other names during sleep were specially potent in leading to arousal, none more so than the name of his recent girl-friend (Figure 6). While Neville slept, the name of his recently acquired heart-throb, *Penelope*, would cause a most violent perturbation in his EEG, and a huge 'psychogalvanic response', or sudden sweating of the palm (itching too, perhaps!).

Many other sources of reticular formation excitement have been discovered, especially chemical ones, such as excess of carbon dioxide in the blood, or a shortage of oxygen. Any interference with breathing will quickly cause awakening. Nevertheless, as we have earlier said, sleep is a condition of inertia and unresponsiveness. That unresponsiveness extends to the normal body reflexes, and the concentration of carbon dioxide in the blood that will be tolerated during sleep, without causing reflexly increased breathing, is much greater than during wakefulness. In natural deep sleep, the concentration rises higher than it does after a large dose of morphia during wakefulness, morphia being a powerful suppressant of breathing reflexes. Adrenalin, too, was found to excite the reticular formation, an illustration of a potential vicious circle, for adrenalin is a chemical released into the blood by the adrenal glands whenever the person is excited or fearful. By an action on the reticular formation it would arouse him even more, and lead to more adrenalin release by impulses passing down from the reticular formation to the spinal cord and the centres in it which control adrenalin release.

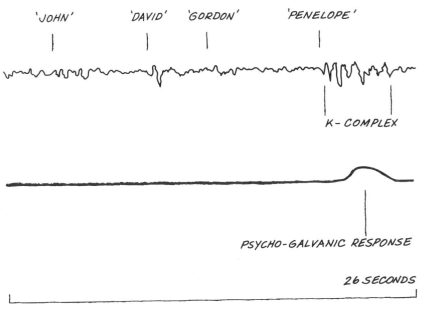

Figure 6

At irregular intervals of four to eight seconds a voice speaks names from an endless list. Big slow waves and spindles were visible in the EEG. The names John!, David!, Gordon! have little effect on the EEG and provoke no psychogalvanic responses. The name of his beloved, Penelope!, provoked a group of big waves forming a 'K-complex' in the EEG and a surge of electric potential at the palm.

If such a vicious circle were to continue unabated, you might expect the poor chap to blow up! Fortunately, regulating devices are present which prevent the development of vicious circles. These 'homeostatic' devices illustrate a common principle, not merely within the nervous system, but throughout the whole of the bodily economy. If some mechanism, through its activity, changes a particular function in a specific direction, the mere occurrence of the change will start up other mechanisms which tend to reverse the direction of change toward the original level of function.

When adrenalin is released into the blood-stream it brings about a rise of blood pressure in the arteries (the blood vessels carrying blood away from the heart). The increased pressure causes a slight stretching of the walls in certain parts of the arterial system, notably the carotid sinus in the neck. Within the walls of the carotid sinus are organs highly sensitive to stretching. When the blood pressure rises these organs send a powerful stream of nerve impulses to the brain-stem which damp down the excited reticular formation. In this way the vicious circle referred to above would be prevented.

There are rare people who, if they twist their necks to left or right while wearing a tight collar, will become unconscious—they fall abruptly asleep because of the distortion of the carotid sinus wall! A subtler but more common sleep-promoting action of the carotid sinus may underlie a relation between atmospheric pressure and the tendency to take a nap. When you inflate a balloon its walls are stretched by a pressure from within, just as is always and quite normally the case with the arteries. If the balloon were placed in a room in which the air pressure was reduced towards a vacuum, the balloon would rapidly expand and soon explode. In the same way, if the atmospheric pressure fell slightly one could expect a very slight expansion of the arteries, particularly the carotid sinus, and therefore a tendency for sleep to be caused. Ordinarily there are a host of factors which act to keep us awake, so that any very mild sleep-promoting influences would be swamped. But what of a gentle rest period? Would resting people fall asleep more easily on low-pressure days?

Airline crew who had routine EEG tests as part of a health check-up were studied in Paris. Keeping still during such a test is a boring but restful occupation. Occasionally people will fall asleep during it, and when, in Paris, the dates upon which airmen fell asleep were checked against the atmospheric pressure, sure enough it was the days on which the barometer was low that sleep usually overcame them.

Homeostatic or regulatory mechanisms are so common in the nervous system that it is not surprising that other means have been discovered whereby the excitement of the reticular formation is damped down. Most important is the degree of pep which the reticular formation itself imparts to the cortex. The more the cortex is pepped up or 'activated', the more strongly it sends down special nerve impulses to damp down the reticular formation. Some beautifully designed experiments in Paris showed that there was no one particular part of the cortex responsible for this. The whole cortex functioned in this way, for when various areas of cortex were prevented from doing so by local, rapid cooling, the damping effect was reduced in accordance with the extent and not the site of the cooling. One would suppose that the cells in the cortex which send down these damping influences to the reticular formation are different from those which can send down exciting impulses (see p. 120), though probably if one increases the other decreases.

CONSCIOUSNESS

To attempt to define consciousness would be to risk the displeasure of philosophers. I am no philosopher. However, most of us know what we mean when we say we are conscious of, or aware of, something whether outside or within ourselves. It will have become apparent from all that has already been written in this chapter, that it is now believed that when human consciousness is lost it is because of failure on the part of the reticular formation to send up a sufficiency of the non-specific or 'activating' nerve impulses to the cortex.

The failure may be for entirely healthy reasons, as in natural sleep, which is a state of unconsciousness from which we can fairly easily be roused. Or it may result from abnormal causes such as pressure upon, or inflammation within, the reticular formation, the state of unconsciousness being one from which the victim cannot be fully roused. It is not strictly correct to call sleep a state of unconsciousness, for at least during some of our sleep we are conscious——not in its full sense, not of the outside world, but of an inner, or dream-world, as we shall be discussing later in this book.

The attributes of consciousness—skilled response, the utilization of former experience, a subsequent statement of having been aware, and being now able to describe what passed—these are not possible without the cerebral cortex or grey matter. Wakefulness, by contrast, is possible without a cortex. Consciousness and wakefulness are not synonymous. Animals from which the cortex has been removed show alternating periods of sleep and activity. While active they move about, eat and excrete and must be considered awake. There are no grounds for inferring the possession of consciousness on their part. The same is true of those human monsters which from birth lack a cerebral cortex. A few of these live, and, if cared for, survive for years, but when awake never reveal any attributes of consciousness—they merely swallow, grunt, and move their limbs aimlessly.

The most common state of human unconsciousness, during life any-way, apart from sleep is that induced by chemical anaesthetics—chloro-form and ether are well-known examples. Most adults today who have general anaesthetics are 'put out' initially and very quickly by an injection into the blood-stream of a barbiturate drug called thiopentone. The drug is quickly carried to the brain by the blood. Using the evoked potential technique new light has been thrown on the action of anaesthetics. Evoked potentials were recorded from both the cortex and the reticular formation while the animals were awake. Then some were put to sleep with ether, others with thiopentone. If a stimulus, such as an electric shock, was now applied to the leg, the evoked potential in the cortex was still present without reduction. On the other hand the evoked potential in the reticular formation of the anaesthetized animals was now very small. Although the cortex still responded to the nerve impulses from the leg, the reticular formation was unresponsive. The anaesthetic drug was showing a predilection for impairing reticular formation function.

When therefore the surgeon sticks a knife into you while you are anaesthetized, your reticular formation is not merely just ticking over quietly, as in sleep, it is also slightly poisoned so that it cannot respond and cause you to awaken. However, we have already seen that numbers of different factors affect the reticular formation, not only anaesthetics. For example, chemicals like adrenalin, and exciting impulses coming down from the cortex. When I was first taught about anaesthetics as a medical student, the role of the reticular formation was not understood and I remember that as we sat in the ante-room to the surgical theatre the anaesthetist told me how puzzling it was that, if one had two people of similar size, and brought about a similar concentration of anaesthetic in the blood of each, if one patient was calm he would be the first to become unconscious. If the other was very apprehensive he would need a much bigger dose of anaesthetic. We can now realize that in the second patient, while the anaesthetic agent was trying to damp down the reticular for-mation, it was all the time being counteracted by adrenalin and by nerve impulses from the cortex which were trying to excite the reticular forma-tion.

Hitherto in this chapter I have written of the reticular formation as if it were a single localized zone in the brain-stem. It is not. It is neither sharply defined anatomically, nor is it uniform in its structure and func-tion. In the last few years the differences of function between various parts of the reticular formation have been proving complex. In this book a single example may serve, an experiment by Italian research workers, of such basic simplicity that, to the scientist, it brings delight as a thing of beauty. Firstly, the connexions between different arteries to the brain were tied off before they reached the brain of the *encéphale isolé*. Then the anaesthetic, thiopentone, discussed above, was injected into the arteries going to the upper brain-stem. The 'waking' *encéphale isolé* passed quickly into the 'sleeping' state. Nothing surprising about that. But if, instead, thiopentone was injected into arteries supplying only the lower brain-stem of already 'sleeping' *encéphale isolé* cats, the EEG quickly changed to a 'waking' one. Just the opposite effect. The most reasonable explanation was that the reticular formation in the lower brain-stem normally has the special function of damping down the upper part (which is the part from which impulses flow up to the cortex to make the EEG of the latter look 'awake' or 'asleep'). Knock out that damping action, by partly poisoning the nerve cells with thiopentone, and the upper reticular formation is allowed to function in a more lively manner. There is little doubt that there are many different functions served by the reticular formation which remain to be revealed. In life, one may be confident, they do not act in isolation and simple opposition, as often appears from laboratory experiments. Each plays an harmonious role within an orchestra.

PROBLEMS IN MAINTAINING CREATIVITY

E. Paul Torrance

chapter eight

CREATIVITY

Not everybody who is "different" is a creative genius, but a lot of creative people seem rather eccentric. Just because they are able to break set and solve problems in ways no one else thinks of, they often are seen as a bit peculiar by their peers. And this "differentness" may cause great problems, one of which is that well-meaning folks—teachers, parents, guidance counselors—may try to get them to fit into the common mold.

The following chapter discusses some of these problems, making them especially vivid through children's stories that present some dilemmas of creativity. In addition, the chapter touches on sex role behavior, deviance, and other topics that relate to maintaining and developing creativity.

PROBLEMS
IN MAINTAINING
CREATIVITY

Inescapably, the individual who thinks of a new idea is in the very beginning a minority of one. Even when matters of demonstrable fact are
involved, as in the Asch (1955) experiments, there are very few people
who can tolerate being a minority of one.[1] Since creativity involves independence of mind, nonconformity to group pressures, or breaking out of
the mold, it is inevitable that highly creative individuals experience some
unusual problems of adjustment. Thus, the highly creative child must
either repress his creativity or learn to cope with the tensions that arise
from being so frequently this minority of one. Repression of creative
needs may lead to actual personality breakdown. Their expression leads
to loneliness, conflicts, and other problems of adjustment. Since teachers,
administrators, and counselors need to understand both types of problems, this chapter will be devoted to a discussion of the problems involved
in maintaining one's creativity and the next to the problems which result
from sacrificing one's creativity. The two chapters which follow will be
given over to a presentation of ideas whereby highly creative individuals
can be aided through sound guidance programs.

In all of the remaining chapters, considerable use will be made of the
imaginative stories of children about animals and persons having some
divergent characteristic. Primarily, these are used to illustrate a principle and make it more vivid. I believe, however, that these stories
provide us with some deep insights into the struggles of children to maintain their creativity and their perceptions of society's treatment of divergent behavior.

Gardner Murphy (1958) has identified the basis of many of the problems of creative people. He points out that they may suffer anguish
arising from specific discoveries, through social disapproval, or through
the fact that the social situation causes preoccupation with a particular

From GUIDING CREATIVE TALENT, *by E. Paul Torrance (Englewood Cliffs,
N.J.: Prentice-Hall, 1962), pp. 104–124; reprinted by permission of the publisher.*

[1]"Length of line" experiments—group behavior chapter in text.

area and leads to poor results. He also explains that an individual may discover that he has found all there is to be discovered at his level of operation or with his opportunities for investigation. The reader will find some of these threads running throughout the problems which I have identified in the Minnesota studies and in the stories of children concerning divergent behavior.

SANCTIONS AGAINST DIVERGENCY

Many of our society's coercive influences against divergency, even against outstanding performance, are reflected in the imaginative stories concerning flying monkeys and silent lions. Many of them sound very much like cautionary tales such as "Tootle," so eloquently attacked by Riesman (1955). The following is an example of one of these cautionary tales, the story of Lippy, "A Lion that Won't Roar":

Lippy Lion, a friend of mine, has a little problem. He won't roar! He used to roar, but now he won't. His name used to be Roarer, too. I'll tell you why.

When Roarer was about your age, he would always roar and scare people. Now this made his mother and father worry. Everybody was always complaining. So they decided they should talk to Roarer.

They went to his bedroom . . . But when they started talking he roared and scared them downstairs. So finally they went to a magician. They talked things over until he had an idea. Then the three went home together.

The magician said his words and said, "He'll never want to roar again."

The next morning he went to scare his mother by roaring, but all that came out was a little squeak. He tried again but only a squeak came out. But he pled and pled to get his roar back, so the magician made it so he could roar. But Roarer didn't believe him. So now that he can roar he won't.

Soon they had to name him Lippy.

Teachers, parents, and peers feel threatened when highly creative children express their creativity. Some of the questioning, experimenting, and wild ideas are annoying. In many respects, however, the annoyance can be tolerated more than the threat which this creative behavior poses. Adults do not know how to evaluate these unusual ideas or respond to the many questions. Creative behavior may be interpreted as aggressive or even hostile, and certainly it soon becomes just that, if ideas and questions are rejected. Thus, one of the problems becomes that of helping the creative child maintain his aggressiveness without being hostile, as Roarer had become.

This tale brings out another problem concerning the parents' expectation of counselors and school psychologists—the expectation that they will use some kind of magic. Frequently, counselors, psychologists, and teachers are expected to play an aversive role, such as that of the magician in the story of Lippy (once Roarer). Such a role is frequently expected of the mental hygiene clinic. Guidance workers must be alert to these expectations and prepared to play more positive roles. This problem will be discussed at length in Chapters 8 and 9.

About two-thirds of the stories about flying monkeys tell similar tales of conformity or of destruction. Some cultures, however, are more indulgent of divergency than others. Stories written by gifted children in special classes are far more hopeful in outlook than those of gifted children in regular classes. In about seventy per cent of the stories of pupils in classes for high achieving children, the flying monkey is in some way able to persist in his flying. The stories written by children in a small Oklahoma town composed of Indians, whites, and a few Negroes also reflect this tolerance of divergency. In seventy-four per cent of their stories, the flying monkey succeeds. He may meet obstacles which may be overcome, but there is little question that "a monkey can fly" and should do so. Some of this spirit is reflected in the following story by an Oklahoma sixth-grade boy:

Once there was a flying monkey named Moonbeam. This monkey had fun every day romping and flying through the trees. One day he was flying around and some men were setting traps for him. As he was walking along, "snap!" the trap sprang. Then the men took him to the alligator pits. They slowly lowered him into the pits. Moonbeam was trying to break out, but the bars on his cage were strong. Suddenly they stopped lowering him. The men started to run. Then they fell into the pits. The men fell on Moonbeam's cage and broke a bar on it. Moonbeam crawled out of the cage and flew out of the pit and went for help. When the men were pulled out of the pit, they were rushed to jail.

The imaginative stories written by French children go even further than those of the Oklahoma children in their willingness to think imaginatively about the flying monkey and the silent lion, never questioning the possibility and never bothering to explain how the monkey learned to fly nor how the lion lost his ability to roar. The stories by Greek children do not question the possibility but are devoted largely to explanations about how the conditions occurred.

The following story by a gifted Long Island boy illustrates some of the dynamics of the plight of the gifted child who lacks some quality regarded as highly important by his society. It especially communicates the depth of the anxiety of the parents under such conditions.

Freddy was born in a cave in the Rocky Mountains. He lived there with his mother and father and his ten brothers and sisters.

The first thing a lion is supposed to learn is how to roar. His ten brothers and sisters learned how to roar very well, but Freddy wouldn't roar because he was a friendly lion. First, his mother tried to teach him. She tried and tried for ten days, after which she fainted. Then his father tried to teach him for eight months, but still Freddy wouldn't roar. So finally they gave up and ordered Freddy to go and find another place to live. . . .

When Freddy walked into the jungle all of the animals ran and hid in the bushes. Freddy was very sad. He tried to make friends with the monkeys but they ran up the trees. He tried to make friends with the zebras but they ran away as fast as possible. All of a sudden there was complete silence as all of the animals waited for Freddy to roar. When he didn't roar, the animals were very surprised. Slowly one by one the animals came out from behind the bushes and down from the trees and started to form a circle around Freddy. Then one of the animals brought up enough courage to go over and touch him. When Freddy didn't do anything, the animals went over to Freddy and started to play with him. Freddy and the animals became good friends. Until this day, Freddy hasn't roared.

This story may possibly reflect the author's childlike optimism that it is possible to escape the rejection of divergency.

MAINTAINING CREATIVITY
MAY ALIENATE FRIENDS

Many highly creative children find quite early that the use of their creative talents alienates them from their friends. In the stories of flying monkeys, the exercise of the talent for flying quite frequently brings about isolation, warnings by parents that the other animals won't like the monkey, and the like. In the stories of silent lions, many are afraid to roar because they will either scare away their friends or alienate others in their society. The following such story illustrates a number of the dynamics of this problem:

One sunny day, the king of the jungle and his wife were blessed with a cub. The king was so happy that he even gave cigars to his enemy, the monkey. Many animals came to see the cub.

The cub was growing and his parents were getting worried. He was five and he hadn't roared once. His father decided that he was old enough to go to school and then maybe he would roar. The king hired a teacher to teach his son, John, who would soon rule the jungle. John did fine in arithmetic, spelling, and other subjects. But in roaring class he refused to roar! His teacher was startled; his mother fainted; and his father was amazed.

That night John and his father went into the study to talk. John's father asked, "Why won't you roar, son?"

John replied, "It scares all of the animals." John then told of his adventure when he was two years old. He had roared his loudest. He saw the monkeys and the other animals he had wanted to be his friends with run away. His father understood and told him that he should learn to roar louder to scare the bad animals. John said that he would make the bad good without roaring.

This story seems to me to duplicate many of the ones which I hear from parents of highly creative children.

The implications of this problem are exemplified in a recent study by Buhl (1961) of creative engineering students. On the basis of the AC Spark Plug Test of Creative Ability, Buhl compared the upper and lower quarters of a sample of 167 freshmen engineering students. He found that the highly creative engineer has a distinct desire to have warm and close personal relationships, to share his ideas with others, to discuss problems, and to find alternative viewpoints. He also wants to be only an average student, apparently because he is afraid that excelling will alienate him from such relationships and rob him of opportunities for the kind of sharing for which he recognizes a need. Buhl sees this desire to be only average a distinct threat to the development of creative engineers. He believes that this unwillingness to show scholastic excellence is due to present-day philosophies of education in elementary and secondary schools. He points out that competition is often discouraged in grading practices and remains only in athletics. Buhl found that the highly creative student admits to being faster than most, due largely to speed competition, but believes that he must conform to the "average," except in matters connected with sports.

In my opinion, this matter of competition is one which needs re-evaluation by teachers and administrators. In my own research, I have found that competition increases tremendously the production and quality of ideas produced by children. "Warm-up" procedures can compensate only in part for these effects.

CREATIVE CHILDREN
MAY NOT BE
WELL-ROUNDED

The highly creative child is likely to have lagged in some phase of his development. Many investigators in a variety of fields have been disappointed in finding that outstanding individuals in the field under study are not well-rounded, "all-American" boys. For example, verbal abilities frequently will be below some of their other abilities. They may even have difficulty in learning to read or write. Perhaps the most inventive and imaginative child we have tested is a boy who has had unusual difficulty in learning to read, yet his store of information and his ability to use it imaginatively in solving problems and developing ideas is fantastic.

This problem is particularly acute at the fourth-grade level. In a number of cases, fourth graders identified by our tests as highly creative have been re-evaluated by teachers. Teachers then discover that these children are far more knowledgeable and thoughtful than they had imagined. I was particularly struck by a comment made by the examiner after testing orally a certain fourth grade boy. The examiner stated: "This boy impresses me as the kind of individual who will become a top executive who can dictate to five secretaries at the same time without becoming confused." The boy's responses gave evidence of high inventivlevel, flexibility, and originality. This boy, however, has a serious reading disability and ranked near the bottom of his class on the written test of creative thinking.

Because verbal skills are highly valued in our society, tremendous pressures are placed on children to be "well-rounded" in this area. The relentlessness of these pressures is symbolized in many of the stories about lions that won't roar, ducks that won't quack, and dogs that won't bark. Some of the authors of the stories deplored the relentless pressures exerted by adults. One referred to those who exert such pressures as "chasers and quackers." Some children resist pressures to become well-rounded because they feel that they can win and maintain respect in more acceptable ways than the commonly approved and expected ways of the society. The struggle involved when this occurs is symbolized in the following story:

In the vast wilds of the Congo jungle came the trumpeting of a bull elephant announcing the coming of a great contest. . . .
It was the message most of the animals had been waiting for. The message that there was to be a new King of the Beasts. The great Bamula had been killed by his enemies and there had been no definite decision about how the new King was to be chosen.
Now at last it had come. There was to be a contest testing the animals' strength and ability to handle all of the most difficult problems. . . . All of the animals, especially the lions went strutting around boasting of their strength and other matters concerning their beauty, intelligence, and swiftness of foot. At night they all sat around the water hole admiring and comparing their images by the light of the silver-blue moon.
All of the animals were excited about the coming event, all but one. As you would least expect, it was a lion. He just sat on the banks of the Chevkrus River thinking and staring into the almost-dry ditch where clear waters used to run. Now and then a tear trickled down his face. . . .
Why was he crying? After all, he was a lion and was as beautiful, intelligent, strong and swift as any of the other animals. For one reason, they thought

he was stupid. They jeered at him and called him names and showered him with remarks such as, "You'd better watch out or you'll trip over your mane" and "Where's your cat food?"

The poor lion hadn't done anything wrong, but the reason they poked fun at him was that he was different from anyone else. He wouldn't roar. . . .

Then he decided, "I guess the only way to show them I'm not an idiot is to win that contest!"

. . . There were 300 contestants, one thousand spectators, and 57 judges. The first part of the contest was held in a gigantic arena. A chill went over the audience as into it tore a gorilla. He was the most brutal beast I have ever seen. . . . Only 249 remained to go on to the next contest. The lion was among them. The next contest was to test their intelligence. Five judges led the remaining contestants into the most savage and unknown parts of the jungle blindfolded and turned them loose. Of the 249 who entered, only 21 returned. The rest were left to die or be eaten by some unknown beast.

The lion was among the 21 and he was still just as determined to win as before. The next contest was to test their swiftness of foot. Two judges told them their route which was to cover 39 miles of rugged country. They would have to go over hot rocks, under waterfalls, and through rivers. The lion and the cheetah tied for first place, but the lion beat the cheetah in the last contest of beauty, for his majestic golden mane and tail and his good posture outdid the cheetah, since he was too bony.

The lion has ruled all of the other beasts to this day and his subjects honor and respect him so much that he never has to raise his voice. He doesn't have to roar.

CREATIVE CHILDREN MAY DIVERGE FROM SEX NORMS

Our over emphasis or misplaced emphasis on sex roles and efforts to establish sex norms during early childhood and throughout the educational ladder makes many problems for highly creative children. We have usually thought that this emphasis takes its toll only on the creativity of women. It has been pointed out frequently that rarely do women become scientific discoverers, inventors, or composers. Over emphasis or misplaced emphasis on sex roles, however, does exact its toll on the creativity of both sexes and does create serious problems of adjustment for highly creative individuals of both sexes.

Creativity, by its very nature, requires both sensitivity and independence. In our culture, sensitivity is definitely a feminine virtue, while independence is a masculine value. Thus, we may expect the highly creative boy to appear to be more effeminate than his peers and the highly creative girl to appear more masculine than hers. Roe (1959), Barron (1957), and I (1959b) have all cited evidence in support of this phenomenon. In our longitudinal studies we are finding interesting examples of children who sacrifice their creativity in order to maintain their "masculinity" or their "femininity," as the case may be.

This cultural block to creativity comes out in many places. We first observed it in our Product Improvement Test in which children are asked to think of all the ideas they can for improving common toys so that they will be more fun to play with. In the first grade, boys excelled girls on the fire truck, but girls excelled boys on the nurse's kit. Many of the boys refused to think of anything to make the nurse's kit more fun, protesting, "I'm a boy! I don't play with things like that!" Some of the more creative boys, however, first transformed it into a doctor's kit and as such were quite free to think of improvements. By the third grade, however, boys excelled girls even on the nurse's kit, probably because girls have been conditioned by this time to accept toys as they are and not to manipulate or change them.

The inhibiting effects of sex-role conditioning also showed up in our experiments involving small groups working with science toys (Torrance, 1960b). Girls were quite reluctant to work with these science toys and frequently protested, "I'm a girl; I'm not supposed to know anything about things like that!" Boys demonstrated and explained about twice as many ideas as girls in experiments involving these materials. We know already, however, that this situation can be modified significantly (Torrance, 1960b). In 1959, we found these phenomena operating quite strongly in one school. Later I had the opportunity to report these and other results to both the teachers and parents in this school. In 1960, we conducted some experiments in this same school in which we used a different but similar set of science toys. This time, we found none of this reluctance on the part of girls; there was no difference in the expressed enjoyment of the activity of boys and girls; the mean performance of girls and boys was almost identical. In one way, however, the situation remained unchanged. The contributions of boys was more highly valued by peers than those of girls. Apparently, the school climate has helped to make it more acceptable for girls to play around with science things, but boys' ideas about science things are still supposed to be better than those of girls.

The social consequences of failure to achieve the behavioral norms associated with sex and social roles are well understood by children by the time they reach the fourth grade, if not before. Such an understanding is reflected in the following story by a young Illinois author:

"No! No! No! I won't roar! I won't! I won't! I won't roar and scare all those little animals," said Roarless, the lion.

"But that is the purpose of roaring," said his mother. "You want to roar to scare the animals. You are the king of beasts and the king of beasts roars."

"No! No! No! I just won't! I won't! I won't! I don't care if I am the king of beasts and can't roar," said Roarless again.

"For the millionth time, Roarless, please roar," said his mother.

"And for the millionth time, I won't roar," shouted Roarless.

That is Roarless and his mother arguing. Ever since he was a little cub he has not wanted to roar because he thought he would scare the other animals. When he was little his father made a roar so loud that it scared Roarless. Now, let's get back to their arguing.

"All right! All right! I won't argue with you," said his mother. "I'm going out for a while. Good bye."

"Good bye."

Then all of a sudden Roarless said, "R-R-R-R-R-R-ROAR!"

Then his mother rushed in and said, "Oh, my baby, at last you have roared. We should call you Roarful instead of Roarless."

"I still think I scared the animals," sadly said Roarless—I mean Roarful.

This tale illustrates two other points of importance in guiding creative children. Counselors and teachers can expect that many highly creative children will be under severe pressure to pursue occupations which will fulfill family expectations. Many of these individuals resist these pressures for a long time, holding out for some occupation in which they can more adequately express their creativity. Unrelenting pressures such as those exerted by the mother of Roarless are extremely stressful. Even the resistant, creative youngster has his "breaking point" and cannot hold out indefinitely.

Another problem may be seen in the negative identification which apparently exists between Roarless and his father. Because of early, unpleasant relationships with the father, Roarless identifies himself as being different from his father. Thus, if roaring makes him like his father, Roarless is motivated to avoid roaring.

CREATIVE CHILDREN PREFER TO LEARN ON THEIR OWN

Many creative children prefer to learn on their own, but schools have been slow in providing such opportunities. Last year we conducted an exciting study in which we found that children would do a great deal of writing on their own, if properly motivated. In another (Fritz, 1958), it was found that gifted children in a split-shift school showed more growth in language development, science, and social studies than they did on a full-day schedule. Only in spelling was there significantly less growth among the split-shift children (seventh graders). In still another, we found that children in a split-shift school engaged in a larger number of learning activities on their own.

Since we have generally assumed that children do not learn on their own, we have seldom provided them with opportunities to do so. I have seen learning situations left "open" a sufficient number of times to have become quite excited about what would happen, if we should do so more frequently. The following story by an Oklahoma Indian girl in the sixth grade, symbolizes this situation.

Once there were some monkeys sitting in a group. They were all alike except three monkeys. They were very different because they could fly.
    One day some men from a park zoo were looking for some monkeys because theirs had died. They came upon the three that flew. So they took them in a cage. The cage didn't have a top to it. They were in the sun one day and the monkey said to the other, "I wish we could get out of here."
    "Then, why don't we fly out of here?" said the other.
    They started to fly out. When they got about half a mile, some men came to feed them. When they couldn't find the three monkeys, they saw them flying away. One of them said, "If we would have put them in a cage with a top, we would have had a real good thing here in the zoo."

One function of the school counselor might be to help highly creative children recognize or discover the "openings" in their cages, or selves, to which they might be blinded.

CREATIVE CHILDREN LIKE TO ATTEMPT DIFFICULT TASKS

Frequently highly creative children strongly desire to move far ahead of their classmates in some areas. They often make their teachers afraid that they are not "ready." Fortunately, however, educators of gifted children are rapidly revising many of their concepts about what can be taught at various levels of education. This terrifies many. The following recent headlines reflect such a fear:

"Caution Urged in Changing Primary into High Schools"
"Can We Rush Primary Education?"
"Don't Turn Grade Schools into High Schools, Educators Warn at Parley"
"Reading for Kindergarten, Languages Too Soon Attacked"

Some of the panic may have been eased by a recent report of the Educational Policies Commission of the National Education Association and the American Association of School Administrators (*Contemporary Issues in Elementary Education*, 1960).

Bruner's (1960) exciting book, *The Process of Education*, should give educators some very useful guidance in working out this problem. Along with revisions about readiness, Bruner develops the concept of "structure of knowledge" and offers interesting ideas about intuition and motivation. About readiness, he says, "Experience over the past decade points to the fact that our schools may be wasting precious years by postponing the teaching of many subjects on the grounds that they are too difficult. . . . The essential point often overlooked in the planning of curricula . . . [is that] the basic ideas that lie at the heart of all science and mathematics and the basic schemes that give form to life and literature are powerful." For this purpose, Bruner suggests "the spiral curriculum," one that turns back on itself at higher and higher levels of complexity.

A very frequent theme in our imaginative stories is related to this problem. The young animal or fowl asks, "When can I roar? When can I crow? When can I quack? When can I fly?" Almost always, the answer is, "When you are a little older." We are always afraid that the young one might not be ready to learn and that he would be forever scarred by even the most temporary failure. On this score, we might note the persistence of the fifth-grade Negro boy from Georgia who wrote the following story:

Once there was a monkey that was very sad. He was sad because he didn't know how to fly. He said to himself, "Why can other animals fly but we can't fly?" Then he began to climb up a tree; he ate some bananas and coconuts. The monkey jumped out of the tree and began to fly. He fell down on the ground. Then the monkey climbed the tree again and began to try to fly. Again he fell to the ground. Again he climbed up and finally he began to fly.

A common experience in the lives of many highly outstanding individuals has been their ability to cope with failure and frustration. Certainly, almost all highly creative scientists, inventors, artists, and writers attempt tasks which are too difficult for them. Had they not attempted such tasks, it is quite unlikely that their great ideas would have been born.

CREATIVE CHILDREN MAY UNDERTAKE DANGEROUS TASKS

In learning on their own and in testing their limits through attempting difficult tasks, creative children may also undertake dangerous tasks. This poses difficult problems for parents, teachers, playground directors, and school administrators who have responsibilities for the safety of children. I have frequently wondered if the solution to this problem doesn't lie in the technique of the parents of the jet aces of the Korean struggle. We found that the parents of these aces both exercised more control and permitted more testing-the-limits and risk-taking behavior than did the parents of the non-aces. They exercised control until skills were adequate and then permitted wide testing of the limits. Their children then could say in sincerity, "This would be dangerous for most boys or most pilots, but for me it is quite safe."

The usual type of control, however, would seem to be more in line with the theme of the following cautionary tale written by a fifth-grade boy:

There was a monkey that liked to tease people. He would pull the lion's tail and would bite the baby tiger cubs. One day he got tired of teasing the same ones. So he started thinking. "I'll tease the crocodile," he thought. The next morning he started working to fix a vine just short enough to swing down on. As soon as he was all finished, he was going to fly down by the crocodile and kick him. He was ready to try it out. He flew right into the crocodile's mouth. Now there isn't any little flying monkey to tease anyone.

This story illustrates another problem of some children in expressing their creativity. Their sense of humor is frequently not appreciated, especially if it has been tinted by hostility and resentment. It may create difficult problems of discipline for the teacher and school administrator.

CREATIVE CHILDREN ARE SEARCHING FOR A PURPOSE

It has been said that most outstanding creative achievers seem to be possessed by a purpose and to be "men of destiny." Creative children need some purpose which is worthy of the enthusiastic devotion they seem capable of giving. Some of this need is symbolized in the following story by a sixth-grade boy:

There was once a South American monkey that didn't know what he was, who he was, or why he was even alive. He decided that he didn't know even the way to figure it out, so he thought he would make up a reason.

He had seen many airplanes overhead. He had seen many ferocious animals, many nice animals, and many machines. He had always thought that it would be nice to fly, so he pretended he was an airplane.

He had also heard that buzzing sound of the engines, so he called himself

"Buzz." He also decided that he was a real fast flyer so that this was the reason he was alive.

Now we all know that monkeys can't fly, but he didn't know this. Why he didn't even know that he was a monkey, so he kept trying and trying—and you know what? He flew!

Perhaps this has some implications not only concerning the need for helping children discover their potentialities but for helping them achieve their self-concepts creatively rather than by authority.

We also need to help highly creative individuals accept themselves, remembering that they may even despise an outstanding "gift," if their giftedness makes them different from others. This makes far too many gifted children willing to emasculate themselves and consciously or unconsciously hide or destroy their talents. The following story by a St. Paul girl illustrates this point effectively:

Once in a big forest lived a monkey. This monkey was very different. He could fly. All the other monkeys in the jungle envied him. . . .

Now one day this monkey was flying over the forest and saw a lion with a big mane. . . . He flew down and asked, "Where did you get that big mane, Mr. King?"

"I don't know," he answered. "I guess it's just a sign of royalty."

Then the monkey was wondering if he could have a mane like Mr. King. He flew home and asked his mother, who couldn't fly. She said, "I wouldn't like to have my son be a flying monkilion." So the monkey walked into his bedroom and sat on the bed. "Why can't I be like other monkeys?" . . .

Then as he was turning his head, he accidentally caught sight of his mother's button box. He got up and walked over to it and took the scissors. Then he took them over to his bed and stuck them under the covers. His mother walked in, and he moved over to where he had put the scissors and said, "Yee-oowww!" as he jumped up and hit his head on the ceiling. After that, he had a big bump on his head.

Later that night his mother asked him what he was going to do with the scissors. Of course he told the truth and said, "I was going to cut my wings off because I don't like to be odd. I want to be like other monkeys."

CREATIVE CHILDREN
HAVE DIFFERENT
VALUES

Counselors and teachers should recognize that the values and attitudes of the highly creative student are likely to be different from those of other students. The very fact that he is capable of a high order of divergent thinking, has unusual ideas, and is independent in his thinking in itself is likely to make his values and attitudes different from the norms of his peer group. Some of these differences have been highlighted in the Getzels and Jackson (1959) study. They found that for the high IQ group, the rank-order correlation between the qualities making for adult success was .81 (showing great similarity); for the high creativity group it was .10 (indicating little or no similarity). Among the highly intelligent, the correlation between the qualities they desired and the qualities they believed teachers favor was .67 (moderately similar); for the highly creative group, it was minus .25 (actually somewhat dissimilar). In other words, the highly creative adolescent desires personal qualities having little relationship to those he believes make for adult success and are in some way opposite those he believes his teachers favor. Thus, counselors and teachers should recognize that the desire to emulate the teacher is absent or weak among creative students. The desire to emulate peers is also weak, as I have found in some of my own studies.

Getzels and Jackson (1959) also found a certain mocking attitude on the part of the creatives toward what they call the "All-American Boy"— a theme almost totally lacking in the stories of the highly intelligent group. This highlights once more the problem of helping highly creative students learn to maintain their creativity without being obnoxious. In some way or other, this rejection of the values and rewards of the majority comes out in most studies of highly creative individuals. Perhaps this too is a function of divergency in general. This rejection of the usual values is illustrated in the following story by a New York boy of a lion that wouldn't roar:

. . . I was on a hike in the forest with the boys in the Boy Scout pack I belong to. . . . This forest was known because some people had seen a lion. We went to prove that there wasn't one. So far there is no proof that there is one. Wait a minute! Look at this footprint! It looks like a lion's! Now that we have proof, let's go. It's funny. No roar.
Here is a lion! A lion! Let's go!
"I won't hurt you," he said.
"A talking lion!"
"Yes, I like to talk. Is there anything wrong with talking?"
"No, but lions are supposed to roar."
"I get a sore throat when I roar, so I gave up roaring and started talking. Old fashioned lions roar."
"No wonder we didn't hear any roar. Will you come back to the city?"
"Not in a cage I won't!"
"If you don't hurt anybody, well-ll, okay."
"But now I am hungry. I want something to eat."
"What do you eat?"
"Canned foods. Mostly beans. I scare hunters. They run and leave their food."

"You can have our beans. After a trip to the city, you can make a million dollars."

"All I want is to go back to a big jungle in Africa and start a tribe of talking lions and have friends. Millions of dollars later, I would buy a ticket to Africa and stay. I have no use for this money so you five boys can have it for helping me."

SOME CREATIVE CHILDREN CAN'T STOP WORKING

Many people misinterpret the motivations of highly creative individuals who can't seem to stop working. Few creative individuals can stand the pressure of working only a forty-hour week. This is interpreted as an attempt to outdo others, rise to a position of power or favor, or such. Creative individuals, however, do not usually care for power and some of the other usual rewards. The exercise of their creative powers is itself a reward, and to them, the most important reward. One sixth-grade Oklahoma boy grasped this truth in the following story of Carlor, a flying monkey who was a fisherman:

There was a flying monkey named Carlor. He was a fisherman. One day they went out for tuna. Carlor flew ahead to have a look. There in front of his eyes was the biggest tuna he had ever seen. Quickly he got his harpoon gun and shot it. Then he took it back to the boat.

The next day they had a feast on the big tuna. Carlor ate so much his sides croaked. The next morning they headed back to land and unloaded their catch.

His wife had come into a fortune of pearls, money, jewels, and other things. . . . But Carlor was very sad because he couldn't work any more now, for they were awfully rich.

The next morning Carlor secretly flew back to his fishing fleet.

The creative individual is unable to stop working because he can't stop thinking. To him, there is nothing more enjoyable than work in which he can use his creative powers.

CREATIVE CHILDREN SEARCH FOR THEIR UNIQUENESS

Counselors and teachers may become irritated with creative children who seem to create problems for themselves by trying consciously to be different—searching for their uniqueness. Barron (1958) maintains that creative individuals reject the demands of their society to surrender their individuality because "they want to own themselves totally and because they perceive a shortsightedness in the claim of society that all its members should adapt themselves to a norm for a given time and place."

Some interesting aspects of this search for one's uniqueness is reflected in the following story by a sixth-grade girl:

There was once a monkey named Holace. Holace was very sad. He sat in his circus cage all day doing tricks when all of his monkey friends were highlights of the Cling Ling Brothers Circus.

His friend, Bayberry, was an organ grinder man while his little friend Stuart was his monkey. My how everyone laughed and clapped at his friends. He rode a bicycle, but Barberry could ride one with no hands. He tried swinging on a bar by his tail but Stuart could do that. . . .

One day he was swinging by his tail thinking of what he could do and he started to fall. Holace didn't want to be ashamed by falling, so he grabbed the bar that was swinging. All the people clapped for it seemed to them that he was flying through the air like a trapeze artist.

When one of the Cling Ling brothers heard the noise, he rushed out. When he saw Holace flying through the air, he gasped in amazement. The next day there was a new sign that said: "The World's Only Flying Monkey." Can you guess who that is? Of course, it's Holace, the new star of the Cling Ling Brothers Circus. Now there are many who do this act, but they are all copying Holace.

As with Holace, one way in which the creative individual searches for his uniqueness is through his vocational choice. Getzels and Jackson (1960), for example, found that their highly creative subjects gave a greater number of different occupations and more "unusual" or rare occupations than their highly intelligent subjects.

THE PSYCHOLOGICAL ESTRANGEMENT OF CREATIVE CHILDREN

From the foregoing it should be obvious that a large share of the highly creative child's adjustment problems are likely to be centered in his psychological isolation and estrangement from his peers and teachers. It will be no news to counselors that peer groups exercise rather severe pressures against their most creative members. In no group thus far studied have we failed to find relatively clear evidence of the operation of these pressures, though they are far more severe in some classrooms than in others.

When we select the most creative members of each sex in each classroom and match them for sex and Intelligence Quotient with other children in the same classroom, as already described in Chapter 4, three characteristics stand out as differentiating the highly creative children from the less creative ones. First, there is a tendency for them to gain a reputation for having wild or silly ideas. Second, their work is characterized by its productivity of ideas "off the beaten track." Third, they are characterized by humor and playfulness. All of these characteristics help explain both the estrangement and the creativity.

Interesting insights are furnished by the clinical data in our longitudinal data. The handling of windows and doors in the drawings of houses suggests some hypotheses concerning the psychological accessibility of highly creative children. According to Buck (1948) the openness of the house through its windows and doors provides an index of the child's psychological inaccessibility. It was noted that some of our most creative children omitted windows and doors altogether in their drawings, drew them abnormally high on the house, or made them extremely small. Of special interest is the house shown in Figure 1, drawn by Subject J, an exceptionally creative third-grade boy. At the time the drawing was done the hypothesis concerning psychological inaccessibility was certainly valid for this subject. The teacher, principal, parents, and school social worker were all greatly concerned about this boy. At times, he would be so preoccupied with his own thoughts that he would be quite unaware of what was happening in the classroom. He was also having difficulty in learning to read and to write down his thoughts. In spite of this, however, it was quite evident that he had amassed a great deal of information, especially in science, and could use it in solving problems and in thinking of new and original ideas of a very high quality. Something of the magnitude of this boy's problem was seen when we found that twelve of his thirty-three classmates nominated him as having ideas for being naughty, and twelve as having wild or silly ideas. No one nominated him as having good ideas, in spite of his truly exceptional talent. Findings from another study by the author indicate that nominations on the "good ideas" criterion is related to percentage of good ideas produced rather than to the actual number of good ideas produced.

The results of an experimental study also helps us to understand this problem. In this study, we formed groups of five children and in each we placed one of the most creative children in the classroom, as identified by our tests. We then placed each group in a situation requiring creative thinking and involving competition among groups. The focus of observation during this hour-long activity was upon the techniques used by the groups to control the most creative member and the behavior of the most creative member in coping with these pressures. Much of the behavior

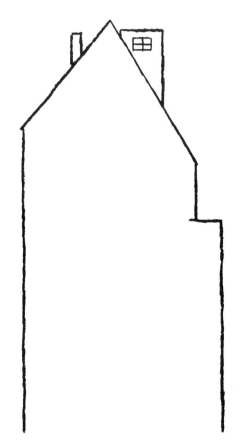

Figure 1

HOUSE DRAWN BY SUBJECT J, AN EXCEPTIONALLY CREATIVE THIRD-GRADE BOY

observed suggests that the highly creative individual may be responsible for many of his own woes.

At the second-grade level, the most highly creative individuals were generally quite unpleasant, showing little consideration for the group, little or no goal orientation, little or no identification with the group and little or no heed to the leadership attempts of their less creative peers. In the third grade, the most creative subjects tended to work independently and were ignored for the most part. This tendency persisted in the fourth grade where the most creative members assumed little responsibility for leadership and were given little credit in the final ratings for the important contributions which they actually made to the group's success. The highly creatives in the fifth grade manifested more leadership attempts than in the fourth grade but brought upon themselves open criticism and attack for "being too scientific," "being too greedy," and such. These tendencies became more pronounced in the sixth-grade groups.

SUMMARY

The fundamental problem of the highly creative individual in maintaining his creativity is in learning how to cope with the discomfort which arises from divergency—of so often being a minority of one. Of the problems which arise in this process some of the more important ones include: coping with the sanctions of society against divergency, the alienation of one's friends through the expression of a talent, pressures to be a well-rounded personality, divergence from sex-role norms, desires to learn on one's own, attempts at tasks which are too difficult, searching for a purpose, having different values and being motivated by different rewards, and searching for one's uniqueness. Running throughout all of these problems, of course, are factors which lead to psychological estrangement from others—parents, teachers, and peers.

EFFECTS OF EARLY EXPERIENCE IN SOCIAL BEHAVIOR AND ORGANIZATION

J. P. Scott

chapter nine

PERSONALITY
AND
EARLY
EXPERIENCE

A bird raised entirely by human beings fails to respond sexually to other birds. A dog raised in isolation does not learn how to fight; he lives peacefully when not attacked by other dogs, and he is unsuccessful in defending himself against attack. An Easter duckling, brought up by children, never learns to quack; when taken to a farm, he stays away from other ducks and refuses to share their food.

These observations of social behavior among animals lead inevitably to some thoughts about human social behavior. What about human infants raised in isolation? What are the effects of lack of social experiences early in life? Just as animal physiology may cast some light on human physiology and functioning (see the fourth selection in this book), so animal social behavior may provide some insights into human behavior in groups. The parallels lead to no firm conclusions, but they are intriguing, as the following selection makes clear.

EFFECTS OF EARLY
EXPERIENCE ON
SOCIAL BEHAVIOR
_____ AND ORGANIZATION

This is a subject which has great practical and clinical interest. Most of our theories concerning education and mental health stress the importance of early, as opposed to later, experience, but only recently have we begun to accumulate a solid observational and experimental basis for these theories. In this chapter, I am going to review these findings in relation to the general principles which they illustrate, using certain species and types of experiments as examples rather than trying to review all of the literature. Many of the species chosen for study belong to the families Canidae (wolves and dogs) and Anatidae (ducks and geese), two highly social families of mammals and birds having close associations with man. The two major types of experimentation are cross-fostering between species and rearing in isolation. Both of these produce major changes in the social environment of the developing young. However, before we can analyze the effects of these experiments, we must understand the nature of the normal behavior which they affect.

SOME FUNDAMENTAL
CONCEPTS OF
SOCIAL BEHAVIOR
AND ORGANIZATION

The most general function of behavior is adaptation to environmental change. All animals which are capable of behavior show such adaptations, and each species achieves adaptations in particular ways. These are called patterns of behavior, and individuals within a species usually have a choice of several. Even in the lower animals there is some variability of

"The Effects of Early Experience on Social Behavior and Organization," by J. P. Scott, in SOCIAL BEHAVIOR AND ORGANIZATION AMONG VERTEBRATES, edited by William Etkin (Chicago: University of Chicago Press, 1964), pp. 231–252; reprinted by permission of the publisher and the author.

behavior, so that if one pattern of behavior does not result in adaptation, another one may be substituted. Such patterns may be extremely complex in higher animals, but any given species still has characteristic ways of behaving.

For example, two male dogs or wolves approach each other for the first time. They walk in stiff-legged gaits with tails erect and tail tips moving slowly from side to side. They may touch noses and then each starts nosing the base of the other's tail, apparently investigating the other's odor. Or, they may suddenly spring at each other, snapping, snarling, and growling. If a full scale fight develops, one of the animals will eventually get hurt and attempt to run away. If he is caught, he will roll on his back, pawing with his legs, and snapping and yelping, whenever the other animal attempts to bite.

These are some of the patterns of agonistic behavior which are typical of the Canidae. In part, they are the result of structure, for the only way in which one dog can hurt another is with his teeth. They also result from learning, an experienced animal being ordinarily superior to one which has never fought before (Scott, 1950).

The most important types of adaptive functions can be classified under nine different headings, as seen in Table 1. This provides an outline for systematic description of a species and also gives a list of the possible ways in which social behavior can be affected by experience.

Table 1
GENERAL TYPES OF ADAPTIVE BEHAVIOR

Type of Behavior	*Synonyms*	*Definition*
Investigative	Exploratory	Investigating social, biological and physical environment
Shelter-seeking	Contactual, Aggregative, Comfort-seeking	Seeking out and coming to rest in most favorable part of environment
Ingestive		Eating and drinking
Eliminative		Behavior associated with urination and defecation
Sexual		Courtship and mating behavior
Epimeletic	Care-giving	Giving care and attention
Et-epimeletic	Care-soliciting	Calling and signaling for care and attention
Allelomimetic	Mimesis, Contagious behavior, Mutual imitation	Doing the same thing, with some degree of mutual stimulation
Agonistic	Conflict, Aggression and defense	Any behavior associated with conflict including fighting, escape, and freezing

A second fundamental concept of social behavior and organization is that of the social relationship, defined as regular and predictable behavior exhibited between two individuals, usually of the same species. One example of such a social relationship is dominance-subordination, described in Chapter 1. This relationship develops gradually in dogs. When young puppies first begin to play with each other they roll over and over, pawing and biting. Sometimes this develops into an actual fight, ending when one puppy gives up and runs away. Thereafter the relationship is likely to develop further along the same lines, so that when we give the two puppies a single bone the dominant puppy takes it and the subordinate one waits until the other is through. This is not the only sort of relationship which may be developed. In some cases, the first puppy to get the bone is allowed to keep it and the other one waits. In still others, the question of dominance is never really settled, and some sort of fight is likely to break out in any competitive situation. Each relationship is thus made up of certain patterns of behavior, i.e., dominance-subordination may include several patterns of agonistic behavior.

Table 2
IMPORTANT TYPES OF SOCIAL RELATIONSHIPS IN VERTEBRATES

Relationship	*Example*	*Type of Social Behavior Involved*
Sexual	Mated pair in doves	Sexual
Care-dependency	Parental care in birds, mammals	Epimeletic plus ingestive, shelter-seeking, eliminative, etc.
Mutual care	Mutual grooming, primates	Epimeletic
Leader-follower	Mother and offspring in sheep	Allelomimetic
Dominance-subordination	Peck order, chickens	Agonistic
Mutual avoidance	Wild deermice	Agonistic

There are many other kinds of social relationships, some of which are outlined in Table 2. An important general principle is that patterns of behavior and social relationships are both developed. The young puppy does not come into the world with either. The capacities for attacking and running away develop slowly as the puppy grows and are modified by learning as well as heredity. In short, the social behavior of an individual changes with time and cannot be considered a constant except in an artificial sense.

BASIC EXPERIMENTS
WITH EARLY SOCIAL
EXPERIENCE

Cross-fostering
between species

This is part of the normal experience of domestic dogs, which are rou-
tinely taken from their mothers as young puppies and reared by human
beings. We might therefore expect that the behavior of dogs would show
the maximum effects of such social experience. One way to find out what
these effects are is to observe the behavior of dogs toward one another
and compare it with their behavior toward human beings. We placed a
number of young dogs in large, open fields where they could live together
and could be observed while entirely separated from people. The idea
was to find out if domestic dogs had developed, either through experience
or through selection, special patterns of behavior toward human beings
different from their responses toward dogs. Actually, these dogs inter-
acted with the same patterns of behavior that they normally exhibit
toward human masters. Furthermore, when dog behavior is compared
with that of wolves, the wild ancestors of dogs, the same sort of behavior
patterns are seen. The chief effect of selection has been to exaggerate or
partially suppress various kinds of behavior in different breeds (Scott,
1950).

Changing the social environment under which they have been raised
for hundreds of generations has not changed dogs into people. They still
act in the same ways that wolves act; the chief differences are that these
reactions are now given to human beings as well as to other dogs and
that dogs are much more variable than their wild relatives. In addition,
these behavior patterns can be suppressed or exaggerated by training.
For example, dogs which react sexually to human beings are punished
and do not show the same type of behavior again.

Dogs are usually not removed from their mothers until they have had
some experience with their own kind, nor are they kept entirely away
from other dogs. However, such separation experiments can be carried
out quite easily with birds hatched in an incubator. One of the commonly
observed effects upon birds reared entirely by humans is that they not
only transfer their usual behavior patterns to human beings but that they
are relatively unresponsive to their own kind. Whenever there is a choice
between another bird and a human being, they choose the person, and

such preferences often render them ineffectual in mating and parental behavior (Lorenz, 1935). Hand-reared male turkey poults respond sexually to the human hand more often than to models of turkeys, whereas the reverse is true of normally reared birds (Schein and Hale, 1959). We can conclude that the major effect of this kind of early social experience is to alter social relationships rather than social behavior patterns. In the many experiments of this type, the adopted animal does not take up the social behavior patterns of human beings but develops social relationships with people on the basis of its own native behavior patterns.

The effects of rearing in social isolation

It is difficult to rear an animal completely apart from all social contacts. However, this is not necessary in order to produce some very striking effects. By the time a young puppy is three weeks of age, it can feed itself quite successfully. If such a puppy is placed in a box and fed so that it never sees or has direct contact with human beings or other dogs thereafter, its behavior becomes very different from that of an animal reared with its own kind. For example, fox terrier puppies, which come from a breed selected for fighting abilities, usually begin to fight with each other at about seven weeks of age if left with their mothers. This becomes so severe that they often have to be separated to prevent their killing each other, although a maximum of two or three can usually get along. If puppies of the same strain of fox terriers are raised in boxes until they are sixteen weeks of age before they are introduced to normally raised fox terriers, they do not attack the other animals and, if attacked, fight back unsuccessfully. They live in peace with fox terriers brought up like themselves and almost invariably get the worst of any encounter with a normally reared animal (Fisher, 1955; Fuller, 1962).

Here we see the general principle that one of the major effects of isolation is to prevent the development of social relationships. The isolated fox terriers had nothing to fight with at the age when fighting normally begins. Some of them bit their food dishes and played with them, throwing them around. As adults, they showed a great deal of this type of behavior, suggesting that they may have attempted to develop social relationships with inanimate objects rather than with their own kind. The experience of isolation thus prevents the development of social relationships. Whether such puppies could still develop normal relationships, given special training, has not yet been determined, but they probably retain some capacity for adaptation. Compared with normal animals, they are greatly handicapped in their capacities for developing social relationships.

THE DESCRIPTIVE STUDY
OF SOCIAL DEVELOPMENT

Before we can experiment intelligently with the development of behavior, we must learn something about its normal course. The best way to do this is to make systematic daily observations of young animals in a reasonably normal environment. This can usually be done more satisfactorily in a laboratory than in the field, because many animals rear their young in holes or nests where observation is difficult. In such cases, the laboratory environment is often no more restricted than that of animals reared in the wild.

Observations should be made systematically and should cover major changes in the capacities of the animals. These include changes in the function of the sense organs, changes in motor capacities such as locomotion, grasping, etc., changes in psychological capacities such as learning and discrimination, and, finally, changes in the major patterns of social behavior. Motion pictures should be made at regular intervals, as this makes it possible to compare different ages simultaneously.

When all the data has been gathered, it can be assembled in the form of a developmental graph or map. This usually shows certain times when a great many changes occur, dividing development into periods (Table 3). From the viewpoint of social behavior, the most important periods are those associated with important changes in social relationships. The following example illustrates the nature of these periods in the development of the puppy.

Neonatal period

The newborn puppy is blind and deaf. Its method of locomotion is a slow crawl while throwing the head from side to side. When it touches anything warm and soft, it attempts to suck; and when it locates a nipple, it sucks vigorously, pushing the breast with its forepaws and pushing forward with the hind paws. If the mother is away, the puppies' movements bring them into contact with one another and they soon settle down in a heap. The mother, coming near them, pokes them with her nose and this contact sets off searching movements and eventual nursing. As they nurse, the puppies touch one another and thus keep themselves stimulated. The mother also licks the puppies in the ano-genital region with

Table 3
PERIODS OF DEVELOPMENT IN THE PUPPY AND SONG SPARROW

Puppy			Song Sparrow		
Name	*Age (weeks)*	*Begins with*	*Name*	*Age (days)*	*Begins with*
Neonatal	0–2	Birth, nursing	Stage 1—Nestling	0–4	Hatching, gaping
Transition	2–3	Eyes open	Stage 2	5–6	Eyes open
Socialization	3–10	Startle to sound	Stage 3	7–9	Cowering—first fear reactions
			Stage 4—Fledgling	10–16	Leaving nest—first flight
			Stage 5	17–28	Full flight
Juvenile	10——	Final weaning	Stage 6—Juvenile	29——	Independent feeding

The periods of development described by Nice (1943) for the song sparrow roughly correspond to similar periods in the puppy. In both species, the young are born in an immature state, require intense parental care and feeding, and go through much the same stages before becoming independent. Development is much more rapid in the bird, although in small mammals such as mice a similar state of maturity is reached within the same time.

her tongue, which sets off reflexes of urination and defecation. She licks up their leavings, and in this way the nest is kept clean. In spite of being deaf, the puppies vocalize loudly in response to pain, hunger, or cold. This usually stimulates the mother to care for the puppy (Scott and Marston, 1950).

Puppies in this period thus show behavior highly adapted for neonatal life and quite different from adult forms of social behavior. Nursing is a neonatal form of ingestive behavior, and reflexive elimination is likewise a neonatal characteristic. The searching movements are a neonatal form of investigative behavior. There is no indication either that the newborn puppies are able to locate the mother through scent or that the performance improves with practice. Learning is extremely slow and uncertain compared to later stages (Cornwell and Fuller, 1961); Stanley *et al.*, 1963).

Transition period

The first change in behavior takes place on the average at about two weeks of age, when the eyes open. During the following week a series of rapid changes take place. At approximately three weeks of age, the ears open, and the animals first give a startle response to sound. When the eyes open, the puppies begin to crawl backwards as well as forwards. By the end of the week they can stand and walk. At the same time, their first teeth appear, and they are able to eat and drink by themselves. At the beginning of the week it requires eighty trials to produce a stable conditioned avoidance response; at its end, the same effect can be produced in less than ten trials (Klyavina *et al.*, 1958). They begin to eliminate by themselves outside the nest by this time. They also begin to take notice of dogs and people at a distance and will approach and investigate them. Some playful biting and pawing, or agonistic behavior, occurs. In short, the puppies have gone through a rapid transition from neonatal to adult capacities in the sense organs, in motor and psychological development, and in many social behavior patterns.

Period of socialization

All of these changes mean that the puppy is now capable of developing true social relationships. During the next few weeks, the puppy shows a typical response to any new individual. For the first few minutes, he is afraid. If no harm comes, he approaches the stranger, sniffing and wagging the tail. Thereafter he is highly responsive, and the further development of the social relationship depends upon the behavior of the stranger. Among themselves, puppies spend a great deal of time in playful fighting: rolling over and over each other, pawing, biting, and clasping. By thirty days of age, the litter moves as a group on many occasions, thus showing allelomimetic behavior. By nine weeks, recognizable sexual behavior can be seen. The only type of social behavior which the puppies do not show in some form is the care-giving behavior typical of parents.

At the same time, the et-epimeletic, or care-soliciting, behavior of whining and yelping has declined a great deal and only appears under certain circumstances. The puppy will still yelp when cold, hungry, or in pain but in many cases can now adapt to these stimuli by its own activities. Other circumstances which now bring out yelping behavior are being caught, being left alone, and particularly being isolated in a strange place.

The puppy's brain is also developing rapidly, as indicated by the electroencephalograph. The newborn pup shows almost no brain waves at all and no distinction between sleeping and waking states. By three weeks of age, the brain waves are beginning to appear, and there is a difference in the sleeping and wakeful conditions. By seven weeks of age, the brain waves are essentially similar to those of the adult (Charles and Fuller, 1956). Since the major brain waves are associated with the development of vision in human beings, it is probable that these changes indicate the development of the visual cortex.

Juvenile period

At seven weeks of age there is an important change in behavior, as this is the time when a mother begins to wean her pups completely. They are still unable to find food for themselves and in a wild state would be dependent on food brought to them by the mother. While they are still nursing, the mother may vomit food for them, and this will be continued for some time after.

The puppies stay closely around their den or nest box for some time, not moving far away until approximately twelve weeks of age. Then they begin investigating nearby areas. They probably would be incapable of any real hunting until after the second teeth appear, beginning about four months of age. Studies of wolves indicate that these animals begin to hunt at about six months of age (Murie, 1944).

Further development

The next major change in social relationships occurs at sexual maturity, when the puppies are first capable of developing sexual relationships. This may occur at anywhere from six months to a year of age in most dog breeds, although the wild Canidae usually do not breed until the end of the second year. The birth of the young initiates a new type of social relationship and the parental period of development.

Comparative study of mammalian development

The dog is an animal which is born in an immature state and which goes through a relatively long period of maternal care. We can now contrast its development with that of the sheep, which is born in a much more mature state and receives relatively little maternal care.

Like the dog, the newborn lamb begins life by nursing, but it begins the transition to the adult type of ingestive behavior earlier, at about ten days of age, when it first begins to graze. Unlike the dog, the period of nursing is a long time, lasting at least three months and requiring close association between mother and lamb.

Most of the transitions that occur in the dog's third week of development take place before birth in the sheep. A young lamb is born with fully developed sense organs and adopts the adult method of locomotion a few minutes after birth. It is probably capable of learning immediately after birth, and experiments show that it can be conditioned within a few days (Moore, 1958).

The formation of social relationships also begins at birth or shortly after. The newborn lamb rises on wobbly legs and approaches the nearest sheep, poking its nose under her body and eventually reaching the nipple where it begins to suck. However, only its own mother will allow it to nurse, and other sheep butt it away (Collias, 1956). This limits its first social relationship to one animal, the mother, and the young lamb follows her closely during the first few days. Likewise, the mother never moves more than a few feet away from her lamb. By ten days of age, the young lamb begins the formation of other social relationships with animals of its own age, following them and showing various playful forms of adult social behavior, such as sexual mounting and butting.

All during the nursing period, the mother and lamb are closely associated, and if they are separated they try to get together again. Usually the mother baas and the lamb comes running, but if the lamb is caught and held in some way, it will call and the mother will come to it. In any frightening situation, the lamb runs to the mother and stays close by her side. In this way a strong habit of following is built up. As a result, in adult sheep the oldest females tend to become leaders of the flock, followed by their respective offspring (Scott, 1945).

The periods of development are not as clear-cut as in the dog. However, changes in social relationships take place at ten days (when there is a shift toward solid food and a tendency to form new social relationships with animals other than the mother), at the time of final weaning, and again in the autumn when the lambs become sexually mature.

Thus there is a recognizable neonatal period and a transition period, but the period of socialization overlaps both of them. We can conclude that these periods can vary greatly in form in different animals and that we are basically dealing not with a time sequence but with certain processes, particularly the processes of transition from the neonatal to the adult forms of social behavior and the process of socialization. These processes do not occur in the same sequence in different species but differ in relation to the type of social organization typical of the adult animals (Figure 1).

In the sheep, the earliest and strongest social relationship is developed with the mother and forms the foundation for leadership in the flock. In the dog, development is such that the strongest social relationships are developed with the litter mates, forming the basis for pack organization of adults. Wolves show a similar type of development, and relationships with the parents are comparatively weak because the adults spend so much time hunting during the period of socialization of the young.

We may also conclude that there is a critical period for the process of socialization (Scott and Marston, 1950; Scott, 1962). In an animal like the sheep, this occurs almost immediately after birth, but in the dog, it comes considerably later in development. In both species, there is a time when it is easy to form a social relationship with the young animal. The period is a critical one, because it determines with which particular members of its own species the animal will develop strong social relationships.

DEVELOPMENT OF
SOCIAL BEHAVIOR
IN BIRDS

In contrast to mammals, birds are primarily animals whose life is spent in the air and whose bodies are adapted for flight. This affects their physical structure, their body covering, their sense organs, and their social behavior (see Chaps. 2 and 4 for general discussion of bird adaptation). An essential part of adaptation for flying is the possession of feathers,

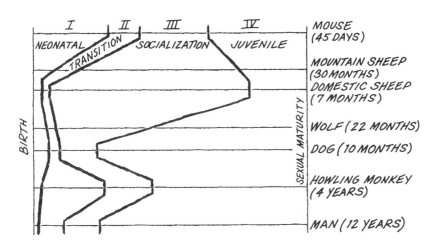

Figure 1
Relative lengths of the first four periods of development in various mammals are shown in this graph. The length of each period is shown as a proportion of the total time required for the attainment of sexual maturity in females of that species as given in the figures on the right. Estimates of the period of socialization are based on the time of weaning. Actually, the period of primary socialization in man begins immediately after the neonatal period (see text). (After J. P. Scott and M. Marston, J. Genet. Psychol. 7 [1950].)

which provide a strong and lightweight means of increasing the surface of the wings and insulating against heat loss. This automatically limits the use of the tactile sense, since any extensive contact ruffles the feathers. With their great rapidity of movement, birds have developed the eyes as the dominant sense organs. Odor is of little importance, and hearing is not highly developed.

The important motor organs are the wings, which means that any manipulation must be done with the feet or beak. This latter organ is again connected with flight, being a lightweight replacement of teeth. Furthermore, birds tend to be relatively small in size compared to mammals.

Another major difference is the fact that all birds lay eggs, which must be kept at body temperature for incubation. This affects both parental behavior and the development of behavior in the young. Compared with mammals, their development is extraordinarily rapid. Smaller birds hatch within twelve to fourteen days and may leave the nest and fly ten days after hatching (Nice, 1943).

Nice (1943, 1950) has carefully described stages of development in passerine birds, particularly the song sparrow (Table 3, p. 158). The newly hatched bird is blind and almost naked. In the first stage, its behavior consists almost entirely of gaping so that it can be fed by the parents. In the second stage, the eyes open and the bird begins to stand up and do some preening. In the third stage, there is a rapid acquisition of adult motor patterns, such as stretching the wings, scratching the head and shaking the body. The fourth stage begins with the most important change—leaving the nest at ten days of age. Along with this come the behavior patterns of hopping, flying, walking, and sleeping in the adult position. Independent feeding does not occur for another two days. The fifth stage begins at seventeen days with the attainment of skillful flight and ends with the complete independence of the young bird and breaking of the parent-offspring relationship at approximately four weeks of age.

Comparing this with the development of mammals, we can see that these birds have a "newly hatched" period comparable to the neonatal period, in which all behavior is of an infantile type and primarily concerned with nutrition. The transition to the adult form of locomotion begins at the second stage, reaching its most important point at Stage 4 when independent flight begins. We could therefore call the second and third stages transition periods. Nice has found that the birds can be socialized to people (i.e., form their first social relationship with the human handler) if they are taken from the nest just before the fourth stage, when they normally leave the nest. It is difficult to tell when the stage of socialization begins, but it is probably as early as the fourth stage. The end of the fifth stage, when the birds achieve complete independence, corresponds to the process of weaning in a mammal and to the beginning of the juvenile period.

Lorenz (1935) reports that the jackdaw, a bird belonging to the crow family (*Corvidae*), will become strongly attached to human beings if hand rearing begins just at the time when the bird is ready for flight. Adoption at a later age produces a less complete social relationship. It seems likely that the process of socialization begins very close to the time of flight, in birds which are hatched immaturely and fly immediately after leaving the nest. This receives some support from observations of development in the cowbird, which does not become attached to the foster parents. However, it is also possible that the formation of social relationships in these parasitic birds is governed entirely by heredity.

Development of behavior in geese and ducks

These birds are hatched in a much more mature state than those described above. The newly hatched gosling has its eyes open, can walk, and even swim. The parent birds may assist the young in finding food but do not feed them. In spite of this maturity, young birds go through a relatively long period before they develop flight feathers and make the transition to the adult pattern of locomotion. By this time they are nearly full sized.

The newly hatched goslings will follow any large, moving object. This is usually the parent bird but may be a boat which comes near the nest of the wild bird, or, in the case of birds hatched in an incubator, may be the person of an experimenter. Once the young goslings have followed an individual for a few hours, it is almost impossible to get them to transfer to another; and they consequently develop their further social relationships with the bird or person to whom they first became attached. This process of primary socialization in birds has been called "imprinting" (Lorenz, 1935), implying that the young birds are in some way permanently impressed or molded by their early social experience. This phenomenon was discussed in some aspects in Chapters 4, 6, and 8, described more extensively in Chapter 7, and will be dealt with here in relation to the formation of the social bond.

The process of socialization normally begins soon after hatching. Most of the transition from infantile to adult forms of behavior has already taken place in the egg, but the most important transition, to flight, takes place at a much later period, at six weeks or more of age. In contrast to the perching birds, in which the transition to flight occurs almost simultaneously with the beginning of socialization, the primary social relationships are formed long before. This is correlated with a different kind of social organization as adults. In geese, ducks, and similar birds, the families stay together at least until the fall migration, with considerable evidence of leadership. Family groups in the perching birds generally break up immediately, and no leadership is apparent.

Experiments with imprinting

Most of these have been done with ducks of various wild and tame varieties and with domestic chickens, whose eggs are more easily obtained (Hess, 1959). The latter have a type of development somewhat similar to that of ducks and geese and pass through the same early period in which primary socialization or imprinting takes place.

Many of these experiments are concerned with the nature of the stimulation which produces imprinting and are done with animated models which bear some degree of resemblance to the parent animals. Fabricius (1951) found that the ducklings would follow a model of almost any shape, including square boxes, and of almost any size, except very small objects. The effectiveness of the model can be greatly increased if some noise accompanies it. This does not have to be the call of the parent bird, almost any monotonous noise being effective, and means that the ducklings respond to a very general sort of stimulation. Once having responded, they rapidly learn to discriminate between the special model and others. Imprinting is thus limited to the parent species by the circumstances of hatching and maternal care rather than any innate response to special stimuli.

Fabricius and Boyd (1954), Hess (1959), and others have found that the young ducklings show the maximum tendency to follow between one and two days of age. Younger and older animals followed much less readily. This confirms the existence of a short critical period for the process of imprinting (Figure 2).

Fabricius also found that the young ducklings showed escape as well as following responses to the model. As the animals grew older, they showed more and more escape responses, indicating that it is the development of fearful behavior which terminates the critical period. In terms of natural behavior, the young ducklings would normally be brooded and protected by their parents during the first few days of life and would have an opportunity to follow only them. Following the parent birds would keep the young ones away from others; but if strange animals did come near, the escape response would prevent the formation of an association. This negative limitation on primary socialization is quite similar to that found in dogs and may be a general one among vertebrate animals (Hess, 1959).

Figure 2

Imprinting in ducks has been analytically studied in the apparatus above. *The decoy "mother" moves around the runway producing the "glock" call. The duckling to be imprinted is placed on the outside runway and allowed to follow the decoy. Among the factors analyzed using this apparatus was the relative sensitivity of animals exposed at different ages to a standard period of imprinting and tested later for their responses. As shown in the chart* (below) *these ducklings were most effectively imprinted when from thirteen to sixteen hours old and were but little affected by the same experience after twenty-four hours. (After E. Hess, in E. Bliss (ed.),* Roots of Behavior, *1962.)*

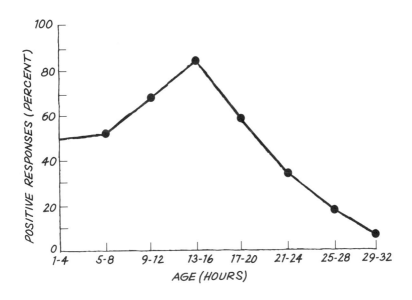

These experiments with models have emphasized the effect of the first social interaction upon the young animal, neglecting the fact that there is a corresponding effect upon the parents. The normal situation is one in which there is interaction between the behavior of parents and young, forming a social relationship involving both animals. Such experiments do show, however, that social relationships of an imperfect sort can be formed with animated or even motionless models, as well as with animals of different species.

THE RESULTS OF EARLY SOCIAL EXPERIENCE

King (1958) has reviewed the factors which must be studied for a complete analysis of the effects of early experience. The age at which the experience is given is extremely important, as is its duration. Furthermore, simple chronological age means little except in relation to the developmental periods of the species studied.

In a satisfactory experiment it must be first established that there is some immediate effect of the early experience. Second, it must be shown by testing at a later date that there is a long-range effect. The age at testing should be primarily related to the periods of development rather than chronological age. Finally, it is not sufficient to show merely that an early experience has a later effect. The test must determine whether the effect was important and whether it will persist if the animal is given a chance to readjust its behavior.

As I said above, the principal types of experiments have been the fostering of young animals by a different species, usually man, and comparing animals raised in isolation with those reared in normal social groups. These treatments have relatively little effect on the patterns of social behavior peculiar to a species but do produce major effects on social relationships. Early social experience thus has a profound effect on social organization.

Sexual relationships

Hand-reared birds of many species tend to transfer their courtship and mating behavior to human beings, resulting in interference with the formation of normal sexual relationships and mating bonds. However, in most experiments there has been little attempt to differentiate between the situations which result in lasting effects and those which might permit some readjustment. In the case of hand-reared mammals, the usual effect is for the hand-reared individual to respond both to human beings and to receptive females of the proper species. Results of this kind are often seen in animals reared as pets.

The other type of experiment (rearing animals in social isolation and comparing them with animals reared in groups) also has effects upon sexual relationships. Beach (1942) found that male rats reared alone after weaning showed more readiness to mate than those reared in groups. Sexual behavior is not otherwise affected, and the explanation seems to be that the young rats reared together form habits of passive inhibition or active play which interfere with sexual behavior later. However, this interference is not serious enough to prevent effective mating. It should be pointed out that the play of young rats is largely aggressive rather than sexual. The sexual responses of females are not affected by isolation (Stone, 1926).

Guinea pigs are much more precocious animals than rats, being able to walk, follow their mothers, and even eat a little solid food at birth. Valenstein and his associates (1955) took male guinea pigs and divided them into two groups. The isolated ones were left with their mothers but away from littermates up to twenty-five days of age, then completely isolated until seventy-seven days, at which time their sexual behavior was tested. The social males were left with their mother and siblings for twenty-five days, then each placed with three to five females up to seventy-seven days. All were then exposed to females in heat, and the socially experienced animals were found to be much more effective in their sexual behavior. The differences were more striking if the isolated males were taken from their mothers at ten days of age, and similar results were obtained for females. In this species of mammal the result of early social experience is to facilitate sexual behavior.

In still another species, mice, isolation has no effect on adult sexual behavior of males (King, 1956). The explanation of the different results in various species of mammals seems to lie in differences in the type of early social experience. In many immature mammals, such as lambs, goats, dogs, and monkeys, a considerable portion of play behavior is sexual in nature. Dr. Albert Pawlowski reared a female puppy at our laboratory apart from dogs but in contact with human beings. When she came into estrus as an adult, she was introduced to several male dogs. Many of her responses were inappropriate, e.g., rolling over in a playful defensive posture when approached by the male. However, an experienced male was able to hold her in the proper position and complete mating.

At the Yerkes Primate Laboratories young chimpanzees are taken from the mother at birth and reared by human beings in a nursery for the first year or two of life. Nissen (1954) placed mixed groups of these young animals together and left them until just before puberty. None of the inexperienced animals were able to complete mating. However, experienced animals were able to mate with members of the group, the males being more effective than the females. Thereafter, the experienced young animals were able to mate with one another. Nissen concluded that in these animals mating behavior has to be learned from older individuals.

Harlow (1963) has obtained equally dramatic results with young rhesus monkeys reared with dummy mothers. Both males and females are completely unable to mate with one another, and Harlow has never been able to induce mating in the males, even with experienced females. In a few cases the females were impregnated by experienced males. The whole difficulty can be averted if the young animals are allowed a few hours of social play during a critical period. Young monkeys normally indulge in a good deal of playful sexual behavior during which the correct adult patterns of behavior are developed.

Thus there are two demonstrated effects of early social experience upon sexual behavior. One is the formation of habits which interfere with later adult behavior, as in male rats. The other and more common effect is practice in playful sexual behavior which facilitates adult behavior. Which of these is most important depends upon the species and the age at which the experience occurs.

Dominance-subordination relationships

Early social experience has a pronounced effect on agonistic behavior. Young animals of many species normally do not fight with the particular adults or young with whom they become socialized. As they grow older, they may form a dominance-subordination relationship with them and continue to live in relative peace, at the same time beginning to fight fiercely against strange animals similar to those with which they were brought up.

Rearing in isolation modifies the development of agonistic behavior in many ways, depending on the species concerned. Guhl (1958) found that young cockerels reared in a group did not begin to form a peck order until they were approximately six weeks of age. However, if he reared them in isolation and put them together at thirty-one days of age, they began to form a peck order immediately.

Among mice, animals reared in the same litter live peaceably together long after they reach the adult stage, and they may never fight at all. If they are exposed to strange animals, however, they begin to fight with them at about thirty-two days of age, when puberty and male hormone production begins. King (1957) studied the effect of early social experience on this tendency to fight strangers. He kept mice with the mother until twenty days of age, which is about a week before the normal weaning time and the first age at which the young animals can survive successfully without the mother. Thereafter he kept some males together for various periods and isolated others. He found that the animals reared with other males attacked strangers much sooner than did the isolated ones. He also found that at least ten days of social experience were necessary to produce the effect and that the same experience as an adult produced no effect at all. There is obviously a critical developmental period for controlling the appearance of this effect. The explanation seems to lie in the fact that isolated males investigate a stranger very cautiously and may never get started fighting at all. Males with social experience seem to recognize the stranger as an enemy immediately and waste no time in starting to fight.

Puppies during the period of socialization exhibit all sorts of playful behavior, including playful fighting. In the more aggressive breeds, this eventually leads to real fights and the formation of definite dominance-subordination relationships between members of a litter. King (1954) tested litters of adult basenjis and cocker spaniels which had been reared in this way, exposing them to strange animals of the same two breeds. He found that they exhibited most aggression against strangers most like themselves; that is, cocker spaniel females tended to attack strange cocker females most severely, and basenji males exhibited most hostility against males of their own breed. The explanation seems to be that the animals recognize the behavior of those similar to themselves but are not inhibited by dominance relationships when the like individuals are strangers.

Wire-haired fox terriers are highly aggressive even as young puppies. By seven weeks of age, they may attack one another so severely as to produce physical injury or even death, although they can form dominance relationships between small groups of two or three pups (Fuller, 1953). As stated above, Fisher (1955) and Fuller (1962) raised such puppies in complete isolation from three to sixteen weeks of age and found that they did not fight when placed together. In this case isolation can completely prevent the development of the dominance-subordination relationship.

As in sexual relationships, there are two effects of early social experience. Socialization can inhibit fighting by the processes of passive inhibition and the early formation of dominance relationships (Scott, 1958). On the other hand, early experience involving mild or playful fighting behavior facilitates fighting against strangers.

Care-dependency relationships

What is the effect of fostering or isolation upon the behavior of an animal which later became a parent and attempts to rear its own offspring? Little work has been done along these lines because the experimental animals must be reared to adulthood. One might expect that a fostered animal would have some difficulty in recognizing its own young. A female sheep was raised apart from the flock and returned at the age of ten days (Scott, 1945). It never became a part of the flock but accepted a male at breeding time and subsequently gave birth to a lamb. The lamb developed the tendency to follow the flock and frequently became separated from its mother. Unlike the normal mothers, the parent showed little anxiety at the absence of her offspring, although the lamb frequently became anxious when the mother was missing. This suggests that such animals might make poor parents.

Among rats, part of the pattern of maternal behavior is building a nest for the young. Riess (1950) reported that rats which were raised on powdered food and given no bedding when young did not build nests for their offspring even though bedding material was provided for this. Eibel-Eibesfeldt (1955) repeated this experiment but only examined nest building of single rats without offspring. He found that if he lowered the temperature, most of the rats without previous nest-building experience built them immediately. Likewise, inexperienced rats were much more likely to build nests when given crepe paper than when provided with straw. It looks as if the nest-building pattern of behavior is organized largely by heredity and that experience chiefly has the effect of making animals respond to a lesser degree of stimulation and a wider variety of materials.

Much more dramatic effects result from isolation of young primates. Harlow (1963) finds that female rhesus monkeys reared with dummy mothers and deprived of contact with other monkeys later become extremely poor mothers. Whereas the normal mother continually holds its baby to her breast and responds to its cries with great solicitude, these orphan mothers are either indifferent to their young or actively reject them, pushing them away and beating them when they cry. In this species, maternal behavior is organized by the combined effects of heredity and early social experience.

**Leader-follower
relationships**

Lorenz' experiments with hand-reared graylag geese showed dramatically how the leadership relationship could be transferred to human beings. As adults, the flock would fly after him as he rode a bicycle or swim after him as he swam in the river.

Similarly, the hand rearing of young lambs transfers the leader-follower relationship to the human handler. If permitted, the young lamb will follow its foster parents everywhere. The relationship between the lamb and its own kind is at first completely disrupted, although a young male forms some tendency to follow through sexual attraction.

In summary, the results of early social experience upon the later development of social relationships can be extremely drastic under certain circumstances. Isolation prevents the normal development of such social relationships. Depending on the species, subsequent development may be completely or only partially disrupted. The normal process of primary socialization may have two conflicting effects. One of these effects is the formation of strong habits of behaving in an immature fashion toward the individuals involved, thus inhibiting the adult behavior toward these same individuals. This plays an important part in the control of agonistic behavior between members of a permanent social group, and it may in some species tend to prevent sexual behavior between closely related animals. The other is the facilitation of development of adult sexual and parental patterns of behavior, this being particularly important in various species of primates.

**THE EFFECTS OF
EARLY SOCIAL
EXPERIENCE ON
HUMAN BEHAVIOR**

It is impossible to perform drastic experiments with young human infants, such as rearing them in isolation or fostering them on different species. There have been a few criminal cases of child abuse involving complete isolation, and various semi-mythical accounts of children reared by animals (Ogburn, 1959). None of these has produced any valid evidence, and we can learn most by a careful study of normal development in human infants (Scott, 1963).

The human infant goes through a neonatal period lasting a month or six weeks during which time its behavior is almost entirely devoted to the infantile mode of feeding. It gives responses to light and sound, but studies with the electroencephalograph show no alpha rhythm, indicating that the visual cortex is undeveloped. Probably the human neonate actually sees very little.

The first change in behavior is the appearance of the ability to form stable conditioned reflexes rapidly. Shortly thereafter, the infant begins to smile at human faces, and the alpha waves appear in the EEG. From this time up until about six months of age, the child will smile at any stranger. After this a fear of strangers and strange situations begins to appear. It looks as if the time from six weeks to six months is the period of primary socialization, although further socialization can take place later, and strangers can form a relationship with the child if they persist in their contacts.

The most important transition processes begin at approximately seven and a half months of age, at the time of the appearance of the first teeth and development of the ability to crawl. By fifteen months of age, the child has the first four grinding teeth and is beginning to walk. This may properly be called a transition period. A further transition takes place in communication, since fifteen months is the time when a child begins to talk. By two years or shortly afterward, he is beginning to talk in short sentences, has a complete set of baby teeth, and can run as well as walk. This is the time when the child first becomes moderately independent of the mother, and thus this point in development corresponds to the age of final weaning and the beginning of a juvenile period in other mammals. All this means that the period of primary socialization precedes the major periods of transition in a human infant and that the first relationships will be developed with the mother or whoever cares for the child.

From a standpoint of practical child care, we can say first of all that the human infant at birth is highly protected from psychological damage, both by the circumstances of normal parental care and by the sensory, psychological and motor immaturity of the infant. Second, the period from six weeks to six or seven months is one in which new social relationships are developed with great ease. We could predict that relationships would be transferred from one person to another with little disturbance of the child, and this seems to be the case with regard to adoptions. We can also conclude that disturbance of primary social relationships during the next period might have much more serious results, and the evidence which Bowlby (1951) and others have gathered from children sent to hospitals at this age indicates serious emotional disturbance, although it may not necessarily have a lasting effect.

Finally, we can say that in attempting to predict the outcome of any social experience, we should keep in mind the kinds of factors which have been discovered experimentally in other animals. The developmental period is very important, and almost equally important is the genetic nature of the child affected. Some individuals are highly sensitive and others relatively insensitive. Early social experience may result either in the improvement of social relationships by practice or the opposite, inhibition of adult behavior by formation of conflicting habits. Finally, we must recognize the ability of a child to learn independently. Two children, given the same experience, may draw opposite conclusions from it. Thus there is no ironclad determination of adult behavior by early experience. We can, however, hope that in the future we may be able to use early experience more intelligently than we now do to promote mutual tolerance and stable conditions of mental health.

REFERENCES

Beach, F. A. 1942. Comparison of copulatory behavior of male rats raised in isolation, cohabitation, and segregation. *J. Genet. Psychol.*, 60: 121–36.

Bowlby, J. 1951. *Maternal Care and Mental Health.* Geneva: World Health Organization.

Charles, M. S., and Fuller, J. L. 1956. Developmental study of the electroencephalogram of the dog. *Electroenceph. Clin. Neurophysiol.*, 8: 645–52.

Collias, N. E. 1956. The analysis of socialization in sheep and goats. *Ecology*, 37: 228–39.

Cornwell, A. C., and Fuller, J. L. 1961. Conditioned responses in young puppies. *J. Comp. Physiol. Psychol.*, 54: 13–15.

Eibel-Eibesfeldt, I. 1955. Angeborenes und Erworbenes im Nestbauverhalten der Wanderatte. *Naturwissenschaften*, 23: 633–34.

Fabricius, E. 1951. Zur Ethologie junger Anatiden. *Acta Zool. Fenn.*, 68: 1–178.

Fabricius, E., and Boyd, H. 1954. Experiments on the following reaction of ducklings. *Wildfowl Trust Annual Report*, 6: 84–89.

Fisher, A. E. 1955. "The effects of differential early treatment on the social and exploratory behavior of puppies." Ph.D. thesis, Penn State University.

Fuller, J. L. 1953. Cross-sectional and longitudinal studies of adjustive behavior in dogs. *Ann. N.Y. Acad. Sci.*, 56: 214–24.

———. 1963. Programed life histories and socialization of the dog, *Proc. Int. Cong. Psychiat.* Montreal (in press).

Guhl, A. M. 1958. The development of social organization in the domestic chick. *Animal Behaviour*, 6: 92–111.

Harlow, H. F., Harlow, M. K., and Hansen, F. W. 1963. The maternal affectional system of rhesus monkeys. In: H. L. Rheingold (ed.), *Maternal Behavior in Mammals*. New York: John Wiley & Sons, Inc.

Hess, E. H. 1959. The relationship between imprinting and motivation. *Nebraska Symposium on Motivation,* 7: 44–77.

King, J. A. 1954. Closed social groups among domestic dogs. *Proc. Amer. Philo. Soc.,* 98: 327–36.

———. 1956. Sexual behavior of C57BL/10 mice and its relation to early social experience. *J. Genet. Psychol.,* 88: 223–29.

———. 1957. Relationships between early social experience and adult aggressive behavior in inbred mice. *J. Genet. Psychol.,* 90: 151–66.

———. 1958. Parameters relevant to determining the effects of early experience upon the adult behavior of animals. *Psychol. Bull.,* 55: 46–58.

Klyavina, M. P., *et al.* 1958. On the speed of formation of conditioned reflexes in dogs in ontogenesis. *Acad. Sci. U.S.S.R. J. Higher Nervous Activity,* 8: 929–36.

Lorenz, K. 1935. Der Kumpan in der Umwelt des Vogels. *J. Ornith.,* 83: 137–213, 289–413.

Moore, A. U. 1958. Conditioning and stress in the newborn lamb and kid. *In:* W. H. Gantt (ed.), *Physiological Bases of Psychiatry.* Springfield, Ill.: C. C Thomas.

Murie, A. 1944. *The Wolves of Mt. McKinley.* (U.S.D.I. Fauna Series No. 5.) Washington, D.C.: U.S. Government Printing Office.

Nice, M. M. 1943. Studies in the life history of the song sparrow, II. *Trans. Linnaean Sec.* (N.Y.), 6: 1–328.

———. 1950. Development of a redwing *(Agelaius phoenicius). Wilson Bull.,* 62: 87–93.

Nissen, H. 1954. Development of sexual behavior in chimpanzees. *In:* W. C. Young (ed.), *Genetic, psychological and hormonal factors in the establishment and maintenance of sexual behavior in mammals.* Lawrence: University of Kansas. (Mimeograph.)

Ogburn. W. F. 1959. The wolf boy of Agra. *Amer. J. Sociol.,* 64: 449–54.

Riess, B. F. 1950. The isolation of factors of learning and native behavior in field and laboratory studies. *Ann. N.Y. Acad. Sci.* 51: 1093–1102.

Schein, M. W., and Hale, E. B. 1959. The effect of early social experience on male sexual behaviour of androgen treated turkeys. *Animal Behaviour,* 7: 189–200.

Scott, J. P. 1945. Social behavior, organization and leadership in a small flock of domestic sheep. *Comp. Psychol. Monogr.* No. 96, 18(4): 1–29.

———. 1950. The social behavior of dogs and wolves. *Ann. N.Y. Acad. Sci.,* 51: 1009–21.

———. 1958. *Aggression.* Chicago: University of Chicago Press.

———. 1963. The process of primary socialization in canine and human infants. *Child Develop. Monogr.,* 28(1): 1–47.

———. 1962. Critical periods in behavioral development. *Science,* 138: 949–58.

Scott, J. P., and Marston, M. 1950. Critical periods affecting the development of normal and mal-adjustive social behavior of puppies. *J. Genet. Psychol.,* 77: 25–60.

Stanley, W. C., *et al.* 1963. Conditioning in the neonatal puppy. *J. Comp. Physiol. Psychol.*, 56: 211–14.

Stone, C. P. 1926. The initial copulatory response of female rats reared in isolation from the age of twenty days to age of puberty. *J. Comp. Psychol.*, 6: 73–83.

Valenstein, E. S., Riss, W., and Young, W. C. 1955. Experiential and genetic factors in the organization of sexual behavior in male guinea pigs. *J. Comp. Physiol. Psychol.*, 48: 397–403.

THE MOOD AND STYLE OF TODAY'S EMERGING ADULTS

John McCabe

chapter ten

YOUTHFUL
REBELLION

Young people, it may be argued, have always *been in a state of rebellion against their elders; today's adolescents are no different from their parents at that age.*

But is this so? Aren't young people today really more aware of what's going on in the world, and more committed to trying to shape world events? Don't they care about substantial issues of war, poverty, race—or do these problems just supply handy ways of showing independence from parents and other oldsters?

The author of the following selection, himself a young man, suggests some issues that face young people nowadays and attempts to define them, if not answer them.

AWARE

Today's youths are very *aware* of the whole world; through TV they are plugged into the problem areas of the entire globe. Every day they are bombarded with Vietnam, China, Lyndon Johnson, Stokeley Carmichael, the U.N., air pollution, treaties with the Soviet Union. The song "Silent Night—Seven O'clock News" of Simon and Garfunkel illustrates perfectly this global awareness.

Though their fears are often not formulated, many know of the movement to automate; it is nearly impossible for them not to learn of the proposed data storage bank, which would include all the available information on each person from many agencies—and they wonder . . .; they hear about Berkeley and about Mississippi, and ponder the wisdom of adult control. This aware generation seems to experience *increased* insecurity. The normal questions of "Who am I?" and "What am I going to do with my life?" are raised, but they are more intense. These questions are intensified because parents seldom offer valid models of what it means to be a responsible person in society. The insecurity is also heightened because we live in a world of fantastic accelerating change; a world of hunger and increasing unemployment, yet of enormous wealth and resources; a world of growing international interrelatedness and, at the same time, of national arrogance—as illustrated by South Africa or our paternalistic relationship with Latin America. In such a world of continuing change, the educational demands become greater and greater.

HUNGRY FOR DEPTH

A signal characteristic of the becoming adults is a great desire for depth. Perhaps it is because they were raised on television that our young people desire deep experience and depth involvement. Some signs of this are

From DIALOGUE ON YOUTH, *edited by John McCabe (Indianapolis and New York: Bobbs-Merrill, 1967), pp. 20–37; reprinted by permission of the publisher.*

the expressive and individually involving dances of our day, the increasing interest in LSD and other sorts of "consciousness expanding" drugs, and the continuing high rates of attendance at significant new and experimental films. Quite possibly, today's mobility and the dispersion of the family add fuel to the search for new relationships and experiences.

The desire for "depth" and "involvement" among the emerging adults puzzles many. The "teeny-boppers" and "hippies" seem opposed to involvement. Yet some would assert that they are involved in their uninvolvement. Marshall McLuhan describes this side of the debate:

The young people who have experienced a decade of TV have naturally imbibed an urge toward involvement in depth that makes all the remote visualized goals of usual culture seem not only unreal but irrelevant, and not only irrelevant but anemic. It is the total involvement in all inclusive nowness that occurs in young lives via TV's mosaic image. This change of attitude has nothing to do with programming in any way, and would be the same if the programs consisted entirely of the highest cultural content. The change in attitude by means of relating themselves to the mosaic TV image would occur in any event. (*Understanding Media*, p. 335).

Some people maintain that the concern for depth is only superficial, representing merely a desire to be passive, to take in, to experience. Those persons describe youth as unwilling to take on the responsibility of relating deeply with other persons. They doubt the worth of that "depth" which seems to rob youths of serious engagement. In response, others argue that today's emerging adults do take responsibility for one another—that the new sexual openness frequently means taking the other person much more seriously than before. Sometimes that means respecting mutual wishes *not* to assume long-term commitments, even though going to bed together. Development of "the pill" has made such new relationships more easily attainable.

The "older" generation tends to insist that real depth means commitment and involvement over a long period of time (as with "study-in-depth"). The underlying question is, perhaps, one of values: What kinds of life-experience do people wish to have? Is the apparent depth experience through drugs, films, etc., genuinely deep and serious? The supporting side says drugs do make them more perceptive of the world, more aware of themselves, more sensitive to others. Their critics say, "It sounds like escape from reality."

It has been suggested by Simmons and Winograd (*It's Happening*) that today's adults are frightened by marijuana and LSD, because they are afraid of their own emotions. Most people have so subjugated their emotions to the rationality of a "technological ego" (cf. Kenneth Keniston, *The Uncommitted*) that they are made anxious by the thought of "a trip," which would take them over and remove them from their comfortable familiar place in the driver's seat. Factual research is needed on this question, though there is already considerable evidence that we are a very repressive culture.

FRUSTRATED

Young people today find many possible paths of action and expression cut short. Frustration is the result of coming up against adult control in many kinds of situations. Barriers of communication are experienced every day: with their parents and with educational administrators; with teachers and employers; with the opposite sex and with themselves— for adolescence is a time of self-discovery and self-definition.

The methods of the educational system, including its segmented curriculum and neatly divided class-hours, are out of tune with the inner drives of becoming adults. They strive for total involvement *now* and for discovering a picture of the *whole* of things. Rather than unfolding as a process of adventure, the education they encounter grows more and more like a dogfight, with competition assuming ever-new forms.

In addition, the ideals of youth—peace, integration, justice—are often betrayed and crushed. Frustration from these many forms of powerlessness shows itself in numerous ways. There is the cynicism represented by Bob Dylan, in the "Ballad of a Thin Man" in which he speaks about Mr. Jones who always shows up never quite knowing what is going on. Then, of course, there are the various kinds of satire carried on by the Beatles, Simon and Garfunkel, and other groups. Perhaps the recent mass murders, sex orgies, and now the most appealing of all frustration outlets, LSD, are stimulated by the social push toward maturity and the isolation which prevents it from being true maturity.

There is, as yet, little clarity about the root causes or effects of experimentation with drugs and sex. However, populations under strict control have in the past been known to restort to these activities as escapes. Among youth, there is the added dimension of rebellion—drugs and sex can be ways of punishing parents who are too restrictive or considered "inadequate."

A further source of frustration among youth is that passage to the status of "adult" is ill-defined. In lower class families, getting a job has been the sign of maturity. But now, due to problems of unemployability from lack of education or training, desirable jobs are often impossible to find. For girls in lower class families, having a baby is the "rite of passage." This, especially for unwed mothers, complicates the economic difficulties and compounds the matriarchal family structure, often encouraging irresponsibility in the young man.

For the middle-class youngster, extended education continues dependency into the twenties. Even after marriage, the parents frequently lend support to their children. Thus, the old image of the child as one who is dependent often is carried on into marriage, leading to feelings of inadequacy and making maturity difficult to achieve.

Frequently, however, the role of wage-earner has shifted to the wife of the undergraduate or graduate student. While this shift has occasioned some struggles over masculine/feminine identity, it has opened up possibilities for changing roles, including the sharing of housework and child-rearing.

It seems imperative that society discover concrete ways in which responsibility can be increasingly granted to the young, or a great deal of creative energy and thought will be lost. In spite of all that has been said, some youths have not chosen complacency, cynicism or escape, but have begun to wrestle with the present structures of society. Cries of "Black Power" and "Freedom Now" indicate a new response to a past heavily burdened with frustration.

Within the "New Left," frequently characterized as anti-institutional, there is a growing concern about the organizational forms of the social order. The Radical Education Project of S.D.S., for example, seeks to discover how to reshape organizations in order to maximize human values.

TENTATIVELY COMMITTED

Among contemporary youths there is a *spectrum of commitments*. Relativism seems to have eclipsed the ultimacy of most causes in our time; therefore, the loyalties of youth are tentative ones. Because adolescence is a time of trying out different identities, what commitments there are tend to change from year to year.

The following continuum is presented as an approximate sketch of the variety of commitments among emerging adults. Not only do individual youths change their views and loyalties over time, but the ratio of commitments is different for each age level. In other words, the balance of sub-groups for 13-year-olds would probably differ from those at 17, and those of the 17-year-olds from those at 21.

This estimated continuum best represents the 17–21 age group:

1. new radical activists   5%
2. concerned liberals   15%
3. hippies and teenyboppers   15%

4. dropouts and drifters   10%
5. delinquents and gang members   10%
6. middle-class complacents   25%
7. concerned conservatives   15%
8. reactionary activists   5%

In spite of this variety of perspectives, there seems to be a large measure of common charactistics among the young. Kenneth Keniston (*The Uncommitted*, p. 402) argues that it is the requirement of technological society for specialized personnel that leads to an enforced alienation, taking the form of a "youth culture." Words such as "teenager," "beat," and "swinger" point to this special world, which is a rather *unnatural* transitional realm. It is almost an isolation ward. Keniston summarizes the shared elements of this sub-culture: "A preoccupation with the present, a concern with the search for identity, many symptoms of continuing problems of dependency, a quest for positive values which aborts in private commitment, and a preoccupation with the ego demands of our technological society" (p. 403). Most of these factors are dealt with at other places in this introduction. However, it is well to point out here that some observers of the youth scene sense a shift beyond the question of identity. These observers judge that the new question is one of vocation: "What am I going to do with my life? Where, when, and how shall I invest it?" It seems evident, on the other hand, that not all emerging adults are seriously raising this question. The disagreement may center on a differing assessment of trends.

Much of the commonness of youth attitudes and drives may be attributed to TV and other mass media. 94% of American homes now in 1967 have television. The aspects of awareness and hunger for depth, explored above, seem especially related to TV. It may also be the case that the encounter with numerous "experts" over TV, often with differing views, has contributed to the distrust of most authorities by the young.

Another significant influence has been the awareness of possible destruction at any moment. The film *Dr. Strangelove* brought this underlying fear into the open. The bomb threat, as well as the historic upsets of the 20th century—Einstein's Theory of Relativity, World War I, the Depression, World War II, Korea, the Civil Rights Revolution, Vietnam, and Kennedy's assassination—have helped to call into question most contemporary myths. As part of this process, Americanism and Christianity have both suffered severe blows. Some, however, prefer to speak of this questioning as a "loss of moral fiber," attributable to the loss of influence of the family, church and school. The disagreement appears to lie in a differing interpretation of the facts. Undoubtedly one's experiences in the home, school, and church are important shapers of his perspectives; but TV is now another potent "window" on the world, challenging these prior authorities.

Two final centers of disagreement about the commitments of youth are:

a. How much are youth today influenced by the drives to earn and consume?
b. What will be the future of the growing group of "hippies"?

(a) Is it possible to be the most important part of the consumer market without being slave to it? Are the emerging adults really free from the selling that confronts them at every turn via TV, radio, billboards, peers, and schools? The folk-rock singers like Pete Seegar ("Little Boxes") and Simon and Garfunkel ("The Big Green Pleasure Machine") point to a significant awareness of the problems.

On the other hand, the number of poverty program graduates grows daily, swelling the army of consumers. Some of the dropouts now involved in job-training centers are unable to sense the satire of a film like *America on the Edge of Abundance*. The film clearly exhibits the ridiculous extremes of consumerism (hair spray for men; ear cosmetics) and salesmanship as "sincere appreciation." The fact that these job-trainees do not sense the humor or tragedy of such scenes indicates that they have bought the Madison Avenue bill of goods, that something more is always needed to make us fully human.

(b) Are the "swinging" successors to the "beatniks" just lazy or cynical, or are they waiting for a new society to be born? There is disagreement here about values and trends. What will happen to the hippies and teeny-boppers who seldom protest and who seem to converse so little, who appear to "hang loose" even when dancing the current contortions? Will they become the complacent citizens of tomorrow, supporters of a repressive Establishment? There are indications that the young radicals engaged in political and social protest frequently become bourgeois with age. But, perhaps today's "happeners" will actually hang loose from the pressure to conform and will constitute the nucleus of a renewed social order. They seem to participate in America's abundance without becoming enslaved by it. Just possibly, they await an effective means of challenge. It is this group of hippies, along with the drifters and dropouts, who seem the most *uncommitted* to American society in its present form, but who may be the most deeply committed to its *ideal* shape.

A NEW MORALITY?

Another important area of disagreement is the range of attitude and behavior related to middle-class standards, often called "the American Way of Life." The concerned conservatives and reactionaries come closest to an embodiment of these middle-class values. They tend to be the legalists or "men of duty," maintaining that certain rules or guidelines are essential for the continued functioning of society. They tend to respond in similar patterns to similar situations. Rather than expecting responsible behavior from youths or the poor, the conservative group wants to *train it* into them through a poverty program imposed from above and through high schools where teachers and administrators are clearly the authorities, imparting middle-class values. To these persons, the idea of deciding anew about each relationship indicates a basic *irresponsibility*. New ideas such as trial marriage seem to them to threaten the very institutions of marriage and the family. They do not see living together on an experimental basis as a possible way of developing genuinely stable marriages.

At the other extreme, are those who actually accept *no standards* or norms. As pure "existentialists," they decide their behavior in the moment with no discernible criteria. Many of the drifters and the dropouts, hippies, and gang members would belong here. Some would also place most of the "middle-class complacents" in this category, arguing that while these give lip service to the American Way of Life, their behavior shows a lack of values. The hippies confront their bourgeois critics thus:

Look at you, blowing up whole countries for the sake of some crazy ideologies that you don't live up to anyway. Look at you, mindfucking a whole generation of kids into getting a revolving charge account and buying your junk. (Who's a junkie?) Look at you, needing a couple of stiff drinks before you have the balls to talk with another human being. Look at you, making it with your neighbor's wife on the sly just to try and prove that you're really alive. Look at you, hooked on your cafeteria of pills, and making up dirty names for anybody who isn't in your bag, and screwing up the land and the water and the air for profit, and calling this nowhere scene the Great Society! And you're gonna tell us how to live? C'mon, man, you've got to be kidding! (*It's Happening*, J. L. Simmons and Barry Winograd p. 28)

Between the extremes is a middle group which feels that this rebuttal by the swingers doesn't excuse the irresponsible behavior, with regard to sex, free speech, etc. which is often their style. The "new morality" or "situation ethics" points to the concerns of this substantial segment of the emerging generation. Some of them are "new radicals" or "concerned liberals," yet others are from the hippy and delinquent populations. Their concern is for specific situations and *concrete responsibility for concrete persons*. They maintain that one cannot know ahead of time how to act in a particular relationship. One does not live life fully by applying a set of principles, but by responding afresh to every situation, without denying a variety of values and norms. This stance appears to demonstrate considerable commitment to the welfare and happiness of others, emphasizing the belief that people should be allowed and encouraged to express themselves, to make their own decisions, to determine their own destinies. Some of these "situationalists," feeling that one can bring about creative change in almost any context, are found at work within "the Establishment."

The basic questions in this area appear to center on the nature of man and the character of responsible action. While the "men of duty" hold that responsibility means fulfilling certain rules, the "irresponsible geniuses" at the other extreme maintain that every specific situation calls for a new, normless response. The situationalists call for a continuing tension between values and circumstances in deciding about action.

FUTURE: CHANGING CONTEXT AND DEMANDS OF TECHNOLOGY

THE TRANSFORMATION OF EDUCATION THROUGH TECHNOLOGY

The increased use of teaching machines for basic routinized types of subject matter appears quite likely, but there is disagreement about whether or not this is a good thing. Those who see further use and development of teaching machines as beneficial argue that it will free teachers from many of their menial tasks to work in more depth with each student.

Other commentators are bothered about the use of machines for teaching, feeling that machines cannot provide the necessary sensitivity to the real needs of the child. These critics fear that all children taught without human dialogue will become depersonalized, that is, less responsive and sensitive to other persons and to human values.

Behind these two views seems to lie disagreement about:

a. the ways in which man learns
b. the manner of using teaching machines.

McLuhan's assertion that the medium or technology itself freights a message would need to be tested out in the former instance, for the effects of learning via teaching machines have not yet been carefully assessed.

With regard to the second question, various models for using the devices could meet the demand for human presence and dialogue. Close supervision, perhaps through closed circuit TV, could enable the teacher to respond personally at any moment. As the student population grows ever larger, sub-professional assistants may be engaged to help spot students having difficulties not sensed by the mechanical teacher. An issue which will continue under exploration for some time is what sorts of material can be effectively taught by machines.

Computers are increasingly being used to store facts and basic information. This stored knowledge is almost instantly available to the researcher who needs it. If this trend progresses it will certainly alter the tasks of education. Those supporting this development state that the learner-researcher spends less time on gathering and mastering basic information and can devote himself more fully to discovering and creating patterns and hypotheses. He also has more time to test alternative hypotheses. Thus, this use of computers will speed up the process of developing comprehensive theories.

Some observers (Paul Goodman, for example, in *Growing up Absurd*) deplore this development. They argue that it is dangerous to formulate generalizations without close work with specifics. The basic questions beneath this disagreement may be a factual matter. How does the mind work in moving from specific to general? Could the computer provide close contact with *more* specifics rather than with fewer aspects of the situation?

Computers are also being used increasingly for registration and record-keeping. Opponents of this development say that it pushes further the already present impersonality of educational bureaucracies. They argue that it is not possible to protest to a machine about a bad schedule, nor can a machine take individual differences and peculiarities into account.

Those supporting greater use of computers say that this method makes possible a *more* individualized treatment of persons, and also helps by speeding up the process of registering, etc., so that there is time for personal attention when needed. Perhaps the conflict here is a matter of facts: what can the computers do and how will administrators use them?

The example of "dating by computer" may shed some light on the issues. Presently computers can provide a person with names and addresses of five or six "dream dates," and within the limits of the request questionnaires, one can select the kind of person he or she wishes to date. People within a region, who very well might never meet, are put in contact with one another.

Some feel that this is a very individualized service. On the other hand, it is argued that, because of the highly selective criteria used, other possible contacts are shut off by one's choices. Thus, if a person goes out with only those who fit his questionnaire categories he loses the opportunity to have his mind expanded and changed. Is man wise enough to choose his potential mates in this fashion, or is there a degree of irrationality and uncertainty which is important in the quest for dates and marriage partners?

THE QUESTION OF A
CENTRAL RECORDS BUREAU

The proposal has recently been made for a national computer center which would maintain a cumulative history of every person, living or dead. Such a center would, of course, be very useful for police agencies —to locate suspects, for universities—to decide about admission, for employers—to learn about skills and reliability, to sales agencies—to uncover the best potential customers.

Those who argue against the data bank fear that it would tend to limit an individual's possibilities for reforming his life style, for simple mistakes and bad ethical judgments would become a permanent part of one's record. This record would probably be available to numerous agencies which determine the destiny of persons. It seems likely that people would try to withhold some kinds of information, through bribery and other means, or attempt to get false information, helpful to them, into the record.

There is *already* a growing records bureau in the United States. Though it is not yet centralized, information on our credit, income, expense accounts, and health histories has been collected for years! The basic issue seems to be that of values or the kind of world we wish to create. Do we want a world where people are hemmed in by what they have done in the past or where persons have the flexibility of some degree of anonymity? The impact of the records center might conceivably be heaviest upon youth. Would they tend to become more fearful of risk-taking, which many psychologists regard as crucial for full self-development? The juvenile court idea may have recognized this basic problem, for juvenile records are less complete and their sentences less severe than for adults. Juveniles are seen as not fully in control of themselves, and their names are withheld from the news media when they are apprehended. No doubt, this sort of consideration could be incorporated in a national records center. Thus, another basic question is *control* of data fed in and taken out.

PROBLEM: THE CREATIVE USE OF LEISURE

Despite disagreements about the speed with which automation will supplant jobs, it seems agreed that youths and adults will find more leisure time on their hands. How will it be possible for people to make creative use of their new-found free time?

Henry Clark has suggested three alternative styles for the use of leisure: engaging in worthwhile service for others, involving oneself in contemplation and reflection, taking part in spontaneous play and celebration. The first two suggestions would involve considerable educational experience and a large measure of motivation, while the latter demands an overcoming of Western rationality and ego-control. Although the education needed for successful service and/or contemplation is a good deal more than many people now get, it is reasonable to expect that in an automated and cybernated age new and satisfying modes of education will be developed to keep people engaged in a continual learning process, rather than a system oriented towards degrees. Still, some observers question our ability to develop these means. A different assessment of trends appears to be the source of this questioning.

It may well be that many members of the emerging generation are already farther along than their elders in realizing the third alternative, that of play. The use of marijuana and the psychedelic drugs frequently serves as a means of play and entertainment, just as participation in films is serious or light-hearted recreation. Perhaps racing miniature slot-cars and adopting more playful views of sex are less irresponsible and empty than they seem to a number of commentators. An "anti-work" ethic has begun developing not only among the hippies, but with the dropouts and drifters who confront a diminishing number of unskilled jobs. These new actions and attitudes may be preparing the way for an otherwise frustrating future.

Once again, the nature of man appears as a basic issue. Is man a creature who must produce things, who must be a reflective being, or who can be satisfied to playfully enjoy himself and others? Which of these dimensions, or what balance between them, is crucial for humanness?

SPACE EXPLORATION AND GLOBAL HUMANIZATION

A final futuric consideration will close this section. Very few persons have contemplated the effects of our space probes on the minds of the young. It can reasonably be asserted that the rising generation takes for granted man's conquest of space. This stance may unleash new powers of imagination or it could lead to over-confidence in the ability of man to control the universe. That is, optimism might develop to such a stage in the new generation that dangerous side-effects of space (and other) technologies would be ignored.

Milan Machovec describes some possible effects of our space research and exploration:

It is quite possible that even the huge proportion of hidden cosmic dangers and risks could have very positive effects on the mentality of earthly inhabitants, that it would strengthen mankind's critical sense of reality and healthy human understanding, that it might even "humanize" politics . . . The eventuality of an atomic, bacteriological, or even cosmic death can be considered a greater danger than that of the so-called "east" to the so-called "west," and vice versa (*Student World*, 4th quarter, 1966, p. 372).

PHYSICAL ASPECTS OF DRUG ABUSE

K. L. Jones, L. W. Shainberg, and C. O. Byer

chapter eleven

DRUGS

INTRODUCTION

Most people nowadays seem to be familiar with the social effects of drug use and abuse. Pot-smoking, whether or not you approve, is widespread social behavior. So is narcotics addiction, a behavior pattern not likely to win much approval. At a party the effects of pot-smoking are obvious and familiar. And the broader social effects of addiction are obvious, too.

What physical phenomena lie behind these behaviors? How do drugs, used and misused, affect the central nervous system? The following selection explores central nervous system responses to varying quantities of stimulants and depressants—hallucinogens, amphetamines, and the like, on the one hand, and tranquilizers, sleeping pills, and heroin on the other. The selection provides more detailed information not only on drug abuse, but also on brain functioning.

PHYSICAL
ASPECTS OF
DRUG ABUSE

Today much of the research into the abuse of drugs is concerned with their biochemical actions. Researchers are attempting to establish the chemical characteristics of drugs which are responsible for the mood, personality, and behavioral modifications or psychotropic (mind changing) actions of specific drugs. In this chapter we will examine drugs that affect the central nervous system and have a potential for being abused by producing personality changes, euphoria, or abnormal social behavior.

DRUG-INDUCED EFFECTS
ON THE CENTRAL
NERVOUS SYSTEM

In this section we will be dealing with areas of the central nervous system and how drug-induced effects take place. These are effects that cause personality changes, euphoria, or abnormal social behavior. Such terms point out the outward signs arising from drug-induced changes on the central nervous system and are not forms of classification. Medically, drugs producing such signs are actually classified as organotropic drugs. As explained in the preceding chapter the over-all actions and effects of these drugs are mainly those of either a stimulant or depressant, acting directly upon the central nervous system to increase or decrease the activity of nerve centers and their conducting pathways.

A central nervous system stimulant is defined as a drug which temporarily increases body function or nerve activity. At times, stimulant drugs produce dramatic effects, but their medical usefulness is limited because of the complexity of their reactions and the nature of their untoward effects. Also, repeated administration or large doses may produce convulsive seizures, alternating with periods of depression ranging from exhaustion to coma.

From DRUGS AND ALCOHOL, by K. L. Jones, L. W. Shainberg, and C. O. Byer (New York: Harper & Row, 1969), pp. 13–27; copyright © 1969 by K. L. Jones, L. W. Shainberg, and C. O. Byer; reprinted by permission of the publisher.

Depressants have the ability to temporarily decrease a body function or nerve activity. Drug-induced depression of the central nervous system is frequently characterized by lack of interest in surroundings, inability to focus attention on a subject, and lack of motivation to move or talk. The pulse and respiration become slower than usual, and as the depression deepens sensory perceptions diminish progressively. Psychic and motor activities decrease; reflexes become sluggish and finally disappear. If a stronger depressant is used or if larger (abusive) doses are consumed, depression progresses to drowsiness, stupor, unconsciousness, sleep, coma, respiratory failure, and death.

The central nervous system consists of several distinct functional components (see Figs. 1 and 2) fulfilling different psychological functions. Consequently, it is quite natural to find that the drugs which act on this system do not act on all parts of it with the same degree of intensity. Also, the specific response of an individual to a drug depends to a large extent on the personality of the individual and a number of other factors as well as the nature of the drug itself.

Cerebral cortex

The cerebral Cortex (Fig. 1) is a vast information storage area. It is the site of consciousness, associations such as memory, perception, and integration of various sensory and motor experiences. Its function is what is spoken of as "higher mental activity." For each part of the cortex there is a corresponding and connecting part to the brain stem (Fig. 1), and activation of a section of the brain stem activates a corresponding and much larger portion of the cerebral cortex.

When sensory areas of the cortex are stimulated, more numerous and more vivid impulses are received and the individual is more alert, responsive, and more aware of his surroundings. When the motor centers are stimulated, he is likely to be more active and restless, but when overstimulated (such as in the abuse of drugs), coordination may be lost and convulsions may result. Cortical stimulation may make someone more talkative, but if the stimulation is excessive, speech becomes incessant and incoherent and the individual becomes delirious. Drugs stimulating specific areas of the cerebral cortex (thinking, reasoning, judgment, will, imagination, attention, etc.) may enable the individual to think faster (not necessarily clearer) and form judgments more quickly. But, at the same time overstimulated sensory areas may produce illusions and flights of imagination. These sensations and motor actions are also evident when lower areas, such as the reticular formation, are stimulated and the stimulation relayed to the cerebral cortex.

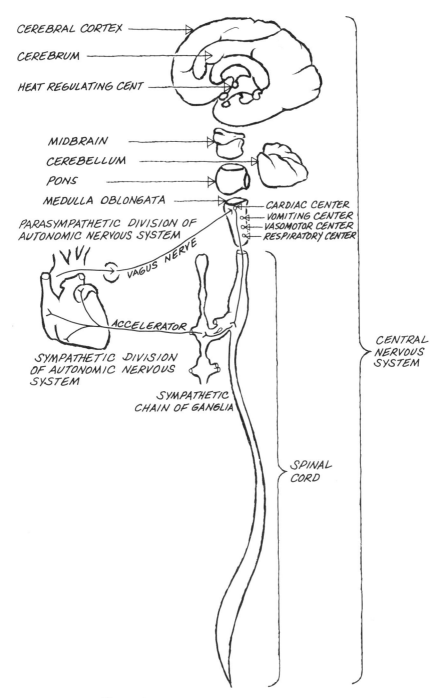

CEREBRAL CORTEX

CEREBRUM

HEAT REGULATING CENT

MIDBRAIN

CEREBELLUM

PONS

MEDULLA OBLONGATA

PARASYMPATHETIC DIVISION OF
AUTONOMIC NERVOUS SYSTEM

VAGUS NERVE

ACCELERATOR

SYMPATHETIC DIVISION
OF AUTONOMIC NERVOUS
SYSTEM

SYMPATHETIC
CHAIN OF GANGLIA

CARDIAC CENTER
VOMITING CENTER
VASOMOTOR CENTER
RESPIRATORY CENTER

CENTRAL
NERVOUS
SYSTEM

SPINAL
CORD

Figure 1
DIAGRAM OF THE FUNCTIONAL COMPONENTS OF THE NERVOUS SYSTEM

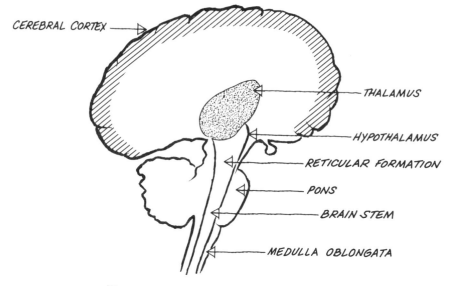

Figure 2
THE RETICULAR FORMATION (RETICULAR ACTIVATING SYSTEM)

Thalamus

The thalamus (Figs. 1, 2) serves as a center for impulses to and from the cerebral cortex. It can relay diffuse signals from the brain stem to all parts of the cerebral cortex and can cause generalized activation of the cerebrum. Or, the thalamus can cause activation of specific areas of the cerebral cortex in distinction to other areas. These activation sections of the thalamus are part of the reticular activating system (Fig. 2) which will be discussed in the next section. The generalized stimulation of the cortex plays an important role in wakefulness and attention. The selective activation of specific areas probably plays an important role in our ability to direct our attention to certain tasks or specific mental activities.

The thalamus is also composed of sensory areas that serve as a center for unlocalized sensation. It gives us our impressions of agreeableness or disagreeableness about a sensation.

Drugs that depress cells in the various portions of the thalamus may interrupt the free flow of impulses to the cerebral cortex. In this way pain can be relieved by drugs. Stimulation of the thalamus actively increases the action of the cerebral cortex.

Reticular formation

The reticular formation is a part of the central nervous system that has increasingly come under study in recent years. Its importance is only beginning to be appreciated. It is made up of cells and fine bundles of nerve fibers that extend in many directions. The formation extends from the upper part of the spinal cord forward through the brain stem (see Fig. 2). It possesses the ability to inhibit or to excite various parts of the nervous system. It receives impulses from all parts of the body and relays impulses to the cerebral cortex to promote wakefulness and alertness, thus affecting many cerebral functions (such as consciousness, perception, and learning). It also inhibits or excites activity in motor neurons, promoting both reflex and voluntary muscle movements. Its over-all function is thought to be that of an integrating system that influences activities of other parts of the nervous system.

General depression of the reticular formation produces sedation and loss of consciousness. Stimulation distorts sensations and motor activity control systems throughout the brain. As you will see later, many highly abused drugs are now believed to exert a major effect on the reticular formation.

The arousal reaction The arousal reaction is the sensory activation of the *reticular activating system*. The reticular activating system must be stimulated into action by signals from other areas. When an individual is asleep, the reticular activating system is almost dormant. Yet any type of sensory signal will immediately activate the system. For instance, proprioceptive signals from the muscles, pain impulses from the skin, visual signals from the eyes, auditory signals from the ears, or even sensations from the intestinal organs can cause sudden activation of the reticular activating system of the reticular formation and arouse the individual. This is called the arousal reaction and has caused the reticular formation to be called the *arousal center*.

Anatomically the reticular formation of the brain stem is well constructed to perform such arousal functions. It receives tremendous numbers of collateral fibers from a number of sensory areas of the body. Almost any sensory stimulus to the body can activate it. In addition, many fibers pass directly from the spinal cord to the reticular formation. It in turn can transmit signals both upward into the brain and downward into the spinal cord. Many of the fibers originating from cells in the reticular formation divide, with one branch of the fiber passing directly upward and another branch passing directly downward.

The cerebral cortex can also stimulate this arousal system and increase its degree of activity. Direct fiber pathways pass into the reticular activating system from almost all parts of the cerebral cortex. Intense activity of any part of the cerebrum activates the reticular activating system and is usually associated with a high degree of wakefulness. For example, a large number of nerve fibers pass from the motor regions of the cerebral cortex to the reticular formation and motor activity or body movement is closely associated with a high degree of wakefulness. This helps to explain the importance of movement to keep a person awake.

Motor control   The reticular formation does not act as one large unit; it has the capability of controlling many discrete functions. Diffuse stimulation in it can cause a general increase in muscle tone either throughout the body or in localized areas. Stimulation of discrete points in any portion of the reticular formation will at times cause discrete muscle contraction or inhibition of a muscle contraction in specific parts of the body. Specific areas control the excitation of an *agonist muscle* (a prime, paired muscle with specific functions) along with simultaneous inhibition of an *antagonist muscle* (muscle with action opposing its paired agonist muscle). This function is extremely important in any body movement or the control of equilibrium and the support of the body against gravity.

Hypothalamus

The hypothalamus is one of the most important areas of the brain for control of autonomic and other involuntary functions of the body. These functions include regulation of arterial blood pressure, body fluid balance, feeding, gastrointestinal activity, and many hormonal secretions of the endocrine glands. The autonomic control impulses are transmitted to the body through two major subdivisions of the autonomic nervous system called the *sympathetic* and *parasympathetic* systems (see Fig. 1).

In addition to these control functions the hypothalamus also has important behavioral functions. As shown in Fig. 2, it is closely associated with, and part of, the reticular formation. Consequently, the autonomic functions and the behavior functions under the control of the hypothalamus are tightly woven into the over-all reticular activating system. This interwoven condition gives rise to the body changes associated with behavioral and emotional changes.

Pain and pleasure (punishment and reward)   The hypothalamus and closely related structures such as the reticular formation are greatly concerned with the effectiveness of sensory sensations, that is, whether the sensations are pleasant or painful. These qualities are also called reward and punishment.

The major centers controlling pain and pleasure have been found to be located in the hypothalamus. These areas are also the most reactive of all the hypothalamic areas. It also seems that stimulation in the pain centers can frequently inhibit the pleasure centers completely. This illustrates that pain can often take precedence over pleasure.

Degree of alertness and excitement Stimulation of specific areas of the hypothalamus greatly excites the reticular activating system causing wakefulness, alertness, and excitement. Such increased stimulation also excites the sympathetic nervous system (Fig. 1) increasing the arterial blood pressure, causing pupillary dilation, and general excitement throughout the organs controlled by sympathetic activity. Also, stimulation of other areas of the hypothalamus or isolated areas of the thalamic portions of the reticular activating system often inhibits this excited state, causing drowsiness and sometimes actual sleep.

Thus, the reticular activating system directly, and the hypothalamus and thalamus indirectly, contribute greatly to the control of the degree of excitement and alertness a person feels.

Rage (affective-defensive pattern) Stimulation of the regions of the hypothalamus that give the most intense sensations of punishment also causes an animal or man to develop a classic emotional pattern called *rage* (development of a defense posture such as: extended claws, lifted tail, hissing, spitting, growling, and wide-open eyes with dilated pupils. Man shows mainly the extended arms, throat sounds and the wide-open eyes with dilated pupils). The slightest provocation, while in this state, causes an immediate savage attack.

Exactly the opposite emotional behavior pattern occurs when the pleasure centers are stimulated, namely, docility and tameness.

Psychological and psychosomatic effects Abnormal psychic states can greatly alter the degree of nervous stimulation to the skeletal muscles throughout the body. This can increase or decrease the skeletal muscle tone. In neurotic and psychotic states, such as anxiety, tension, and mania, generalized overactivity of both the muscles and sympathetic nervous system often occurs throughout the body. The hypothalamus and reticular activating system undoubtedly help to maintain the extreme degree of wakefulness and alertness that characterizes these emotional states. Also, the docility and somnolence characteristic of extreme depression shows the abilities of the hypothalamus and reticular activating system to decrease the muscle tone throughout the body.

Many psychosomatic abnormalities (ulcers, rashes, etc.) result from hyperactivity of either the sympathetic or parasympathetic systems. Emotional patterns controlling the sympathetic and parasympathetic centers of the hypothalamus can cause wide varieties of peripheral psychosomatic effects.

Medulla oblongata

The medulla oblongata contains the so-called vital centers, the respiratory, vasomotor, and cardiac centers (Fig. 1). If the respiratory center, for example, is stimulated, it will discharge an increased number of nerve impulses over nerve pathways to the muscles of respiration, thereby increasing respiration. If this center is depressed, it will discharge fewer impulses, and respiration will be correspondingly reduced. Other centers in the medulla that respond to certain drugs are the cough center and the vomiting center. The medulla, pons, thalamus, reticular formation, hypothalamus, and other areas of the midbrain constitute the brain stem and contain many important correlation centers, other than the ones we have talked about, as well as ascending and descending nerve pathways.

Cerebellum

The cerebellum is the center for muscle coordination, equilibrium, and muscle tone. It receives impulses from the reticular formation, the organs of equilibrium (semicircular canals), as well as the cerebrum. The cerebellum plays an important role in the maintenance of posture as well. Drugs that disturb the cerebellum usually cause loss of equilibrium and dizziness.

Spinal cord

The spinal cord is the center for reflex activity and the transmission of impulses to and from the higher centers in the brain. It may be affected indirectly by the drug actions on higher centers or directly by drugs such as spinal stimulants, which may cause convulsions when given in large doses or may just increase excitability when given in smaller doses. When a drug is described as having *central action* it means it has an action on the brain and spinal cord.

SPECTRUM AND CONTINUUM
OF DRUG ACTION

The degrees of depression and stimulation of drugs affecting the central nervous system are not discrete actions. As shown in Fig. 3, the spec-

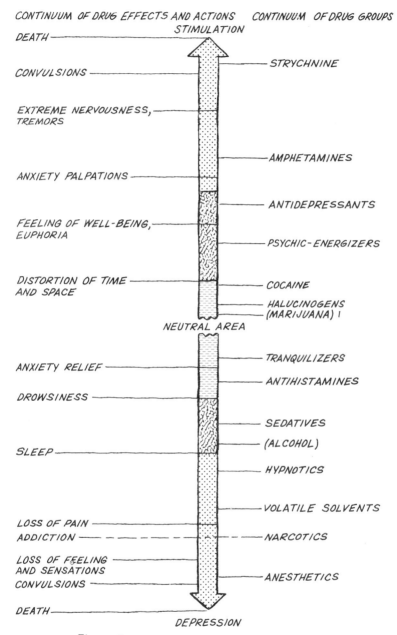

CONTINUUM OF DRUG EFFECTS AND ACTIONS   CONTINUUM OF DRUG GROUPS

STIMULATION

DEATH

CONVULSIONS ———————————— STRYCHNINE

EXTREME NERVOUSNESS,
TREMORS

———————— AMPHETAMINES

ANXIETY PALPATIONS

———————— ANTIDEPRESSANTS

FEELING OF WELL-BEING,
EUPHORIA

——————— PSYCHIC-ENERGIZERS

DISTORTION OF TIME
AND SPACE ——————— COCAINE
———— HALUCINOGENS
———— (MARIJUANA) I

NEUTRAL AREA

———————— TRANQUILIZERS
ANXIETY RELIEF

———————— ANTIHISTAMINES
DROWSINESS

———————— SEDATIVES

———————— (ALCOHOL)
SLEEP

———————— HYPNOTICS

———————— VOLATILE SOLVENTS

LOSS OF PAIN
ADDICTION — — — — — — — — — — — NARCOTICS

LOSS OF FEELING
AND SENSATIONS
CONVULSIONS ——————— ANESTHETICS

DEATH

DEPRESSION

Figure 3

SPECTRUM AND CONTINUUM OF DRUG ACTION

(Robert W. Earle, Ph.D., Senior Lecturer, Department of Medical Pharmacology and Therapeutics, University of California at Irvine, California College of Medicine.)

[1]Dr. Earle has suggested recently that marijuana may belong among the sedatives (personal communication, 1971).

205

trum of drug actions can be set into a continuum of effects and actions. The continuum of drug effect extends from overstimuluation of the nervous system to death at one extreme to severe depression of the nervous system to death at the other extreme. The central or neutral area of this continuum is the degree of stimulation and depression usually encountered in everyday living.

The drug groups are placed along the continuum according to the actions or effects that they produce when normal therapeutic (minimal) dosages are consumed by an individual. The action of a drug used for this classification or grouping is called its *major action*. Drugs in different groups may have similar side (or untoward) actions even though their major action differs. For example, narcotics are used to relieve pain (major action), but they may also cause a person to be drowsy or sleepy (side action). Barbiturates are used for their ability to produce sleep (major action), but they do not have the ability to relieve pain and cannot be used as a narcotic. Thus, sleep-producing effects of these two depressants, narcotics and barbiturates, overlap on a continuum of action chart (see Fig. 4). All of the drugs that affect the central nervous system have similar properties. These actions were used by Dr. Earle to produce the continuum shown in Fig. 3. As we progress along the chart from the neutral area, specific points marked on the chart show where we move from the area of one group of drugs in terms of its major action into the area of another more powerful group of drugs. The weaker groups of drugs are nearer the center, while the most powerful drugs are at the two extremes.

If dosages are increased from minimal to maximal, to toxic, to abusive, to lethal, any drug group listed in Fig. 3 is able to produce the complete range of effects of stimulation on one hand or depression on the other. This overstimulation or extreme depression produces the effects the drug abuser is seeking. Consequently, dosages used by drug abusers are far in excess of the dosages normally used in medical practice. A complete range of effects, produced by increased dosages, is presented in Fig. 5. An example of the relationship between dosage and effects for one group of drugs, the hallucinogenic drugs, is given in Fig. 6.

Drugs can be arranged in such a continuum because the effects a person is seeking, when abusing drugs, are extremely similar. For example, any of these drugs will produce hallucinations at some dosage. This is why individuals, while preferring one drug over another, will abuse any drug within these groups if it becomes available. As the specific actions of a drug become more familiar and less spectacular, the individual may experiment with new ways to use the drug. He may progress from taking the drug orally to injecting it under the skin or into a muscle

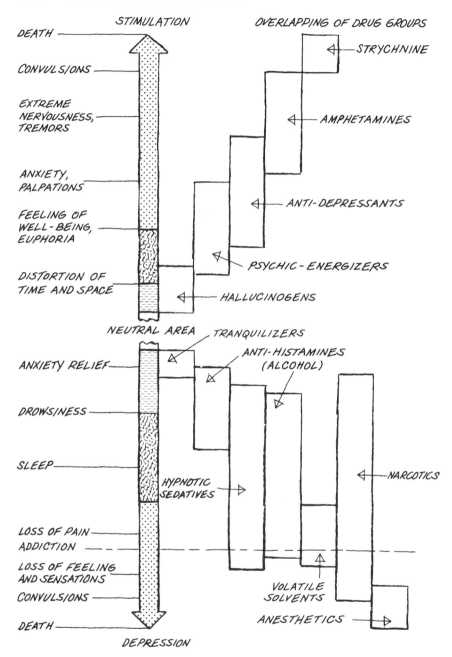

CONTINUUM OF DRUG EFFECTS AND ACTIONS

STIMULATION

OVERLAPPING OF DRUG GROUPS

DEATH

CONVULSIONS

EXTREME NERVOUSNESS, TREMORS

ANXIETY, PALPATIONS

FEELING OF WELL-BEING, EUPHORIA

DISTORTION OF TIME AND SPACE

STRYCHNINE

AMPHETAMINES

ANTI-DEPRESSANTS

PSYCHIC-ENERGIZERS

HALLUCINOGENS

NEUTRAL AREA   TRANQUILIZERS

ANTI-HISTAMINES (ALCOHOL)

ANXIETY RELIEF

DROWSINESS

SLEEP

HYPNOTIC SEDATIVES

NARCOTICS

LOSS OF PAIN
ADDICTION

LOSS OF FEELING AND SENSATIONS

CONVULSIONS

DEATH

VOLATILE SOLVENTS

ANESTHETICS

DEPRESSION

Figure 4
OVERLAPPING ACTIONS OF DRUGS

207

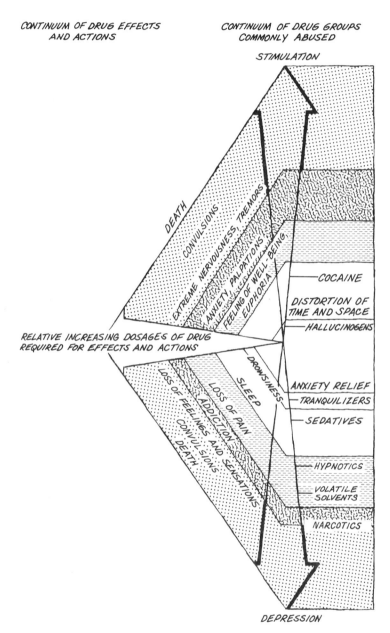

Figure 5

RELATIONSHIPS OF INCREASED DOSAGES TO CONTINUUM OF DRUG EFFECTS

As dosages of drugs are increased the effects progress along a continuum of effects until a lethal dosage, producing death, is taken.

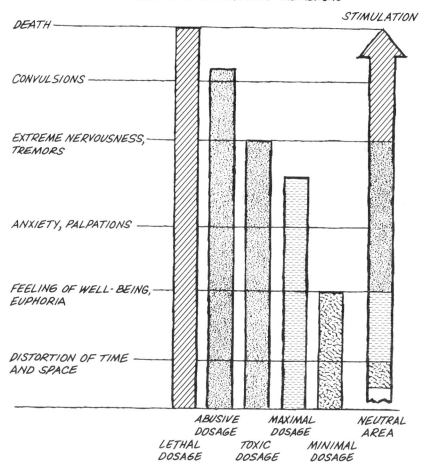

Figure 6
RELATIONSHIP OF INCREASED DOSAGES OF HALLUCINOGENS TO
CONTINUUM OF DRUG EFFECTS

("skin popping") to injecting it directly into a vein ("mainlining"). Or, he may seek stronger and stronger drugs to produce more vivid effects, quicker actions, or longer lasting experiences. Very few drug abusers are satisfied with experiences from just one drug. Most often they will move toward the extremes of the continuum. If they were first introduced to a drug in a group somewhere in the middle of either the stimulant or depressant column, they continue on toward the extremes from there. They do not regress to a less potent drug group.

The more commonly abused drugs, such as marijuana (a hallucinogen) or the barbiturates, are close to the center of the chart when used in minimal dosages. The strong preference for these drugs lies in the abilities of an individual to control the amount and consequently the relative effect of the drug. In a highly emotional state a user is able to increase the dosage or consume more of the drug to reach a more intense effect. If he is less emotionally disturbed at the time of abuse he is less concerned and often content with a reduced consumption and effects. This ability to control drugs is offset when addiction levels (Fig. 3) are reached with the depressant drugs. At addiction levels the dose must be increased regularly to keep the body from entering withdrawal, regardless of the individual's emotional state. This increasing dosage level is required to keep the individual at his normal or neutral level. Thus, he has built himself into a constantly changing artificial continuum of effects. The minimal dose must be used daily to maintain a neutral level and then additional abusive dosages are needed to reach the levels of effects to satisfy his emotional states.

When abusing stimulant drugs, which do not have the addictive properties of depressant drugs, an individual may not progress from the relatively mild drugs (hallucinogens) because he is better able to control the effects by controlling the amounts consumed. However, some who start on weaker drugs do progress to stronger ones because of the slight differences in the quality or intensity of effects.

The drugs within each group do differ slightly in their effects. This is why different drugs are used for different therapeutic uses. These differing effects are regulated by the areas or routes of action within the central nervous system. All of these drugs either stimulate or depress the functions of cells, tissues, or organs. For instance, caffeine stimulates the function of nerve cells, while barbiturates depress their function. Because of the complexity of the body organization, drug action is often complex. This complexity of action, at times, makes it extremely difficult to place a group of drugs on a progressive continuum chart. This is more of a problem with the stimulant drugs than with the depressant drugs. Also, at times the complexity of actions leads to apparent paradoxes. For example, if alcohol is a depressor of nerve function, why do people seem stimulated by a small amount of alcohol? The answer is that the brain contains a group of cells whose function is inhibition—cells that normally keep us from acting irresponsibly on every passing impulse. These inhibitory cells are more sensitive to alcohol and similar drugs (such as barbiturates and solvents) than are the other brain cells. As the alcohol concentration in the blood begins to rise, the inhibitory cells are depressed and cease to function properly, so that many impulses which would otherwise be suppressed are acted upon. Therefore, moderate amounts of alcohol, a depressant drug, can cause excitation by depressing an inhibitory function.

RELATIVE EFFECTIVENESS OF ONE-SIDED AND TWO-SIDED COMMUNICATIONS IN COURTROOM PERSUASION

Robert G. Lawson

chapter twelve

PERSUASION
IN
THE
COURTROOM

In reading Psychology, the Hybrid Science, *you may have been struck by the lack of "jargon"—terms and expressions peculiar to psychology, which ordinary mortals may not understand. Or, better yet, maybe you didn't even notice the language used in the textbook (that was certainly my hope when I wrote it).*

The next selection, an article from a professional journal, will give you an idea of how psychologists communicate with each other. The topic of the article is interesting: Are people persuaded better by hearing a strong argument on one side of an issue, or does bringing in the opposing arguments and then refuting them help to strengthen the case? You will have to do some intellectual work to grasp the author's evidence and conclusions.

RELATIVE EFFECTIVENESS OF ONE-SIDED AND TWO-SIDED COMMUNICATIONS IN COURTROOM PERSUASION

A. INTRODUCTION

In the presentation of persuasive communications to jurors at the trial level and to judges at the appellate level of litigation, a lawyer is always confronted with the question of whether to limit his communication to strictly supportive material or to "anticipate in an attempt to demolish his opponent's argument before it is raised" (1, p. 334). Efforts of the better trial lawyers to answer this question have resulted in substantial disagreement. Some (8, p. 121) suggest the use of a one-sided argument (one that mentions only those ideas supportive of the position advocated):

With regard to the content of your summation [jury argument], it should contain enough for you to complete a full and clear presentation of *your own case*. Ordinarily, it is not advisable to waste any time pointing out the deficiencies in your opponent's case.

Others (3, p. 626) agree that a one-sided argument is more effective but for a different reason than that contained in the above quotation. Their reasoning is as follows:

There are many attorneys who spend much time on the points they expect their adversary to urge against them. This is often a mistake if for no other reason than that these points are thereby unduly emphasized, and strengthened by double exposure, so to speak.

Still another group of lawyers assert that a two-sided argument (one that mentions both supporting and opposing arguments) results in "a greater opinion change in the desired direction" (1, p. 334). This group (16, p. 319) describes its assertion in these words:

"Relative Effectiveness of One-Sided and Two-Sided Communications in Courtroom Persuasion," by Robert G. Lawson, in THE JOURNAL OF GENERAL PSYCHOLOGY, 82 (1970), 3–16; reprinted by permission of the Journal Press, Provincetown, Mass., and the author.

The opening argument should seek to anticipate your opponent's contentions, since there is a definite advantage in having the Court know the answers to and weaknesses in his arguments before he makes them.

These conclusions, like many others derived from legal reasoning, are based on logic and a rather haphazard study of human nature, and are totally unblemished by scientific data. Upon the one-sided *versus* two-sided issue, such conclusions are especially unfortunate in view of the fact that a substantial amount of scientific research is available. For the last several years, the relative effectiveness of these two types of persuasive communications has been a subject of special interest to social psychologists. Yet, no effort has been made to apply the findings of this research to what may be its most important application, the administration of justice through the judicial process. In this article an attempt is made to review the part of this research that is relevant to persuasive communications in the courtroom, and to offer some observations concerning its effect upon a fair administration of the law. The end toward which the article is directed is the stimulation of additional thought on this subject by those who have conducted the research.

B. REVIEW OF THE RELEVANT EXPERIMENTAL STUDIES

1. Studies involving "controversial" issues[1]

The first experiment on the effectiveness of one-sided and two-sided persuasive communications was conducted by Hovland, Lumsdaine, and Sheffield during the latter part of World War II (4). The subject matter of this experiment, and the position toward which the persuasive communications were directed, was the proposition that "the job of finishing the war [against the Japanese] would be tough and that it would take at least two years after VE Day." (The experiment was conducted at a time when the war against Germany was nearing its completion.) With this proposition as the final conclusion, the experimenters prepared two argumentative communications, one of which was two-sided, the other one-sided. The content of the latter included only those arguments which indicated that the war would be long and difficult. The content of the former included these same arguments plus some consideration and refutation of several arguments supporting an antithetical proposition: i.e.,

[1]Understanding these arguments may involve making up a simple chart that shows what arguments were presented to whom.

that the war against Japan would be easy and of short duration. The experiment was then administered in three steps: (*a*) a preliminary survey was taken to determine the pre-experiment opinions of the subjects as to the expected length of the Pacific War; (*b*) the communications were presented to the subjects with half receiving the one-sided argument and half receiving the two-sided argument; and (*c*) a second survey was taken for the purpose of measuring the relative shifts in opinion resulting from the two types of communications.

The findings of this experiment are significant in at least two respects to the question of one-sided *versus* two-sided communications in the courtroom. The first concerns the relative impact the communications had on two classes of subjects, those initially opposed to the position advocated and those initially favorable to that position. As summarized by the experimenters: "The program giving some of the U.S. advantages in addition to the difficulties was more effective for men initially opposed. . . . On the other hand the program giving the one-sided picture was more effective for men initially favoring the stand taken" (4, p. 213). [This finding was later confirmed in a similar experiment conducted by McGinnies (10).] The second significant finding of the Hovland, Lumsdaine, and Sheffield study concerns the relative effect of these two types of communications on individuals with different amounts of education. It was described in this manner: "When the results were broken down according to education level, it was found that the program which presented both sides was more effective with better educated men and that the program which presented one side was more effective with less educated men" (4, p. 214).

In this initial study, no attempt was made to measure the relative effectiveness of the two types of communications after exposure of the subjects to a countercommunication. A subsequent study conducted by Lumsdaine and Janis was designed to add this additional factor (9). As with the first experiment, this one involved the use of a controversial public issue: "Russia would be unable to produce large numbers of atomic bombs for at least the next five years." (The experiment was conducted several months before the announcement of Russia's first atomic explosion.) Two communications were prepared to advocate the affirmative of this proposition. One of the two consisted of a one-sided argument, the other a two-sided argument. A third communication was prepared to advocate the negative of the above proposition. The latter was largely a one-sided argument which "consisted of playing up and elaborating the opposing arguments that had been mentioned" in the two-sided affirmative communication. Four groups of high school students were used as subjects. One of the four received only the one-sided affirmative communication; another received only the two-sided affirmative communication. A third group received the one-sided affirmative communication followed by the negative communication, while the fourth group received the two-sided affirmative communication followed by the negative communication. All four groups were surveyed before and after the presentation of the communications to measure the resulting shifts in opinion.

The results of this experiment generally support the findings of Hovland, Lumsdaine, and Sheffield. With the additional factor of a counter-communication, of the two affirmative arguments the two-sided one was found to be decidedly superior. This superiority was described with this statement (9, p. 318):

Regardless of initial position, a convincing one-sided communication presenting only positive arguments will tend to sway many members of the audience farther in the direction advocated by the communicator. However, when these persons subsequently hear the opposite point of view, also supported by cogent sounding arguments, their opinions tend to be swayed back in the negative direction, especially if the new arguments appear to offset the previous positive arguments. But if the initial communication is, instead, a two sided one it will already have taken into account both the positive and negative arguments and still have reached the positive conclusion. When the listener is then subsequently exposed to the presentation of opposing arguments in the counter propaganda, he is less likely to be influenced by them.

Application of these findings, as well as those of the initial experiment, to the persuasive communications presented by lawyers is reserved at this point for subsequent discussion.

2. Studies involving "noncontroversial issues"

Subsequent to the studies of Hovland, Lumsdaine, and Sheffield, and Lumsdaine and Janis, a group of experiments dealing with the problems of inducing resistance to persuasion through prior refutation of counter-arguments was undertaken by McGuire and Papageorgis (12, 13, 14, 15). The relevance of these experiments to the present discussion may be demonstrated in part by a description of their subject matter and experimental design. As to the former, cultural truisms such as the following comprised the topics for the investigations: "Everyone should get a chest X-ray each year in order to detect any possible tuberculosis symptoms at an early stage"; "the effects of penicillin have been almost without exception, of great benefit to mankind"; and, "everyone should brush his teeth after every meal if at all possible." As to procedural design, the experiments consisted of two sessions. In the first, the subjects were presented communications which were devised to immunize them from attacks against their beliefs on the "truisms." The first-session communications were of two types, designated by the experimenters as "supportive" and "refutational." The former consisted *only* of arguments supporting the cultural truisms; the latter consisted *only* of exposure to possible counterarguments against the truisms together with refutations of those counterarguments. In the second session of the experiments, the subjects were presented persuasive communications containing strong arguments against the truisms. In some of the experiments, these communications contained only those counterarguments which had been refuted by the first-session "refutational" communication; in others they contained novel counterarguments. Measurements of the subjects' beliefs on the truisms were taken before and after each experiment to determine the relative effect of the two types of immunization communications.

In many respects these experiments are quite similar to those discussed in the preceding section. As stated by McGuire and Papageorgis (14, p. 332):

The supportive *vs.* refutational manipulation . . . is quite similar to the one-*vs.* two-sided argument manipulation in previous studies (Hovland, Lumsdaine, and Sheffield, 1949; Lumsdaine and Janis, 1953). Their one-sided condition is much the same as our supportive; their two-sided condition is, however, a less close analog to our refutational. While their two-sided defense involved the supportive arguments plus some lesser mention of counterarguments either unsupported or refuted, our refutational defense involved no supportive arguments, only some mention of counterarguments with detailed refutations thereof.

Perhaps a more significant connection between the two is the fact that in one sense the "truism" studies served to test the theoretical analysis of the one-sided *vs.* two-sided experimental results. This analysis, as stated by Lumsdaine and Janis, was to the effect that the two-sided communication inoculated the listeners by giving them "an advance basis for ignoring or discounting the opposing communication" (9, p. 318). As subsequent discussion will indicate, this interpretation was supported by the findings of the experiments described in this section.

Before particularizing these findings, an important difference between the conditions of these two types of experiments should be mentioned. This difference pertains to the fact that the subject matter of the "truism" experiments was generally devoid of controversy. As a consequence of this characteristic, the issues involved in these studies were much less likely to have been exposed to pre-experiment persuasive appeal than were the issues involved in the one-sided *versus* two-sided studies. And in respect to this difference, the significance of which has been expressed by McGuire (11), the condition under which persuasive communications are presented in a courtroom is like that of the one-sided-two-sided studies and unlike that of the "truism" studies. Despite this difference, the "truism" experiments have at least some application to the one-sided *versus* two-sided question in court-room communications, and, therefore, merit consideration in this discussion.

Now, on the basis of the experimentation conducted by McGuire and Papageorgis several hypotheses concerning the creation of immunity against persuasion have been confirmed. Those which have practical implications for the persuasive situation of the courtroom may be summarized as follows: (*a*) The supportive approach "of pre-exposing a person to arguments in support of his belief has less immunizing effectiveness than the 'inoculation' procedure of pre-exposing him to weakened, defense stimulating forms of the counterarguments" (14, p. 327); (*b*) pre-exposure to weakened counterarguments via the refutational type communication produces resistance not only to the counterarguments specifically refuted but also to subsequent strong forms of novel counterarguments (15); and, (*c*) the supportive communication, in addition to being inferior in the amount of immunity to counterarguments initially created, will decay more rapidly than that conferred by the refutational communication (12). The first of these findings lends support to the superiority of the two-sided type of argument demonstrated by the experimental studies described in the preceding section. The second is significant to those persuasive situations, frequently confronting lawyers, in which the opponent's argument cannot be anticipated with precision. The third will be applied to legal arguments following a description of one other type of experiment, that which has controlled prior familiarity with the subject matter of the persuasive communications.

3. Studies involving
controlled prior familiarity

The first experiment of this type was conducted by Insko and involved as subject matter an issue much like those which confront jurors in the courtroom (6). The question to be decided by the subjects was the guilt or innocence of an accused in a criminal case involving a charge of bigamy. (With this issue, prior unfamiliarity by the subjects was assured.) Upon this question, the experimenter prepared four communications patterned after those presented to juries in actual trials, with equal division between one-sided and two-sided arguments. The prosecution and the defense were favored by one argument of each type. After their preparation, the communications were presented to eight separate groups of subjects. (See Table 1.) Following the communications the subjects were asked to mark a nine point rating scale as to guilt or innocence of the accused.[2]

Insko (6) had predicted that under the one-sided *versus* one-sided and the two-sided *versus* two-sided conditions neither primacy nor recency effects would occur. This prediction was supported by the experimental results. He had also predicted that in the one-sided *versus* two-sided condition recency would occur and that in the two-sided *versus* one-sided condition primacy would occur.[3] This prediction was based upon the

Table 1

PRESENTATION OF COMMUNICATIONS TO EIGHT GROUPS

Order of Presentation	Group 1	Group 2	Group 3	Group 4	Group 5	Group 6	Group 7	Group 8
Prosecution—1st	1-sided vs.	1-sided vs.	2-sided vs.	2-sided vs.				
Defense—2d	2-sided	2-sided	1-sided	2-sided				
Defense—1st					1-sided vs.	1-sided vs.	2-sided vs.	2-sided vs.
Prosecution—2d					1-sided	2-sided	1-sided	2-sided

projected superiority of a two-sided communication. However, it was supported by the results only as to the one-sided *versus* two-sided condition. The two-sided *versus* one-sided condition did not result in a primacy effect. An inconsistency between this finding and a finding of an earlier experiment (9) led Insko to conduct a second experiment, with only one change in experimental procedure. Prior to the presentation of the persuasive arguments described above, the subjects were familiarized to a limited extent with the subject matter. They were presented a one-page summary of half of the one-sided prosecution and defense arguments. With this change in the conditions, all of Insko's predictions were confirmed, leading him to suggest that "prior information has an important effect upon the relative impact of subsequent communications on attitude change" (6, p. 205).

The second experiment of the "controlled familiarity" type[4] was conducted recently by Chu (2) and patterned after the experiment of Hovland, Lumsdaine, and Sheffield (4). The most significant difference between these two experiments was that the subject matter of the former was relatively unknown to the subjects prior to the experimental com-

[2]A scale with nine marks on it, running from "very guilty" to "innocent." The subject marks the point along the line which indicates how strongly he feels.

[3]Primacy means occurring first in time. Recency means occurring most recently.

[4]That is, the experimenter controlled how familiar the subjects were with the issue.

munications. With this difference it was possible to test the effect of prior familiarity upon the relative persuasive force of one-sided and two-sided arguments. The subjects of Chu's experiment were high school students in Taiwan, while the topic of his communications concerned the advisability of creating an international free trade zone in that country. In support of the proposition that the free trade zone would be advisable, the experimenter prepared two communications. One of the two discussed only those arguments favoring creation of the zone (one-sided); the other mentioned the arguments against the trade zone, refuted them, and then presented the favorable arguments used in the first communication (two-sided). Before the presentation of the communications, the subjects were divided into four groups. Two of the groups were given a standardized lecture on the economic problems of Taiwan, including discussion of a proposal for opening an international free trade zone. During the course of the lecture, the pro and con arguments for the proposal were mentioned but not supported by the lecturer. The other two groups received no information about the topic used in the experimental communications. After this step, the one-sided persuasive communication was presented to one group with and one group without prior familiarity, and the two-sided persuasive communication was presented to the other two groups, one with and one without familiarity.

The results of this experiment confirmed the findings of Insko, and confirmed and extended the findings of Hovland, Lumsdaine, and Sheffield. To those subjects who were initially favorable to the conclusion of the communications, the type of argument, as well as the extent of familiarity with the subject matter, made little difference. Of those who were initially opposed to the conclusion of the communications, the ones unfamiliar with the subject matter were more influenced by the two-sided communication. These results were explained in terms of the extent to which the subjects detected bias in the presentation of the communications. (Bias was measured by checking the degree to which the subjects detected omission of relevant arguments, pro or con, from the communications.) Among the initially favorable subjects, there was no difference in the detection of bias by those receiving one-sided communications and those receiving two-sided communications. (It was suggested that this resulted from the absence of motivation to question the communicator's fairness.) Among the initially opposed, there was a difference in the detection of bias aroused by the two types of communications, a difference related to the listener's prior familiarity with the subject matter. Those who had been familiarized with the issue were more aroused to detect bias in the one-sided communication and were, therefore, less influenced by that type of argument than those who had not been familiarized with the issue.

From the experimentation described in this section, it is possible to conclude as follows: (a) When an audience is familiar with an issue and initially opposed to the position advocated, a two-sided communication will be more effective in persuasion than a one-sided one; and, (b) when an audience is familiar with an issue and initially favorable to the position advocated, no difference in effectiveness will exist between a one-sided and two-sided communication. The importance of these conclusions to a selection of the most effective type of legal argument will be made apparent in the following discussion.

C. APPLICATION OF THE EXPERIMENTAL FINDINGS TO COURTROOM COMMUNICATIONS

1. Arguments before appellate courts

One of the two most important types of legal arguments is that which occurs in the appellate courts of the state and federal judicial systems. The subject matter of this type of argument is always one of law as distinguished from one of fact, and in many respects is similar to the subject matter of the above described experiments. This similarity may be observed from an examination of some typical issues which have confronted appellate judges in recent years. For example: (a) Should a Negro citizen have the right to purchase property from a white citizen who is unwilling to sell except to another white citizen; (b) should an individual have the right to burn his draft card in exercise of his freedom to protest his nation's involvement in war; and (c) does capital punishment of a convicted criminal offender constitute cruel and unusual punishment? All of these issues at the time presented for decision were subject to substantial controversy, and upon each of them the judges who were exposed to the persuasive communications obviously had pre-existing opinions as to how the issue should be decided. Both of these factors were present in the experiments of Hovland, Lumsdaine, and Sheffield, and Lumsdaine and Janis. One or the other of the two was present in the remainder of the experiments described above.

In like manner, there is similarity between the conditions under which appellate arguments are presented and those under which the experimental communications were presented. Perhaps the most important likeness concerns the extent to which appellate judges are familiar with the pro and con arguments on the issues presented for decision. The significance of this condition was demonstrated by the studies of Insko and Chu. A second similarity in conditions is related to the fact that appellate judges are compelled by the rules under which they operate to expose themselves to persuasive communications on both sides of each issue. The influence of this factor was tested by the experiment of Lumsdaine and Janis. Of less importance but still worthy of mention is a condition tested by one of the experiments conducted by McGuire (12). Frequently, a decision by an appellate court occurs several days or weeks after the presentation of the persuasive communications. During this interval, it is likely that the judges of that court will expose each other to additional argumentation on the issue involved. Thus, the persistence of the persuasion induced by the appellate argument becomes a consideration of significance.

Considering the nature of appellate issues and the conditions under which communications on those issues are presented, it is possible to make some tentative predictions concerning the most effective type of appellate argument. Although not without uncertainty, the experimental findings seem to support the conclusion that a two-sided communication will be more effective in shifting and maintaining opinion in the desired direction than a one-sided one, if the appellate judges are initially opposed to the position advocated. Likewise, they support the conclusion that if the judges are initially favorable to the position advocated, neither of the two types of communications will be more effective than the other. The reason for the unbalanced effectiveness of a two-sided argument under the first situation could be one of several. Since appellate judges are fully aware of both pro and con arguments on most issues, a one-sided communication might be expected to make them "feel the presentation was invalid because biased" (4, pp. 270–71), or to cause them to rehearse the opposing arguments during the presentation and thereby "learn less of the content of the communication because of the distracting effects of their preoccupation with implicit incompatible responses" (4, p. 271). Or, in line with the reasoning of Lumsdaine and Janis, a two-sided argument might have an advantage not possessed by a one-sided one of giving the judges "an advance basis for ignoring or discounting the opposing communication" when it is presented (9, p. 318).

The uncertainty left in the above conclusions exists because of the presence of some conditions under which appellate arguments are presented that have not been tested by any of the experimental studies. Probably the most important of these concerns the attitude of judges toward those who present persuasive communications of this type. One of the most fundamental characteristics of one lawyer's attitude toward another lawyer is an expectation that the latter will be an advocate, that he will present biased viewpoints in behalf of his cause. Such bias is a demand of the adversarial system of justice, one that is not only understood but encouraged by all lawyers, including those serving as appellate judges. Now, if Chu's theoretical interpretation of the one-sided-two-sided differential is accepted: i.e., that the detection of bias by the listeners accounts for the advantage of two-sided communications, this first untested condition could be a significant factor in deciding which, if either, of the two types of communications would be more effective in appellate argument.

A second condition of appellate argument that is experimentally untested relates to the amount of knowledge possessed by the judges prior to the presentation of the persuasive communications. In some of the experiments described above the subjects had limited knowledge of the subject matter (4, 9); in others the subjects had only such knowledge as was provided by the experimenter (2, 6). But with respect to none of the experiments can it be said that the subjects possessed the amount and kind of knowledge about the subject matter of the communications that is possessed by appellate judges. On most appellate issues, it is likely that the judges were initiated during their law school days. It is possible that they practiced cases involving such issues prior to appointment to the court, and since that time have discussed such issues with other judges and lawyers. As a consequence, they probably know almost as much about the topic of the communications as the communicators. In accordance with the finding of the initial one-sided *versus* two-sided experiment that a two-sided argument is more effective with better educated listeners, the expertise possessed by judges might support the conclusion that a two-sided communication is more effective in appellate argument. However, when this expertise is accompanied by an expectation of bias on the part of the communicators, a different relative effect of the two types of communication might result.

One other untested condition of appellate argument should be mentioned before concluding this part of the discussion. In the experimental laboratory, the decisions by those who are exposed to the persuasive communications possess no actual, real-life consequences. On the other hand, the decisions made by appellate judges are always of consequence to the litigants before the court, and, because of their application as "legal precedent" under the common law system, of consequence to all of society. An awareness of these facts by the listeners of the two situations should have an effect upon their responses to the persuasive messages. Whether or not such awareness would play a part in the one-sided *versus* two-sided issue is an open question.

It is doubtful that any one of these untested conditions would cause a one-sided communication to be more effective in persuasion that a two-sided one. However, they could operate to reduce or eliminate the unbalanced effectiveness of a two-sided argument shown to exist under certain conditions. Such an effect, of course, would in turn reduce the importance of selecting one or the other of the two types of appellate argument. Until a study of the effect of these conditions is made, any prediction as to the relative effectiveness of one-sided and two-sided appellate communications must be accepted with caution.

2. Arguments before juries in trial courts

The type of persuasive communication presented to a jury is vastly different from that presented to an appellate court. The conditions under which it is presented are also different. With regard to subject matter, jury communications involve controversial issues of fact rather than controversial issues of law. Issues such as the following are typical topics of jury communications: (a) Was the act which resulted in the death of the victim committed by the accused; (b) was this act committed at a time when the accused was mentally incompetent; and, (c) was the act committed by the accused in self-defense? The principal difference between these issues and those which are presented to appellate courts is the absence of pre-existing opinion by the jurors. The existence of this state of mind is a prerequisite to service on a jury.

With regard to the comparative conditions under which appellate and jury arguments are presented, there are two significant differences. The first relates to the relative familiarity of the decision makers of the forums with the adversarial system of administering justice. Jurors are not nearly as aware as judges of the expectation that lawyers be biased in favor of the cause of their clients, and are more likely, therefore, to react to a detection of bias in the communications. The second difference relates to the context in which the two types of legal arguments are made. In appellate courts, the decision makers receive nothing but persuasive communications on the issues involved. In trial courts, the decision makers receive much more than the persuasive arguments. At the outset of the trial, they receive from each of the litigants a narrative statement of the basic facts giving rise to the litigation. These communications, presented through the attorneys, are known as "opening statements" and are required to be devoid of persuasive appeal. Following these communications, the jury is presented the testimony of all witnesses, this consisting of examination by the litigant calling the witness and cross-examination by the opposing litigant. It is only in the context of these prior communications that the parties are permitted to present their persuasive messages.

Considering these differences in subject matter and conditions, a prediction as to the most effective type of persuasive argument before a jury can be made with considerably less uncertainty than was the case with appellate arguments. The studies of Insko and Chu make such a prediction possible. The conditions under which Chu's persuasive communications were presented were similar to those under which jury arguments are presented, especially with regard to the important factor of prior familiarity with the subject matter. Insko's second experiment was even more duplicative of courtroom conditions than that of Chu. His subjects had no knowledge of the subject matter prior to the experiment, no pre-existing opinion as to the appropriate decision, and were familiarized with the pro and con arguments prior to the presentation of the persuasive communications. The results of this experiment, along with those of Chu's experiment, strongly suggest that a two-sided jury argument possesses a significant advantage over a one-sided one.

D. CONCLUSION

The most important implication from the experimentation described in this paper for courtroom communications relates to jury arguments, and is suggested by the study conducted by Insko. In his second experiment, he was able to generate an advantage in a two-sided argument over a one-sided argument by familiarizing the subjects with the subject matter prior to the presentation of the communications. An advantage of this kind in a jury trial—i.e., one resulting from the use of a two-sided argument by one party and a one-sided argument by the other party—would be a contributing factor to the final judgment, totally unrelated to the substantive merits of the issue. Despite this, such advantage could be tolerated by the law as a consequence of the adversarial system of justice, which demands that each litigant do whatever is necessary to maximize the probability of a favorable result, including selection of the most effective type of persuasive argument.

The significance of Insko's study is that he was able to generate this advantage with relatively little prior familiarity. He presented a summary of only one-half of the pro and con arguments on the issue. What would have happened if his subjects had been as thoroughly familiarized with his subject matter as jurors are with the subject matter of the communications which they receive? By the time litigants are permitted to make their persuasive arguments, jurors have been exposed to every possible shred of data bearing upon the disputed issue. The law assures this by prohibiting the advocates from mentioning in their arguments any data not already presented to the jury by witnesses. Is it possible that under these circumstances, a two-sided communication presented *first* would be more effective in persuasion than a two-sided communication presented *second*? An advantage of this type could not be dismissed as a consequence of the adversarial system. The studies on order effects in persuasion by Hovland, Mandell, Campbell, Brock, Luchins, Cohen, McGuire, Janis, Feierabend, and Anderson (5), did not answer this critical question. A study conducted by Lana suggests the possibility that such an advantage may exist (7). It should be possible to design an experiment that would provide a more reliable answer. The importance of such to a fair administration of law is obvious.

REFERENCES

1. Cone, A., & Lawyer, V. The Art of Persuasion in Litigation. Boston, Mass.: American Trial Lawyers' Association, 1966.
2. Chu, G. C. Prior familiarity, perceived bias, and one-sided *versus* two-sided communications. *J. Exper. Soc. Psychol.*, 1967, 3, 243–254.
3. Goldstein, I. Trial Technique. Chicago: Callaghan & Company, 1935.
4. Hovland, C. I., Lumsdaine, A. A., & Sheffield, F. D. Experiments on Mass Communications. Princeton, N.J.: Princeton Univ. Press, 1949.
5. Hovland, C. I., Mandell, W., Campbell, E. H., Brock, T., Luchins, A. S., Cohen, A. R., McGuire, W. J., Janis, I. L., Feierabend, R. L., & Anderson, N. H. The order of presentation in persuasion. New Haven, Conn.: Yale Univ. Press, 1957.
6. Insko, C. A. One-sided *versus* two-sided communications and countercommunications. *J. Abn. & Soc. Psychol.*, 1962, 65, 203–206.
7. Lana, R. E. Familiarity and the order of presentation of persuasive communication. *J. Abn. & Soc. Psychol.*, 1961, 62, 573–577.
8. Lorry, W. A Civil Action, The Trial. Philadelphia, Pa.: American Law Institute, 1955.
9. Lumsdaine, A. A., & Janis, I. L. Resistance to "counterpropaganda" produced by one-sided and two-sided "propaganda" presentations. *Publ. Opin. Quart.*, 1953, 17, 311–318.
10. McGinnies, E. Studies in Persuasion: III. Reactions of Japanese students to one-sided and two-sided communications. *J. Soc. Psychol.*, 1966, 70, 87–93.
11. McGuire, W. J. Inducing resistance to persuasion. *Advances in Experimental Social Psychology*, Vol. 1 (Ed. Berkowitz). New York: Academic Press, 1964.

12. ———. Persistence of the resistance to persuasion induced by various types of prior belief defenses. *J. Abn. & Soc. Psychol.*, 1962, 64, 241–248.

13. ———. Resistance to persuasion conferred by active and passive prior refutation of the same and alternative counterarguments. *J. Abn. & Soc. Psychol.*, 1961, 63, 326–332.

14. McGuire, W. J., & Papageorgis, D. The relative efficacy of various types of prior belief-defense in producing immunity against persuasion. *J. Abn. & Soc. Psychol.*, 1961, 62, 327–337.

15. Papageorgis, D., & McGuire, W. J. The generality of immunity to persuasion produced by pre-exposure to weakened counterarguments. *J. Abn. & Soc. Psychol.*, 1961, 62, 475–481.

16. Stern, R., & Gressman, E. Supreme Court Practice. Washington, D.C.: Bureau of National Affairs, Inc. 1950.

THE GERMAN CONCENTRATION CAMP
Paul Chodoff

chapter thirteen

GROUP
BEHAVIOR
AND
PSYCHOLOGICAL
DEFENSES

Not all writers in the field of psychology speak the same language. Compare the next selection, which is taken from a professional journal, to the one you just read. The article on German concentration camps is about as concrete and human as writing can be.

In addition to style, consider the substance of the material, which demonstrates in a real-life situation (unfortunately) how phychological defenses operate to protect people threatened by the group. The article leaves one amazed at the ability of the human psyche to survive.

THE GERMAN
CONCENTRATION CAMP
AS A PSYCHOLOGICAL
STRESS

Homo homini lupus (*Man is a wolf to man*).

The bloody chronicles of recorded history have, time after time, demonstrated the truth of this bitter adage, but never more clearly than in the treatment of the Jewish minority under their control by the German Nazis of the hitlerian reich. Therefore, in a symposium on the psychological aspects of stress, the concentration camp experience can serve as a paradigm of how the human organism reacts to stressful conditions which approach the outermost limits of human adaptability.

All of the concentration camps set up by the *Geheime Staats Polizei* (SS) in Germany and occupied Europe were not alike and the differences between extermination camps and labor camps were certainly significant. However, the conditions faced by the inmates of all concentration camps can only be described, in the words of A. P. J. Taylor, as "loathsome beyond belief." In addition to the out-and-out extermination measures, the physical stresses endured by the prisoners included malnutrition, crowding, sleeplessness, exposure, inadequate clothing, forced labor, beatings, injury, torture, exhaustion, medical experimentation, diarrhea, various epidemic diseases, and the effects of the long "death marches" from the camps in the closing days of the war. The physically depleted state of the prisoners, the brutal and primitive conditions in which they lived, and the entirely inadequate medical facilities were responsible for an extremely high death rate, and also had the effect of increasing the susceptibility of the inmates to the nonphysical stresses which they had to face. Chief among these latter was the danger to life, everpresent and unavoidable. It is possible, to some degree, for a healthy personality to defend itself against a peril which, though very grave, is predictable, and is at least potentially limited in time, as in the case of soldiers in

"The German Concentration Camp as a Psychological Stress," by Paul Chodoff, in ARCHIVES OF GENERAL PSYCHIATRY, 22 (January 1970), 78–87; reprinted by permission of the author and the publisher.

combat who can at least hope for relief and rotation out of the fighting zone, but for the concentration camp inmate, as has been described by Viktor Frankl from his own experiences in Auschwitz,[1] the absolute uncertainty of his condition was a barrier to the erection of adequate psychological adaptive measures. In addition to the threat to life, the prisoners had to face the catastrophic trauma of separation from their families and, consequently, to the agonizing uncertainty about their own future there were added equally agonizing doubts as to whether they would ever see their relatives again. The very least price one had to pay to survive in the camps was to suffer the grossest kind of daily humiliation at the hands of an organization superbly qualified to mete out humiliation. Massive frustration of their basic drives had the apparent dual effect of driving the sexual life of the prisoners underground and of rendering the insistent demands of hunger all-dominating so that fantasies about food occupied much of their conscious awareness. If not himself the victim of casual violence or deliberate cruelty, the prisoner at least frequently witnessed such exhibitions. Since it was impossible to retaliate effectively he had to smother his aggressive feelings, for even the appearance of resentment against the torturers could lead to his own destruction. Regimented, imprisoned, without a moment of privacy during the 24 hours, the prisoner's human worth, and even his sense of an individual human identity, was under constant and savage assault. His entire environment was designed to impress upon him his utter protoplasmic worthlessness, a worthlessness which had no relationship to what he did, only to what he was. Reduced from individual human status to the status of a debased being, identified not by name but by a number and a badge of a particular color, a conviction of his ineluctable inferiority was hammered into the prisoner by the SS jailers who needed to justify their own behavior by convincing themselves of the inferior, subhuman status of the Jews in their charge. The concentration camp inmates lived in a kafkaesque world in which the rules governing their existence were senseless, capricious, and often mutually contradictory, as, for instance, when impossible standards of cleanliness were demanded, while, at the same time, the inadequate opportunities and senseless rules about toileting made even an elementary decency impossible.

At this point, I am going to interpose exerpts from a description—recorded in her own words at my request—of some aspects of life at Auschwitz by a former inmate who has also been a patient of mine. I believe that this account will convey to you something of the physical and psychological stresses which confronted the concentration camp inmate, as well as a suggestion of the adaptive measures called forth by these stresses.

LIFE IN A
CONCENTRATION CAMP

"We arrived to Auschwitz in the early part of April. That's a story by itself—the arrival and the happenings. We lived in blocks. It's called a block in German but it's a barracks and it has 1,500 people and the barracks had rows and rows of three-tier bunk beds—they were very poorly built, out of just boards and lumber and each bunk bed had 12 people—in our case 12 women, and we happened to choose the upper bunk because we thought it would be the best. It was OK for us but it caused an awful lot of heartache afterwards because, as I said, the bunk beds were not built very well and the boards broke under the weight of us in the beginning before we started losing weight and there were many broken or fractured skulls or bones below us.

"Each person was supposed to have a blanket. It so happened that the blankets were stolen so we never ended up with enough blankets for all of us. Maybe by the end of the evening we would have two or three blankets left for 12 people. I think the biggest crisis after the day's hardship was finding a blanket to sleep on and the fights we had keeping the blanket. I must say I was one of the lucky (I say lucky) or exceptional persons who was an assistant to the Capo. It came in very handy at the time. I suffered an awful lot because of it later, but it gave me protection. Maybe I had the blanket . . . I don't even remember because all this did not matter.

"Anyway, we got up at two o'clock in the morning. We were awakened by the girls who brought the coffee in big barrels. It was black and it had charcoal in it and maybe chicory. It was rather lukewarm and they thought it was enough to hold us through the day. And no one wanted the coffee. You would rather have an hour sleep or so, but you had to have it. The barracks had to be emptied, and we had to get back and line up for the *appel*—roll call—and that was my job, getting people up. I was assigned to three or four bunks and that means I was assigned to wake-up approximately a 150 to 200 people who did not want to face the day's reality. I mean, because we knew what was coming. So I was up, pulling blankets off of people—'get up,' screaming, carrying on, even hitting. Once I hit someone and she looked at me and it was one of my mother's friends. I apologized. I felt terribly bad. I kept on doing it. I got them up. I think the whole process took nearly half an hour to make 1,500 people get out of the block. We were up but there was no question of dressing because we got one dress when we entered Auschwitz and I got a very, very long petticoat. It came all the way down to my ankles.

It came in very handy because I was able to use it little by little as toilet tissue which was nonexistent, 'till there was nothing left. So I just had a dress to wear and I think most people, that's all they had, and shoes and a toothbrush that hung around my neck. It was my most prized thing . . . a toothbrush.

"I know I got out of my bunk a half an hour earlier than anyone else because we were determined to keep clean and we went to the washroom that was at least, oh, two or three bunkers away from us and we stripped ourself completely naked and scrubbed ourselves with cold water because we didn't want any lice on us. We checked our clothes for lice, because typhus was spreading already at that time and, anyway, we had to line up for *appel*—and the 1,500 people were divided in three groups so that means I had 500 people to line up and in each line I think there were maybe 10, 15, I'm not sure. But somehow, I don't know how the rumor started, but someone gave the word that they were going to pick so many people to be cremated—that the first four or five rows are going to be taken to be cremated. Well, I tried to get anyone to get in the first five rows. It was impossible. I had to make them do it. I was shoving and pushing. But we were lined up around two-thirty in the morning and the Germans did not come out till five or six o'clock I think it was for the *appel* and there were 30,000 people in the c lager and it took them a while. They always miscounted because, after the first counting was over we were being punished for someone was missing. We had to get down on our knees with our hands up and wait till they counted over and over and over and over till they decided that they had a number. But meantime, we didn't have the big selections as when Dr. Mengele came around. Just the little officers did their jobs and decided a girl with a pimple on her face, someone who was a little bit more run down than should be, or someone with a little bandage were selected. Naturally those people were taken out automatically to the crematorium. So we had to be very careful that you shouldn't have any scars showing or you should look fresh and not unwell. Well, by 11 or 12 we were allowed to come in to our bunks and then lunchtime came.

"It is very hard for me to recall food—what we ate or not because I decided that all those things are unimportant. That I am going to have control over my body, that food is not important, so I can't remember, but I think it was one slice of bread and a slice of margarine on it, and some kind of jelly made out of red beets.

"I think in all my eight months that I have been there, maybe twice we were able to take a walk—because we were being punished for one reason or the other and we had to stay in our bunks, or a new transport came in and they would not allow us out to watch the transport coming in so we were locked in our block or barracks. So the days were spent in the barracks.

"Then came the evening roll call. That started about two o'clock in the afternoon and then again the same circus-lining up, waiting, miscounting and counting, and counting, and counting, and it was seven to eight o'clock in the evening before the evening meal came and before we were allowed to come in—sometimes nine-thirty or ten o'clock. If someone was missing we were punished by kneeling. Otherwise we stood—and we had to stand sometimes in hot sun and sometimes in rain.

"Anyway, evening came around and then we had our meal. The meal consisted of mush. It was some kind of a liquid, thickened with something. It had a few potatoes in the bottom of the barrel and then it had some kind of a chemical taste to it so that the women decided it was some kind of a tranquilizer, but I doubted the Germans spent money on putting tranquilizers in. But another thing, we stopped menstruating and they thought that, whatever chemical taste it had in it, this is the thing that stopped us from menstruating so we didn't menstruate at all.

"Again, I was one of the lucky ones who distributed food. I think I was fair when it came to distributing food—I did not, I would not allow myself to bring any more up to my bunk than we were allowed to except for my mother who was quite ill—she had diarrhea and she could not digest the food. She was getting weaker and weaker day by day. You know she was at that time 43 years old and it is hard to think that I have reached that age. How would I have been able, how would I have reacted under the circumstances that she did at this age. I feel very young, by the way. But she seemed to me very old at that time and well anyway, evening meal over, we were allowed to take a walk. But again, when transports were coming in they locked the doors and there was complete curfew and we were not allowed to go out and we were just well, listening to the screams or the silence or the smell of the burning flesh and wondering what tomorrow was going to bring to us. Some were wondering. I knew I was going to make it. The human torture, getting up in the morning and things, smelling the burning flesh and the flying soot. The air was oily, greasy. There were no birds."

"I think they were very worried about our physical well-being and cleanliness so we had to be shaved. That's right, several times while I stayed in Auschwitz, we were shaved of hair—head, under arms and intimate parts of our body by Jewish inmates—standing. We were standing on a stool so that the Jewish inmates would be able to reach us easier and we were surrounded by SS men who seemed to enjoy it very much. Well it didn't bother me either. I had no feelings whatsoever. I couldn't care less at this point of the game. It really didn't matter."

"As I said, we had selections every single day—some just slight—just picking people out as I mentioned before because of scars, because of pimples, because of being run down, because of looking tired or because of having a crooked smile, or because someone just didn't like you. But then they were beginning to liquidate Auschwitz and we had major selections where you were selected either to go to work or to the crematorium and in this case Dr. Mengele was involved in it. He was quite an imposing figure and his presence—I don't think everybody was scared because, rather I wasn't. I was hypnotized by his looks, by his actions.

"The barracks had two massive doors and we were inside. They did not let us out. It was in October and it was rainy and we were holding pots of water—we didn't sleep because of the rain because we had to keep ourselves dry . . . and then the doors swing open quite dramatically . . . great entrance with Mengele in the center accompanied by two SS women and a couple of soldiers . . . he stands with his whip on one side and his legs apart. It's unbelievable. It looked like Otto Preminger arranged the theme for the whole thing. It seems to me now that it was like a movie.

"Anyway the Capo came out and she gave us orders to undress and line up in front of the barracks. It had two rooms. One was a storage room and one was the Capo's room—and Mengele stood in between and he had one leg lifted on a stool, his right leg, and he was leaning on his knee and he had a switch in the same hand and while we were lining up I was able to observe what he was doing. Till I had to face him I really had no feelings. I couldn't describe how I felt but I saw the switch go. It was a horsewhip—left, right, and I noticed that those who were motioned left were in better condition, physical condition than the ones who were motioned to go right. Anyway, this went on and on and not a sound, even if it meant life or death. I don't know how other people felt about it, but I was quite well informed, I was accused of being able to face the truth, of being able to know because I had my mother with me. The others said it was easy for me to believe all this because I had my mother with me. I had no great loss. They loved their mothers, they cared, and they wanted to believe their mothers were safe somewhere in another bunk, somewhere in another camp. It made them stronger, knowing their parents were not cremated, but I had my mother and I knew my father was OK at that time in another bunk at camp.

"Anyway, my turn came. I had a choice to make. Not only Mengele had a choice to make, I had. I had to make up my mind. Am I going to follow my mother or is this it? Am I going to separate from her? The only way I was able to work out the problem was that I was not going to give myself a chance to decide. He will have to decide. I will go ahead in front of my mother—that was unusual, she being my mother, out of courtesy I followed her all the time in any other circumstances—but in this case I was going first and my mother followed me and I went. I think my heart was beating quite fast, not because I was afraid—I knew I would come through, but because I was doing something wrong. I was doing something terribly wrong. Anyway I passed Mengele. I didn't see him. I just passed and I was sent into the room where I would be kept alive and I turned around and my mother was with me, so this was a very happy ending.

"As I said in the evenings if I had a chance I went over to talk to my friend . . . to the fence, to the electric fence, and at each end of the fence they had the watchtowers where the Nazis were able to observe us and . . . just for the fun of it . . . the girl who was right next to me—I think they just wanted to see if they can aim well because I don't know why— they shot her right in the eye, and she lost her eye. Another time another girl was at the same place. Her friend threw a package of food over to her and she ran towards the fence to catch it and she touched the wire and there she hung. She looked like Jesus Christ spread out with her two arms stuck to the wire."

"In the end, people were losing weight, and they were getting skinnier and skinnier and some of them were just skeletons but I really did not see them. I just wiped the pictures out of my mind. I was able to step over them and when I came out from the concentration camp I said I did not see a dead body—I mean, I feel that I didn't see them. Even if I can see them. This is what's killing me now that I have never felt the strain, the brutality, the physical brutality of the concentration camp. I mean like my aunt, my young aunt. She was 13 or 14 when she was exposed to brutality and death and she talks with a passion of what they did to her. Then when I meet another woman who is in her 60's and she will tell me her sufferings, I can't stand them. I broke all the friendship up with them. I don't want them. I can't stand them, because they bore me. I just can't stand listening to them, and I have nothing to do with them."

COMMENT

What enabled a man or woman to survive such a hell? We have no real answers to this question and must resort to such generalizations as the almost miraculous and infinite adaptability of the human species. It needs to be emphasized that while particular varieties of individual defensive and coping behavior played a role in whether a prisoner would live or die, such behavior was far less important than were such chance factors as where the prisoner happened to be when a "selection" for the gas chamber was taking place or the mood of the selector at the time.

However, accounts by survivors do agree in describing a fairly consistent sequence of reactions to concentration camp life. This sequence was inaugurated by a universal response of shock and terror on arrival at the camp, since the SS made it their business to impress the new prisoner with their malevolent power, while many of the old prisoners, displaying "the camp mentality," manifested by irritability, egotistical behavior, and envy, were often cold and unsympathetic to new arrivals. This fright reaction was generally followed by a period of apathy, and, in most cases, by a longer period of mourning and depression. The period of apathy was often psychologically protective, in that it served to provide a kind of transitional emotional hibernation, but, in some cases, apathy took over to such an extent that the prisoner became a "mussulman," who gave up the struggle to live and did not survive very long.

Among those prisoners who continued to struggle for life, certain adaptive measures gradually gained ascendancy and came to be characteristic of the long-term adjustment. Regressive behavior, of greater or lesser degree, was almost universal, being induced in the prisoners by the overwhelming infantilizing pressures to which they were subjected and by the need to stifle aggressive impulses. As a consequence of the complete reversal of values in the camps, it is likely that such behavior served an adaptive function, since regressive prisoners immersed in fantasies were likely to be docile and submissive toward the SS and thus to have a better chance of escaping retaliatory measures. A consequence of such regression was that many prisoners, like children, became quite dependent on their savage masters, so that attitudes toward the SS were marked more by ambivalence than by conscious overt hostility. Some prisoners went so far as to employ the well-known mechanism of identification with the aggressor, imitating the behavior and taking on the values of the SS. In the dreams of more than one female survivor whom I have examined, SS troopers were always tall, handsome, and god-like figures, and I believe you will be able to detect elements of such a reaction in the description of my patient's encounter with Dr. Mengele. Those who have seen or read the play, *The Deputy*, will remember the satanic figure of "The Doctor" who was modeled on the same Dr. Mengele, "The Angel of Death of Auschwitz," whom I have heard described in such awed terms by survivors of Auschwitz that I—who have never seen him—can visualize his tall, radiant, immaculately dressed figure sitting nonchalantly astride a chair as—like Osiris, the judge of the Kingdom of the Dead—he gestures with his riding whip, selecting the prisoners lined up in front of him for either death or life.

It appears that the most important personality defenses among concentration camp inmates were denial and isolation of affect. As might be expected in the case of this probably most ubiquitous of all defenses, there was widespread employment of denial as manifested by my patient who would not see the corpses she was stepping over, and by the poignant picture of her fellow inmates who refused to believe that the smoke arising from the crematorium chimneys came from the burning corpses of their mothers. Isolation of affect, which could be so extreme as to involve a kind of emotional anesthesia, seemed to have functioned particularly to protect the ego against the dangers associated with feelings of hostility toward an external object which treats the self as if it were an inanimate thing and not a person. My patient who says, "It didn't bother me. I had no feelings whatsoever" when being shaved while naked in front of SS troopers, was certainly isolating her affect from her cognition. When combined with an ability to observe themselves and their surroundings, this kind of tamping down of affect along with sublimatory processes helped such gifted individuals as Frankl,[1] Cohen,[2] and Bettelheim[3] to produce some rather remarkably objective reports of life in the camps. Some form of companionship with others was indispensable, since a completely isolated individual could not have survived in the camps, but the depth of such companionship was usually limited by the overpowering egotistical demands of self-preservation, except in certain political and religious groups. Daydreams of revenge served the purpose of swallowing up some of the submerged aggression, while aggression could also be discharged through quarrelsome and irritable behavior toward the other prisoners, as illustrated by the description of the fighting over food and blankets, and by projection on the SS who were then seen as even more formidable, endowed as they thus were with the unexpressed hostility of the prisoners. Since the existence of mental illness of any degree of severity would have been incompatible with survival, an interesting adaptive consequence of imprisonment was that new psychosomatic or psychoneurotic disorders rarely developed while already existing ones often markedly improved, and suicide—except under conditions as to be almost indistinguishable from murder—was also an infrequent phenomenon.

As soon after the end of the war and liberation as the recovery of some physical health permitted, most survivors made their way back to their homes. More often than not, their worst fears were confirmed, and they usually found that not only had their relatives and friends perished in the holocaust but they also found their homes and communities destroyed or uninhabitable. Such frustrating and disappointing aspects of post-liberation reality were responsible for the inevitable disruption of the rosy fantasies of postwar life which had proliferated during the imprisonment and which have been called "the post-disaster Utopia."[4] In the regressed state of most of the exprisoners at this stage, such a narcissistic blow, as well as real disappointment of their idealistic hopes that a better world would now arise from the ruins of Europe, resulted in much bitterness, resentment, and depression, even, in some cases, in temporary flurries of antisocial or paranoid behavior. A large number of the liberated prisoners, homeless, alone, bewildered, and without resources, took refuge in the displaced person (DP) camps which were set up in various parts of Europe, and, in some cases, remained in them for years with the result that their neurotic symptoms became fixated because of the monotony of DP camp life and its fostering of passivity and hypochondriacal preoccupation.

As the immediate postwar epoch drew to a close, the surviving remnant of concentration camp prisoners gradually settled themselves in more or less permanent abodes in their own countries of origin, or in other lands, especially in the United States and Israel. For this latter group, to the multiple traumata they had already endured there was now added the need to adjust to a new environment, to new customs, and to a different language.

At this point one might expect the grisly story to come to an end for most of the survivors, with the passage of time allowing the gradual envelopment of their fears and memories in psychic scar tissue. This is not what happened, however, for, as I have described in another publication,[5] in the late 1950's and early 1960's articles began to appear in the medical literature of many countries describing features of personality disorder and psychiatric illness still present many years later in a large number of these survivors of the holocaust, in some cases cropping up after latent periods of months or years after the persecution.

Although figures are not available for the overall incidence of psychiatric sequelae among the survivors of the Nazi persecution, it is clear, judging from reports from many countries, including Germany, the United States, Israel, Poland, and Norway,[5] that they are of high frequency.

Long-term, unfavorable personality alterations in survivors have taken two widely overlapping directions. Some individuals develop tendencies toward seclusiveness, social isolation, helplessness, and apathy. They are passive, fatalistic, and dependent, wanting only to be taken care of, and to be let alone by a world whose requirements they are no longer interested in trying to fulfill. Other survivors regard their environment with suspicion, hostility, and mistrust, reflected in their attitudes toward other people which range from quiet, envious bitterness to cynicism and quarrelsome belligerence.

The most distinctive long-term consequence of the Nazi persecution, however, is the concentration camp syndrome. Invariably present in this syndrome is some degree of felt anxiety along with irritability, restlessness, apprehensiveness, and a startle reaction to such ordinary stimuli as an unexpected phone call or a knock at the door. These anxiety symptoms are almost always worse at night and are usually accompanied by insomnia and by nightmares, which are either simple or only slightly disguised repetitions of the traumatic experiences. Psychosomatic involvement of almost all the organ systems has been reported, the most common being weakness, fatigue, and gastrointestinal troubles. A very characteristic feature is an obsessive ruminative state in which the individual is preoccupied with recollections of his own persecutory experiences and with the often idealized life with his family before the persecution began. Interviews with concentration camps survivors often leave the interviewer with the uncanny sensation that he has been transported in time back to, say, the gray inferno of Auschwitz, so vivid and compelling is the wealth of detail with which they describe the events which befell them and which they witnessed, so that the interviewer gets the impression that nothing of real significance in their lives has happened since the liberation. This feeling, that life was permanently interrupted by the concentration camp period, may be why my patient still feels "young" at her present age. Most individuals find their memories unwelcome and obtrusive, but there are a few who actually appear to derive pleasure from them. Depression, at times associated with "survival guilt," is also a very common manifestation of the concentration camp syndrome.

Studies dealing with the very few surviving individuals who were infants or very young children in the concentration camps are particularly interesting. Anna Freud and Sophie Dann have made a fascinating study of a group of six children who had all been in the concentration camp at Theresienstadt before the age of 3 years.[6] When seen in England after the liberation, these children showed severe emotional disturbances and were hypersensitive, restless, aggressive, and difficult to handle, but they had also evolved a remarkably stable sibling group and a group identity during their internment which seemed to protect them against the worst pathogenic effects of the absence of a maternal figure. A follow-up of the later fates of these children indicates that, though they all had stormy experiences during adolescence, most of them achieved some degree of stability by early adulthood. Sterba has reported on a group of 25 displaced children and adolescents[7] who had lost both parents and had been in concentration camps or in hiding for three to five years. She describes how attempts to place these children with foster parents were greatly hampered by the disappointment and dissatisfaction, expressed by the children toward whatever was done for them. They, too, displayed a desperate need to cling together, apparently deriving more security from these peer relationships than from even the most benevolent relationship with the adults on whom they were displacing all the angry fear engendered in them by the loss of their parents. Among my own cases, there were six who were 5 years of age or younger in 1939, and who therefore underwent the experiences of the persecution at an extremely early period of their lives. In addition to various degrees of overt psychoneurotic symptomatology, I found them all to be emotionally volatile people whose moods fluctuate markedly and who react to a mild degree of stress, such as an unexpected event, with exacerbations of anxiety. Their personalities are marked by various admixtures of a bitter, cynical, pessimistic attitude toward life and a child-like and total kind of emotional dependency. Although intimacy and closeness are of the greatest importance to them, they tend to show self-defeating patterns of excessive expectation and bitter or despairing withdrawal when these expectations are disappointed. They are extremely sensitive to actual or threatened separation from those on whom they have become dependent. It seems clear that the most damaging consequences to the personality maturation of these individuals resulted from the absence of a reliable and secure interpersonal environment, particularly the lack of adequate mothering in the early years. This applies not only to those children who lost both of their natural parents but also to those whose mothers were forced to appear and disappear actually by force of necessity but certainly, to the perception of the children, in a cruel and capricious manner.

To return to the concentration camp syndrome, its nature has been the subject of some controversy but, on the whole, it appears reasonable to regard at least the anxiety core of the concentration camp syndrome as a special variety of traumatic neurosis resembling in some respects the ordinary combat stress reaction, which is the paradigm of the traumatic neurosis. A more interesting analogy is the Japanese A-bomb disease or neurosis described by Lifton in survivors of the Hiroshima bombing,[8] who for many years afterwards have suffered from vague and chronic complaints of fatigue, nervousness, weakness, and various physical ailments, along with characterological changes and feelings of what Lifton calls "existential" guilt. Also, although the analogy is not as direct, it is possible, without stretching the bounds of imagination beyond credibility, to draw significant parallels between the concentration camp experience and the poverty ghettos of our great cities.[9]

Although there can be no doubt that the primary cause of the concentration camp syndrome is the multiple, massive emotional and physical stress to which the prisoners were exposed during internment, these stresses cannot alone account for the origins and development of the later added features of the syndrome or of the persistence of these symptoms in many cases in spite of the passage of time and infinitely more favorable circumstances. For such secondary developments, which differ in character and intensity in different patients, other, additional explanations must be invoked. One theory seeks to ascribe not only the immediate postwar, but also the chronic persistent symptoms of the concentration camp syndrome to organic brain disease resulting from injury, illness, and malnutrition incurred during the internment. However, my own experience is in agreement with that of a majority of observers who have reported that brain injury was relatively unimportant in their cases, and that the development and persistence of certain features of the concentration camp syndrome are far more dependent on the immediate and later postwar experiences of the survivor than on organic factors. It is during this postwar period, too, that basic personality strengths and weaknesses would have their effects on the ability of the survivor to cope with what fate might bring his way. Postwar experiences having a significant influence on the ultimate adjustment of the individual include loss of immediate members of family, relatives, homes, and livelihoods, a dashing of the inflated hopes for a postwar Utopia, a long and debilitating residence in DP camps, downward change in socioeconomic status, and emigration to strange lands with different language, tempo of life, and customs.

I will conclude with a consideration of depression and guilt among concentration camp survivors, because these symptoms seem to me to strike to the core of the psychopathology they display, and to constitute a kind of existential signature of the persecution. Depression is one of the most characteristic symptoms of concentration camp survivors, and, along with the traumatogenic anxiety state and the obsessive rumination over the past, is a hallmark of the concentration camp syndrome. More likely to occur is an unvarying feeling of emptiness, despair, and hopelessness in older people; most of the survivors become depressed episodically, particularly at holidays, anniversaries, and in connection with events which remind them of the past, like the Eichmann trial. It has been suggested that depression may represent a delayed mourning reaction, particularly insistent in its demands because the concentration camp prisoners had been unable to engage in ceremonial mourning for their dead.[10] Certainly the brutal destruction of so many family members, relatives, and friends needs no explanation as a cause for depression, but it is not so obvious why the depression of the concentration camp survivors is so often tinged with feelings of guilt. In some cases, such feelings are attributed to specific episodes, such as when a prisoner had taken an action which led to the saving of his own life at increased risk to another and in such instances it may be possible to detect the predisposing influence of insufficiently resolved earlier conflictual experiences. This was true in the case of the patient whose account of life at Auschwitz you have heard and certainly in general it would be difficult to devise a more diabolical environment than the concentration camp for fostering guilt-producing conflict over agressive drives or between self-preservative and superego impulses. However, there remain a significant number of ex-concentration camp inmates whose guilt and depression are attached to nothing more specific than the very fact that they survived when so many were lost. My encounter with a large number of survivors of the persecution has left me not completely satisfied that the depression and guilt they feel can be explained entirely by the usual combination of precipitating stress and morbid predisposition which psychiatrists invoke to explain such symptoms. Perhaps this is because the immense scale of the tragedy in which these survivors were immeshed seems to render the ordinary language of psychopathology inadequate and invites a grander, more transcendent dimension of explication. The stubborn, even prideful, refusal to forget displayed by certain survivors seems to involve something more than masochistic personality mechanisms or a revival of past, incompletely resolved emotional conflicts, and, instead, suggests a desperate attempt to rescue their dead from the limbo of insignificance to which they have been consigned by bestowing upon their destruction a benison of meaning.

Viktor Frankl himself emerged from Auschwitz with the conviction that the need to find some meaning in an otherwise incomprehensible universe constituted an elemental human hunger equal in importance to other such putative primary motivational forces as the pleasure principle of Freud.[1] In a similar vein, Lifton found[8] in his study of A-bomb survivors in Hiroshima that for them the order of the universe had somehow been violated and that they continued to identify themselves with the dead and be unable to resolve their guilt through the usual mourning experiences because they could find no spiritual or ideological explanation, no "reason" to explain the disaster and thus to release them from this identification with the dead.

There is an ancient Talmudic legend of the Lamed-Vov, the 36 just men who take upon themselves the sufferings of the world. Perhaps those concentration camp survivors who ceaselessly lament the past are performing a similar function and their sufferings can be thought of both as a memorial to their dead and as an act of existential expiation for a species capable of such an outrage upon a common humanness.

REFERENCES

1. Frankl, V. E.: *Man's Search for Meaning*, Boston: Beacon Press, Inc., 1959.
2. Cohen, E. A.: *Human Behavior in the Concentration Camp*, New York: W. W. Norton Company, 1953.
3. Bettelheim, B.: *The Informed Heart*, New York: Free Press of Glencoe, 1960.

4. Wolfenstein, M.: *Disaster*, New York: Free Press of Glencoe, 1957.
5. Chodoff, P.: "Effects of Extreme Coercive and Oppressive Forces," in Arieti S. (ed.) *American Handbook Psychiatry*, New York: Basic Books, Inc., Publishers, 1966, vol 3.
6. Freud, A., and Dann, S.: An Experiment in Group Upbringing, *Psychoanal Stud Child* 6:122, 1951.
7. Sterba, E.: Some Problems of Children and Adolescents Surviving From Concentration Camps, read before the Second Wayne State University Conference on the Late Sequelae of Massive Psychic Traumatization, Detroit, Feb 21, 1964.
8. Lifton, R.: Psychological Effects of the Atomic Bomb in Hiroshima, *Daedalus* (summer) 1963.
9. Chodoff, P.: "The Nazi Concentration Camp and the American Poverty Ghetto: A Comparison," in the *Proceedings Psychiatric Outpatients Centers of America*, 1967.
10. Meerloo, J.: Delayed Mourning in Victims of Extermination Camps, *J Hillside Hosp* 12:96, 1963.

PSYCHOTHERAPY IN AMERICA TODAY
Jerome D. Frank

chapter fourteen

THE
PSYCHO-
THERAPISTS

The patient lies on the psychoanalyst's couch and explores the dark regions of unremembered childhood. Or —the witch doctor wraps his patient's body in wet leaves and pronounces an incantation over him. Or—an actor, an unemployed school teacher, a veterinarian, and a woman lawyer get together with a psychologist once a week to talk, argue, cry, shout, embrace, stamp out of the room.

Therapy has innumerable styles, because its basic ingredients are simple and endlessly flexible: a healer who has a method and enjoys the approval of people; a person who wants to be healed and believes in the healer's ability to help; a series of encounters between them that are designed to relieve the sufferer's problems and render him better able to lead a satisfying life.

The following essay tells something about modern therapy, about the special qualities of those who practice it, and about some of the people who benefit from it.

"What is it you want to buy?" the Sheep said at last.
. . . "I don't *quite* know yet," Alice said very gently. "I
should like to look all round me first, if I might."
(Lewis Carroll, *Through the Looking Glass*, 1872, Chapter
5)

Throughout his life every person is influenced by the behavior of others
towards him. His relationships with his fellows shape his own behavior,
attitudes, values, self-image, and world view and also affect his sense of
well-being. It is customary to classify different forms of personal influence in accordance with their settings and the role of the influencing
figure. Thus we say that a person is brought up by his parents in the
family, educated by his teachers in school, and led by his officers in
battle, for example.

Attempts to enhance a person's feeling of well-being are usually
labeled treatment, and every society trains some of its members to apply
this form of influence. Treatment always involves a personal relationship
between healer and sufferer. Certain types of therapy rely primarily on
the healer's ability to mobilize healing forces in the sufferer by psychological means. These forms of treatment may be generically termed psychotherapy.

Although psychotherapeutic methods have existed since time im-
memorial and a vast amount of accumulated experience supports a belief
in their value, some of the most elementary questions about them remain
unanswered. Research has not yet yielded sufficient information to permit description of the different methods in generally acceptable terms,
specification of the conditions for which different methods are most
suitable, or comparison of their results. These difficulties spring largely
from persisting lack of precise knowledge concerning the nature of psychotherapeutic principles.

From PERSUASION AND HEALING: A COMPARATIVE STUDY OF
PSYCHOTHERAPY, *by Jerome D. Frank (Baltimore: The Johns Hopkins
Press, 1961), pp. 1–17; reprinted by permission of the publisher.*

The purpose of this book is to review data from various sources that may help to identify and clarify the active ingredients of various forms of psychotherapy in our own and other cultures by searching for their common features. If these features can be found, they will presumably include the active components since they would otherwise be unlikely to reappear under so many guises and circumstances. In embarking on this review, it seems appropriate to begin with a definition of psychotherapy, followed by a brief consideration of its historical roots and its place in America today, and a brief consideration of the problems involved in the evaluation of the relative efficacy of its different forms.

WHAT IS PSYCHOTHERAPY?

Since practically all forms of personal influence may affect a person's sense of well-being, the definition of psychotherapy must of necessity be somewhat arbitrary. We shall consider as psychotherapy only those types of influence characterized by the following features:

1. A trained, socially sanctioned healer, whose healing powers are accepted by the sufferer and by his social group or an important segment of it.

2. A sufferer who seeks relief from the healer.

3. A circumscribed, more or less structured series of contacts between the healer and the sufferer, through which the healer, often with the aid of a group, tries to produce certain changes in the sufferer's emotional state, attitudes, and behavior. All concerned believe these changes will help him. Although physical and chemical adjuncts may be used, the healing influence is primarily exercised by words, acts, and rituals in which sufferer, healer, and—if there is one—group, participate jointly.

These three features are common not only to all forms of psychotherapy as the term is generally used, but also to methods of primitive healing, religious conversion, and even so-called brain-washing, all of which involve systematic, time-limited contacts between a person in distress and someone who tries to reduce the distress by producing changes in the sufferer's feelings, attitudes, and behavior. By this definition, the administration of an inert medicine by a doctor to a patient is also a form of psychotherapy, since its effectiveness depends on its symbolization of the physician's healing function, which produces favorable changes in the patient's feelings and attitudes. Our search for the active ingredients of psychotherapy, then, will require exploration of these activities, as well as a consideration of experimental studies of the transmission of influence.

HISTORICAL ROOTS OF PSYCHOTHERAPY

Since at least part of the efficacy of psychotherapeutic methods lies in the shared belief of the participants that these methods will work, the predominant method would be expected to differ in different societies and in different historical epochs. This is, in fact, the case. Modern psychotherapies are rooted in two historical traditions of healing—the religio-magical and the naturalistic, or scientific. The former, originating before recorded history, regards certain forms of suffering or of alienation from one's fellows as caused by some sort of supernatural or magical intervention, such as loss of one's soul, possession by an evil spirit, or a sorcerer's curse. Treatment consists in suitable rites conducted by a healer who combines the roles of priest and physician. These rites typically require the active participation of the sufferer and members of his family or social group and are highly charged emotionally. If successful, they undo the supernaturally or magically caused damage, thereby restoring the victim's health and re-establishing or strengthening his ties with his group. As we shall see, the religio-magical tradition is still influential, even in secularized Western society, and many of its principles have been incorporated into naturalistic forms of psychotherapy.

The earliest surviving account of these principles is in the writings attributed to the Greek physician Hippocrates in the fifth century B.C. He viewed mental illness, like all other forms of illness, as a phenomenon that could be studied and treated scientifically. Though largely eclipsed in the Middle Ages, this view has come into increasing prominence since the early nineteenth century and is the dominant one today in the Western world.

Like the religio-magical view, the naturalistic view originally did not clearly distinguish mental illness from other forms of illness, and treatment for both was essentially similar. The emergence of psychotherapy as a distinctive form of healing probably began with the dramatic demonstration by Anton Mesmer, in the late eighteenth century, that he could cause the symptoms of certain patients to disappear by putting them into a trance. Though his particular theories and methods were soon discredited, mesmerism was the precursor of hypnotism, which rapidly became recognized as a method of psychotherapy. Through the use of hypnosis, Sigmund Freud and Joseph Breuer discovered, towards the end of the nineteenth century, that many symptoms of their patients seemed to be symbolic attempts to express and resolve chronic conflicts that had their roots in upsetting experiences of early life. This led Freud to develop a form of treatment based on minute exploration of patients' personal histories, with emotional reliving of childhood experiences in the treatment setting. From the information thus gained he formed a theory of human nature and mental illness known as psychoanalysis, which supplied a rationale for his psychotherapy. During the same period the Russian physiologist I. P. Pavlov demonstrated by experiments with conditioned reflexes that dogs could be made "neurotic" by exposing them to insoluble conflicts, and this led to a "conditioned reflex" theory of mental illness and treatment.

In recent years American experimental psychologists have developed various theories of learning based on experiments with animals and humans. Some of these concepts seem applicable to mental illnesses conceived as disorders of the learning process. Thus most current naturalistic theories of mental illness and its treatment represent various combinations and modifications of ideas derived from Freud, Pavlov, and experimental studies of learning. Fortunately these three conceptual schemes are not incompatible, despite differences in terminology. They supply a scientifically respectable rationale for contemporary naturalistic methods of psychotherapy. In America, which accords high prestige to science, this probably contributes to their efficacy.

CULTURAL ASPECTS OF
MENTAL ILLNESS
AND PSYCHOTHERAPY

As the preceding discussion implies, the definition of mental illness depends heavily on the attitudes and values of the society or group in which it occurs. For example, the same symptoms that in the Middle Ages were viewed as evidence of demoniacal possession to be treated by exorcism are now regarded as signs of mental illness to be treated by a psychiatrist. In World War II Russian soldiers were never classified as having psychoneuroses, which can only mean that the Russian army did not recognize this condition. Presumably soldiers with complaints that we would term psychoneurotic were regarded either as malingerers subject to disciplinary action or medically ill and therefore treated by regular physicians. In the American army, by contrast, many commonplace reactions to the stresses of military life were initially regarded as signs of psychoneurotic illness, warranting discharge from the service. Today many of these same soldiers would be promptly returned to duty.

Similarly, whether or not a person is sent to a mental hospital for treatment depends at least as much on the attitudes of those around him as on his symptoms. Many actively hallucinating persons function in the community because their families, neighbors, and employers are willing to put up with their eccentricities, while other persons, especially among the elderly, wind up in the hospital largely because the family want to rid themselves of responsibility for their care.

Contemporary America has gone far in the direction of regarding socially deviant behavior as illness, which requires treatment rather than punishment. This is probably partially attributable to the strong humanitarian trend in American society and the high value it places on the welfare of the individual.

Probably more significant, however, is the recognition that certain criminals, alcoholics, and sex deviates, for example, appear to be attempting to cope with the same types of conflicts and other stresses as other persons who are regarded as mentally ill, but their efforts take the form of deviant behavior rather than symptom formation.

An interesting, if somewhat unfortunate, consequence of the fact that social attitudes play such a big role in the definition of mental illness is that mental health education may be a two-edged sword. By teaching people to regard certain types of distress or behavioral oddities as illnesses rather than as normal reactions to life's stresses, harmless eccentricities, or moral weaknesses, it may cause alarm and increase the demand for psychotherapy. This may explain the curious fact that the use of psychotherapy tends to keep pace with its availability. The greater the number of treatment facilities and the more widely they are known, the larger the number of persons seeking their services. Psychotherapy is the only form of treatment which, at least to some extent, appears to create the illness it treats. It can never suffer the unfortunate fate of Victor Borge's physician uncle who became despondent on realizing that he had discovered a cure for which there was no disease.

Cultural values influence not only the definition of mental illness but also the nature of its treatment. Psychotherapies in societies or groups with a primarily religious world view are based on religio-magical theories and healing rituals merge with religious rites. The scientific world view of Western societies is reflected in the tendency to regard psychotherapy as a form of medical treatment, based on scientific understanding of human nature. Furthermore, naturalistic psychotherapies tend to express the dominant values of their cultures. Thus, methods of psychotherapy in Germany and the U.S.S.R. tend to reflect the authoritarian values of these societies. In the United States, permissive, democratic therapies have a higher prestige, consistent with the high value placed on individual freedom and responsibility.

Within a given society, the dominant type of treatment depends in part on the class position and group affiliation of the recipient. In America, religio-magical forms of healing are practiced by certain religious groups. Lower-class patients, who view treatment as something the doctor does to one, are more likely to receive directive treatment, often accompanied by physical measures of medication. Middle- and upper-class patients, who put a high value on self-knowledge and self-direction, are more likely to receive permissive forms of treatment stressing insight.

In mid-twentieth-century America, mental illness has not fully shaken off its demonological aura, as evidenced by the stigma still attached to it. In the minds of many it implies moral weakness. The insane still tend to elicit a kind of fascinated horror, reflected in their being shunted off to isolated hospitals on the one hand and being objects of morbid curiosity on the other, as shown by the popularity of novels, plays, and films about them. Nevertheless, all forms of suffering or troublesome behavior that involve emotional or psychological factors are viewed as treatable by psychotherapy. This is reflected in the great variety of recipients and purveyors of psychotherapy and its settings. To reduce this chaotic scene to some sort of order, we shall describe it first from the standpoint of those receiving psychotherapy and then from the standpoint of those offering it.

WHO RECEIVES PSYCHOTHERAPY?

The many thousands of Americans who undergo some form of psychotherapy cover an extraordinarily broad range. At one extreme are some who are best characterized as mental hypochondriacs, searching for someone to lift the normal burdens of living from their shoulders. At the other are persons who are severely ill with disturbances of thinking, feeling, and behavior. They constitute the populations of our mental hospitals. In between is a vast group of persons suffering from chronic emotional stress produced by faulty patterns of living.

The most clearly definable recipients of psychotherapy are persons who are regarded by themselves or others as patients. Candidates for psychotherapy are distinguished from those who do not receive this type of treatment by the presence of a recognizable emotional or psychological component in their illnesses. The difficulty here is the word "recognizable." As the contributions of unhealthy emotional states to all forms of illness and disability are becoming increasingly recognized, psychotherapeutic principles are being incorporated into all forms of medical healing. It is possible, however, to distinguish four classes of patients for whom psychotherapy constitutes the entire treatment or a major part of it.

The first class comprises the hospitalized insane, patients who are so disturbed that they cannot carry out the ordinary tasks of life and need to be protected. The bulk of these are senile and schizophrenic patients. Both can be helped by psychotherapy, but it can do more for the former, because their adaptive capacity has not been irreversibly reduced by brain damage. The second class of psychiatric patients consists of neurotics, whose distress seems clearly related to chronic emotional strain and often involves some disturbance of bodily functioning. Akin to these is the third group, patients with so-called "psychosomatic" illnesses such as asthma, peptic ulcer, and certain skin diseases, in whom definite and chronic disorders of bodily organs seem related to emotional tension. The fourth group of patients in whose treatment psychotherapy should play a prominent part are the chronically ill. This category cuts across the other three and also includes those with chronic disease or disability that was initially unrelated to psychological causes, such as loss of limb, epilepsy, rheumatic heart disease, and so on. Since the emotional stresses created by chronic disease probably contribute more to the distress and disability of these patients than their bodily damage, increasing use of psychotherapeutic principles is being made in rehabilitation methods.

No one questions that psychotics, psychoneurotics, the psychosomatically ill, and the chronically ill are suitable candidates for psychotherapy, but from this point on confusion reigns. The difficulty is that many emotional stresses result in misbehavior, which comes into conflict with the standards and values of society, so that its moral and medical aspects are inseparable. Alcoholics, drug addicts, and sexual deviates are clearly sick in the sense that they are caught up in behavior patterns they cannot control, but they also offend against social standards, which brings them to the attention of the legal authorities. Their deviant behavior often seems attributable to emotional difficulties related to disturbing childhood experiences, such as parental mistreatment or neglect, broken homes, and lack of adequate socialization, suggesting that they might respond to psychotherapy. Modern criminology is increasingly emphasizing the use of psychotherapeutic principles in the rehabilitation of offenders, but much work remains to be done to determine which approach is more suitable for different types of criminals. Current views distinguish the socialized criminal, who represents the values of his own deviant group and is a well-integrated member of it, from the so-called sociopath or psychopath, who cannot get along with anyone and is always in trouble. The proper handling of offenders is a knotty problem requiring cooperation of the healing, legal, and corrective professions.

A large and heterogeneous group of people who may receive psychotherapy may be termed "misfits." Their distress results from failure to cope satisfactorily with their environments, yet they are not severely enough out of step to be considered either ill or criminal. The failure to adjust may be temporary or permanent, and sometimes the chief fault lies in the environment, sometimes in the patient. Misfits include those who seek help or are brought to it because of difficulties on the job, at home, or, in the younger age groups, at school. They include tired business executives, married couples on the verge of divorce, unruly or emotionally disturbed children and their parents, and the like. In this category may also be included members of the intelligentsia or middle and upper classes who have leisure to worry about themselves and who look to psychotherapy to solve their general state of dissatisfaction, malaise, spiritual unrest, or feeling that they are not living life to the full.

Finally, mention must be made of psychotherapists in training who are required to undergo psychotherapy as part of their training program. Although these are in no sense patients and represent a very small proportion of persons receiving psychotherapy, they are of some importance in the total scene because their psychotherapy occupies a large proportion of the time of some of the most able and experienced psychotherapists at the expense of the patients who might receive their services.

WHO CONDUCTS PSYCHOTHERAPY?

The variety of practitioners of psychotherapy in one form or another is almost as great as the range of persons they seek to help. Psychotherapists in the naturalistic tradition include a relatively small group specifically trained for this art, and a much larger number of professionals who practice psychotherapy without labeling it as such in connection with their healing or advisory activities. The largest group of professionals trained to conduct psychotherapy are psychiatrists, numbering about ten thousand. Their ranks are supplemented by well over four thousand clinical psychologists and five thousand social workers.

Psychologists enter the field of psychotherapy through the scientific study of human thinking and behavior, and they supply most of the sophisticated researchers in this field. In clinical settings such as hospitals and psychiatric clinics they carry out diagnostic tests and do therapy under the more or less nominal supervision of psychiatrists. The major institutional settings in which they work independently are schools and universities. Increasing numbers, especially in the larger cities, are going into independent private practice as both diagnosticians and therapists.

Psychiatric social workers are specialists within the helping profession of social work. Like clinical psychologists, they are members of treatment teams in hospitals and clinics under psychiatric supervision, but they also operate independently in social agencies, family agencies, marriage counseling centers, and so on, and as private practitioners.

Psychotherapy in one guise or another forms part of the practice of many other professional groups. An indeterminate number of America's approximately 215,000 nonpsychiatric physicians use psychotherapy with many of their patients, often without recognizing it as such. To them must be added osteopaths and healers on the fringes of medicine such as chiropractors, naturopaths, and others. The effectiveness of these latter, especially with emotionally disturbed persons, probably rests primarily on their intuitive use of psychotherapeutic principles.

In addition to the healers more or less linked to medicine a wide variety of counselors and guides may use psychotherapeutic principles with their clientele. These include marriage counselors, rehabilitation and vocational counselors, parole officers, group workers, clergymen, and others.

Members of different disciplines tend to describe their activities in different terms. For example, medical and quasi-medical healers treat patients, psychiatric social workers do case work with clients, clergymen offer pastoral counseling and group workers do group work. For obvious reasons, each discipline tends to emphasize the special features of its approach, leading to a greater appearance of difference than may actually exist. In all likelihood their similarities far outweigh their differences.

The distinction between different healers and advisers lies less in what they do than in the persons with whom they do it, and this, in turn, depends largely on the settings in which they work. Certain settings sharply limit the kinds of persons who seek or receive psychotherapeutic help. Thus the bulk of the population of mental hospitals consists of the insane; those using the services of social agencies tend to be persons struggling with economic, social, marital, or parental problems. The school psychologist inevitably deals with children with school problems, the prison psychologist or psychiatrist with offenders, and so on.

The private office of the independent practitioner, however sets no such limits on the kind of person who comes to him. A person may wind up in different hands depending on the referral channel he happens to pick, or the way in which he defines his problems. The very same patient might be treated by a psychiatrist, a psychologist, a psychiatric social worker or even a clergyman, depending on where his feet carry him. As a result, the relationships among the different professions that conduct psychotherapy are in a state of flux. Clergymen and psychiatrists have formally recognized their field of common concern by forming the Academy of Religion and Mental Health. Jurisdictional problems are most acute in the larger cities where, in response to the increasing demand for psychotherapy, psychologists and psychiatric social workers have gone into independent private practice in direct competition with psychiatrists, resulting in attempts by the various groups involved to settle the issue by legislation.

This review of psychotherapeutic practitioners would be seriously incomplete without mention of the thousands of religious healers who are members of established sects such as Christian Science and New Thought, and, on their fringes, cultists of all sorts whose claim to healing powers rests solely on their own assertions. Though there is no way of counting these last, they must treat vast numbers of troubled people indistinguishable from those receiving more recognized forms of psychotherapy.

WHAT ARE THE EFFECTS
OF PSYCHOTHERAPY?

The ever-increasing investment of time, effort, and money in psychotherapy and its steadily increasing popularity imply that both its recipients and its practitioners are convinced that it does some good. Patients must believe it to be helpful or they would not seek it in increasing numbers, and every psychotherapist has seen permanent and striking improvement in a patient following some occurrence in psychotherapy. To date, however, although proponents of every method present persuasive accounts of their successes and vast amounts have been spent on research in psychotherapy, convincing objective demonstration that one form of psychotherapy produces better results than another is lacking.

Statistical studies of psychotherapy consistently report that about two-thirds of the neurotic patients and 40 per cent of schizophrenic patients are improved immediately after treatment, regardless of the type of psychotherapy they have received, and the same improvement rate has been found for patients who have not received any treatment that was deliberately psychotherapeutic. Thus about 70 per cent of neurotic patients who received only custodial care in state hospitals are released, and the same percentage of patients with neurotically based disabilities treated by insurance doctors have returned to work at the end of two years. Similarly, the few follow-up studies that exist fail to show differences in long-term improvement from different types of treatment. Indeed, with hospitalized psychotics, although certain procedures such as electroconvulsive therapy seem able to accelerate improvement of certain illnesses, no procedure has been shown to produce five-year improvement rates better than those occurring under routine hospital care.

The question of the relative effectiveness of different forms of psychotherapy is also puzzling when viewed from the standpoint of the amount or duration of therapeutic contact. Within wide limits, these seem to depend largely on the therapist's notion of how much treatment is necessary, rather than on the patient's condition. With respect to amount of contact, an eminent psychiatrist has pointed out that when psychoanalysis was transplanted from Europe to America, the frequency of sessions soon dropped from six times a week to five, then to three times a week or even less. There is no reason to think that this reduction depended on differences in the severity of illness between European and American patients, and the writer suggests that it was probably a reflection of the increasing demands on the therapists' time created by the growing number of patients seeking help. Yet "in actual duration of treatment, in terms of months or years, the patient going five times a week takes about as long to be cured as the patient going three times."

Duration of treatment also may be more closely related to the therapist's conception of how long treatment should take than to the patient's condition. Practitioners of long-term therapy find that their patients take a long time to respond; those who believe that they can produce good results in a few weeks report that their patients respond promptly. There is no evidence that a larger proportion of patients in long-term treatment improve or that improvement resulting from long-term treatment is more enduring than that produced by briefer treatment.

However, psychotherapy has tended to become increasingly prolonged in settings where there are no external obstacles to its continuance. Psychoanalysis that originally lasted a year or two at most now often lasts five to six years. At one university counseling center the average number of sessions increased from six in 1949 to thirty-one in 1954. It is hard to believe that the lengthening of treatment reflects changes in the severity of patients' or clients' illnesses. More probably it reflects certain changes in the therapist's attitudes produced by increasing experience.

At this point it must be emphasized that the failure to find differences in improvement rate from different forms or amounts of psychotherapy is a sign of ignorance, not knowledge. These negative results may well be due to lack of criteria of improvement that would permit comparison of different forms of treatment. In many reports improvement is left undefined, so that there is no way of knowing precisely what the therapist had in mind, or whether or not he shifted his criterion from one patient to another.

When improvement is defined, the relationship between criteria used in different studies is usually unclear. Criteria determining the discharge of patients from state hospitals, the resumption of work by patients receiving disability payments, and the diagnosis of "recovered" by a psychoanalyst obviously may have little in common.

The problem of lack of comparability of measures of improvement is most acute in studies that define improvement in terms of a particular theory of psychotherapy. Criteria based on such definitions often can be precisely measured, but their relevance to clinical improvement may be problematical. Moreover, in order to get precise quantitative results, the research must confine itself to special types of patients. One such study, for example, compared changes on certain psychological test scores in a group of outpatients who received eight months of psychotherapy with a matched group who received no treatment over seven months, and found no differences between them. But the experiment had to be confined to persons who were able to do the test, and also were willing to forego treatment for seven months, so one can draw no general conclusion from the negative findings.

In short, the inability to prove that a phenomenon exists is quite different from proving that it does *not* exist. The difficulty in demonstrating by statistical or experimental methods that therapy works or that one form is superior to another may lie in our inability to define adequately any of the variables involved. We cannot yet describe patients, therapies, or improvement in terms that permit valid comparison of the effects of different therapies on the same class of patient.

In the present state of ignorance, the most reasonable assumption is that all forms of psychotherapy that persist must do some good, otherwise they would disappear. Furthermore, it is likely that the similarity of improvement rate reported from different forms of psychotherapy results from features common to them all. The improvement rate for each form, then, would be composed of patients who responded to the features it shares with other forms and therefore would have improved with any type of psychotherapy, plus, perhaps, some patients who would have responded favorably only to the particular type of psychotherapy under consideration. If this were so, it would be hard to tease out the unique considerations of different forms of treatment until the features they share—and the attributes of patients that cause them to respond favorably to these features—were better understood.

The purpose of the book is to try to define these shared active ingredients, looking for features common to many different forms of interpersonal healing, and then seeing if these features also are present in psychotherapy. This exploration will lead quite far afield, and into some largely uncharted areas. Therefore, before setting out, it seems desirable to identify home base more clearly. To this end, the next chapter outlines a theoretical framework for psychotherapy.

SUMMARY

This chapter has attempted a general definition of psychotherapy, briefly reviewed its historical roots, and described the types of patients, therapists, and settings characteristic of psychotherapy in America today. It appears that many thousands of troubled people of all sorts seek psychotherapy or have it thrust upon them, and its practitioners are almost as varied as its recipients. Despite this feverish activity, there is little established knowledge about the relative efficacy of various forms, and the therapist's expectations seem to influence the length and amount of treatment required to produce improvement. These observations lead to the tentative conclusion that the features common to all types of psychotherapy probably contribute more to their efficacy than the characteristics that differentiate them.

EMERGING CONCEPTS OF MENTAL ILLNESS AND MODELS OF TREATMENT: THE MEDICAL POINT OF VIEW

Roy R. Grinker, Sr.

EMERGING CONCEPTS OF MENTAL ILLNESS AND MODELS OF TREATMENT: THE PSYCHOLOGICAL POINT OF VIEW

George W. Albee

chapter fifteen

PSYCHOLOGISTS AND PSYCHIATRISTS

Is mental illness a sickness, in which weakness must be diagnosed and treated? Or is it a social-developmental problem in which strengths must be sought out and reinforced, and prevention practiced on a large scale?

Like any field, psychotherapy has its internal disputes. The one examined in these two essays is between the medical view of mental illness and the psychological view of the same phenomenon—which the psychologist might be unwilling to call either "mental" or "illness."

Beyond giving some insight into this controversy, the essays will, I hope, enrich your understanding of the variety of ways in which emotional difficulties may be diagnosed and treated.

EMERGING CONCEPTS OF MENTAL ILLNESS AND MODELS OF TREATMENT: THE MEDICAL POINT OF VIEW

In accepting an invitation to participate in this discussion I emphatically rejected the role of a debater. In my opinion the conflicting views of two professional disciplines, or perhaps we may call them two sciences, can never be resolved by debates, which in the recent past have engendered more heat than light(1, 5, 11, 13, 15). Instead, I propose a serious discussion about our agreements, disagreements, and misunderstandings in the hope that some compromises may be reached.

Perhaps it would be better to say that clearer recognition may develop that we are discussing two professions in the process of rapid evolutionary changes, moving partly toward and partly away from each other but inevitably tied together by mutual concern with problems of human mentation and behavior. Since some of our objectives are nearly or actually identical, how do we get along with each other?

Two elements of this problem need little discussion. The first, payment for services, I believe has been resolved by national agencies, insurance companies, and the private sector. No one should deny the right of a professional to receive just and equitable remuneration for services rendered.

Second is the problem of prestige and status in accordance with functional positions. The clinical psychologist is called "doctor" in every position except perhaps in his own university. He is an absolutely essential and respected staff member in our state and Veterans Administration mental hospitals and clinics. Finally, on the modern bandwagon of community mental health centers, he is just as frequently the director as is a professional of any other discipline since not one of them has all the knowledge and skills necessary to administer community resources or to carry out so-called social engineering. I view the "top dog" conflict as argued by both psychiatrists and psychologists to be nonprofessional and unworthy of people who aspire to teach others adjustment to realities, compromise, and rational behavior(1, 6).

From "Emerging Concepts of Mental Illness and Models of Treatment: The Medical Point of View," by Roy R. Grinker, Sr., in AMERICAN JOURNAL OF PSYCHIATRY, *125 (1969), 865–869; reprinted by permission of the publisher and the author.*

THE MEDICAL MODEL

It has been stated frequently that psychiatrists operate within a medical model inasmuch as they treat patients, and the words "treat" and "patients" belong to the realm of medicine. Albee(1) argues with Szasz(18) that mental illness is a myth; it is not a disease and therefore physicians are not necessary. This seems to be only semantic gymnastics. Instead of disease, the argument continues, there is only faulty education which should and can be corrected by reeducation, a task for which psychologists are eminently fitted.

I would agree that all of psychotherapy has a strong reeducational element, but it must include methods oriented toward making the subject *capable of learning* in depth: that is, the education must be more than cognitively directed. These two concepts of "helping," education versus education-plus, are certainly susceptible to scientific study and require no acceptance on faith. Actually there is a sense of closure in the term education, as if we knew what to teach. Treatment is a more open and flexible concept, yet there is at present no *hard* evidence that any form of psychotherapy versus any other form or versus none is curative or ameliorative.

All forms of psychotherapy (even those in which the psychological aspects are not admitted or are denied, including drug therapy) on the one hand, and psychoanalysis on the other, utilize behavioral and learning theory and methods. None is objective since all operate through personal relations or, in our terminology, some elements of transference.

The essential question, however, is what the term "medical model" means, and I confess to some confusion about it. Does it mean treatment by a doctor of medicine? Does it mean treatment by drugs in whole or part? Does it mean that what is treated is called a disease—a term literally meaning dis-ease? I care not whether we change the term *disease*, because of fees, position under the law, or whatever, to *disturbance*; it is still the same euphemistic attempt to define the indefinable(17).

In understanding an unhappy, ineffective individual who is seeking help, systems of communication, understanding, and then interpretation —or supportive, educational, or directive techniques—are appropriately utilized. With full sanction these are employed in varying depths or degrees of intensity by middle-aged housewives, pastors, nurses, social workers, and psychologists as well as by psychiatrists. It is therefore clear that of all therapies psychotherapy is the least medical. The problem rests on the fact that the persons enumerated above utilize, with varying degrees of skill, the same general method of treatment for all conditions.

The truly medical model is one in which psychotherapy is only a part. The total field in terms of therapy includes differential diagnosis involving consideration of organic brain disease and other somatic afflictions; diagnosis of specific nosological[1] categories about which something of the natural history and prognosis is known; the choice of therapeutic environment such as home, clinic, or hospital; the choice of therapy such as drugs, shock, and psychotherapy; orientation toward individuals, groups, and families; and such choices as behavioral therapy or psychoanalysis, etc.

Indeed, psychiatry as a whole constitutes an expanded field that can be envisaged best as a system(8) without sacrificing any of its parts: "Whether we view categories of mental illness or mental health, or for that matter, any living process, each constitutes a large field containing a large number of variables, the permutations of which enable us to observe combinations and recombinations that determine types or subcategories"(10).

In defining kennetic inquiry, Bentley(2) stated, "this is a name proposed for organized investigation with the problem of knowing and knowns, where this is so conducted that the full range of subject matters —all the knowings and the knowns—form a common field." Shands(16) pointed out that if mental illness is a disorder of knowing, then a theory of learning should be integrated with empirical observations, and that knowing develops from primary body contact and physiological satisfactions and requires continuous participation of motor and sensory components. This viewpoint is indeed the prototype of unified theory, sometimes called psychosomatic.

Behavior and mentation cannot be separated and, as Kaufman(11) has clearly stated, from another aspect the biopsychosocial field cannot be fractured into the social *or* medical. Since no one person can encompass all of the kennetic field, some disciplines have established "parcels" by "squatters' rights" instead of multidisciplinary cooperation.

Albee's suggestion(1) that psychologists withdraw from psychiatric institutions and profess psychology in their own centers is a dangerous goal for psychology. Where it has been tried in client counseling centers, disastrous results have accrued to staff and clients. An overview of the entire field will be lost and the traditional medical methods of research will be abandoned. This includes the study of pathology in order to understand health better. The overlapping of psychology and psychiatry is clearly exemplified in that the former contributes greatly to the field of psychopathology and the latter to the study of normality or health(14).

Education, or nurture, will be fractured from the nature-nurture sys-

[1]Classifications of mental illness, e.g. obsessive-compulsive.

tem as a reversion to an obsolete dichotomy. There will be estrangement from the real problems of life as seen in the psychiatric clinic and a reversion to that dominated by projects suitable for Ph.D. theses. The universities, having farmed out their students to psychiatric centers as an admission of their own failures in clinical training, will have to assume a responsibility which for now at least seems unfeasible.

The greatest danger as I see it has been before our eyes for several decades in another isolated discipline, that of psychoanalysis(7). Isolated, utilizing its own language, developing a closed system, and specializing in a single therapeutic technique, psychoanalysis has organized itself into a self-destructive posture. Some analysts have escaped into departments of psychiatry where they have learned and contributed much that is applicable to the problems of the larger field. No profession can endure for long on the basis of a therapeutic method, even if it be called education.

When a psychology center becomes isolated from the main body of psychiatry there is a tendency to utilize monolithic approaches, making the therapist appear as the sole or most important element of what should be a therapeutic transaction. Concomitantly, diagnosis is depreciated and becomes irrelevant.

In a sense many contemporary psychiatrists have been working upstream against the forces opposing concepts of syndromes and accurate diagnostic criteria. The unpopularity of diagnosis and knowledge of the life history of describable entities is a reaction against the "disease" concept in psychiatry and the overemphasis on individual dynamic processes. Yet the pendulum has swung too far away in the direction of concern only with "the problem" of a specific patient (or client). In truth there can be no science without classification and no sound classification without modifying the repetitive old observations and descriptions. Psychiatry and psychology need to take a fresh look at modern theories of ego functions in process and new methods of description, rating, and statistical analysis(10).

Let us be absolutely clear when we talk about psychotherapy that we are not discussing psychiatry, within which the former is only a small technical part. Psychiatry as a branch of medicine is heavily dependent on the basic, the behavioral, and the social sciences. For this field, which encompasses all of life, a broad education is necessary. Efforts to provide it are often woefully inadequate in our universities, but also in our medical schools and psychiatric training centers. Training in techniques that can be learned by rote or by imitation during the processes of supervision does not furnish either true understanding of the totality of the field or the ability to create and contribute to progress and to teach others. These require some degree of knowledge of the total biopsycho-social field(7). To this academic psychology has contributed and will continue to do so. In isolation, however, clinical psychology can only lose the roles which it laboriously and slowly acquired.

HISTORICAL PERSPECTIVES

Some of the statements made today by leading psychologists have a peculiar sound: "Psychology should not lay its eggs in other birds' nests." "Psychologists have been brainwashed into using the values and languages of their masters." This is a far cry from the 1920s, when psychologists competed vigorously for positions in psychiatric clinics. At that time they were mostly people with master's degrees employed as technicians. We *ordered* IQ tests or Rorschach tests and read written reports without much communication. In the 1940s Ph.D. clinical psychologists began to replace the technicians because they needed the kind of training the universities could not offer. They felt themselves to be part of the psychiatric team and participated in service, teaching, and research.

As their service orientation lessened they became our consultants. We explained our puzzling cases to them and discussed their test results. They formed independent autonomous sections in the departments of psychiatry and had their own teachers and separate as well as mixed courses, seminars, and conferences.

Their research usually began by following the pattern of their Ph.D. theses, which were usually insignificant problems devoid of contact with important clinical questions, unless they were adequately directed by working clinicians. They then also prospered as members of interdisciplinary research teams.

In the 1950s psychologists pushed for therapeutic training and experience and with exceptions were successful: I have not found in my supervisory work that individual psychologists are deficient in concern for patients in spite of lack of formal training in medical ethics. In fact they are more careful not to do harm than are many psychiatric residents. They asked for and thrived under psychiatric supervisors and recognized the limited goals of psychotherapy. Because of their scientific training they were somewhat rigid and less intuitive than psychiatrists, who to the contrary were too loose and credulous. I doubt whether many psychology fellows, if not exhorted to rebel, would state that their training is inadequate and want to return to the university.

Another discipline also shifted its major tasks to psychotherapy. The psychiatric social workers are now "psychosocial therapists." After World War II we needed them as therapists and took many of them out of casework. Gradually they learned the whole range of psychotherapies, but they did not develop pressures to detach themselves into independent centers. When they work in independent social agencies, they always cooperate with a staff of working psychiatric consultants. We may be their ego ideals but never their masters. Without revolution or conflict, social workers have evolved into a comfortable position within the psychiatric field.

As I wrote in discussing the current dilemma of the psychiatric social worker, "contrary advice from academic teachers of social work theory and practical chiefs of psychiatric social services . . . resulted in a victory for the latter"(9). This resulted in a transposition into collaborative psychotherapy.

CLEAVAGES

As Chein(4) pointed out, the *scientists* in psychology form the "in" group. They use scientific methods, conduct themselves as scientists, and use appropriate language. They experiment, use quantitative analysis, favor prediction based on hypothetical inductive methods, and are in general reductionistic. Yet I believe that their research is restricted unless they have contact with psychiatry in order to attack meaningful research problems with appropriate techniques.

On the other hand, the "outs," or *practitioners*, who treat patients or "clients," according to Chein, are empirical, nonstatistical, use probabilistic statements with free terminology, and are intuitive. Yet they are depreciated by the leaders of the field of psychology, more than by psychiatrists, as deviants who should go back to the university. Others, like Dunnette(6), plead for more eclecticism and less pretense. That practitioners among clinical psychologists want to treat patients exclusively and tend to reject their research training makes one wonder what is wrong with their academic models.

My own experience in a psychiatric institute with staff psychologists and postdoctoral psychology fellows reveals a wide diversity of interests. Although each seems to have his favorite area of interest, there exists a climate of eclecticism conducive to healthy collaboration in research, teaching, diagnosis, and treatment. It is true that specific and specialized activities are pursued by psychologists carefully selected for this purpose. In the field the working psychologists are only moderately interested in and often resistant to the clarion call of their leaders to withdraw from general psychiatry into an isolated discipline of therapeutic reeducation.

For the good of all concerned there should be a moratorium on debates, conflicts, and exhortation by armchair psychologists as well as parochial psychiatrists, since nothing new has been added for some time and the discussions are redundant, as I can attest from surveying the literature. Albee is correct when he writes, "Back to the drawing board." I would add, "Back to work."

In truth we need working psychologists as viable therapists in our large mental hospitals, and the profession of psychology needs these many positions for the economic security of members of the American Psychological Association. On the other hand, in our private hospitals, our institutes, and in our medical school departments of psychiatry the need for psychological services has sharply decreased as we have observed the evolution in their diagnostic skills replacing the supposedly exact or deeper penetrating instruments. As psychologists have learned that these instruments constitute the framework for diagnostic interviews we have developed more reliance on our own psychiatric skills. Nevertheless we will always need the psychologist in our multidisciplinary research teams and as colleagues in teaching.

THE SOLUTIONS

I believe that the solution to what has become an endless and sometimes bitter verbal controversy, with threats and lawsuits, is not revolutionary change but rather evolutionary experimentation. All of the mental health disciplines psychiatrists, psychologists, social workers, and nurses— should be cooperatively involved in the processes of allocated individual as well as overlapping functions. The 1964 position statements of both the American Psychiatric Association and the American Psychological Association include the mutual recognition of competence and genuine collaboration. These words have real meaning and in no way can be defined as depreciatory. The alternative is to follow the plan proposed by Kubie(12), Mariner, and Charney(3) of developing a new discipline with a special degree under university auspices.

Both models should be studied scientifically. Collaborations between psychology and psychiatry as well as between psychiatry and medicine require study, not explosive disruption. Under any circumstances, standards must be maintained and regulatory devices set up in practice for psychology and psychiatry because practitioners of both professions, isolated from hospitals and clinics in office practice, are hidden from professional scrutiny and are equally open to criticism.

REFERENCES

1. Albee, G. W.: Give Us a Place to Stand (editorial), The Clinical Psychologist 20:51–53, 1967.
2. Bentley, A. F.: Kennetic Inquiry, Science 112:775–783, 1950.
3. Charney, N. H.: Education in Flux (editorial), Psychology Today 1:16, 1967.
4. Chein, I.: Some Sources of Divisiveness Among Psychologists, Amer. Psychol. 21: 333–342, 1966.
5. Cohen, N.: The Cold War Between Psychiatry and Psychology: A Psychologist's View, Psychiatric Opinion 4:10–14, June 1967.
6. Dunnette, M. D.: Fads, Fashions, and Folderol in Psychology, Amer. Psychol. 21: 343–352, 1966.
7. Grinker, R. R., Sr.: A Struggle for Eclecticism, Amer. J. Psychiat. 121:451–457, 1964.
8. Grinker, R. R., Sr.: Normality Viewed as a System, Arch. Gen. Psychiat. 17:320–324, 1967.
9. Grinker, R. R., Sr., MacGregor, H., Selan, K., Klein, A., and Kohrman, J.: Psychiatric Social Work: A Transactional Case Book. New York: Basic Books, 1961.
10. Grinker, R. R., Sr., Werble, B., and Drye, R.: The Borderline Syndrome. New York: Basic Books, 1968.
11. Kaufman, M. R.: Psychiatry: Why "Medical" or "Social" Model? Arch. Gen. Psychiat, 17:347–361, 1967.
12. Kubie, L. S.: Need for a New Subdiscipline in the Medical Profession, Arch. Neurol. Psychiat. 78:283–293, 1951.
13. Levine, A.: The Cold War Between Psychiatry and Psychology: A Psychiatrist's View, Psychiatric Opinion 4:6–10, June 1967.
14. Offer, D., and Sabshin, M.: Normality. New York: Basic Books, 1967.
15. Pearlman, S., and Williams, A. V.: The Relationship of Clinical Psychology to Psychiatry, Psychiatric Opinion 4:15–18, June, 1967.
16. Shands, H. C.: personal communication.
17. Simon, L. J.: On Honesty and Subsidized Psychotherapy, The Clinical Psychologist 20:92–102, 1967.
18. Szasz, T. S.: The Myth of Mental Illness. New York: Hoeber Medical Div. (Harper & Row), 1964.

EMERGING CONCEPTS
OF MENTAL ILLNESS
AND MODELS OF
TREATMENT: THE
PSYCHOLOGICAL POINT
OF VIEW

In preparing this presentation I had to choose between either: 1) developing a psychological model for disturbed behavior and then spelling out its implications for intervention and prevention or 2) discussing the shortcomings of the sickness model in order to provide a logical groundwork for the subsequent development of alternative models. I chose the second alternative because I have spent more time thinking about this problem and also because I do not think the alternative to the sickness model is likely to be a psychological model! Indeed I believe the new approach will be social-educational, and it is more likely to develop out of the fields of special education or social work than out of psychology.

WHAT IS THE
"SICKNESS MODEL"?

This explanation of disturbed behavior, briefly stated, holds that "mental illness is an illness like any other." The very fact that strenuous efforts, made for a century and more, have achieved only limited acceptance of this slogan suggests that it is not entirely creditable.

Attempts to explain the origins of neurotic and psychotic behavior, addiction to alcohol, juvenile delinquency, mental deficiency, and even such peripheral problems as marital maladjustment and school learning difficulties as sicknesses inside the person make them discontinuous with normal beravior. The sickness model suggests that these conditions are among a number of separate, discrete mental illnesses, each with a separate cause, prognosis, and potential treatment. We have seen this theme in some of what Dr. Grinker had to say.

The sickness model further suggests that the treamtent of these "illnesses" is properly the function of a physician specially trained in their

From "Emerging Concepts of Mental Illness and Models of Treatment: The Psychological Point of View," by George W. Albee, in AMERICAN JOURNAL OF PSYCHIATRY, 125, no. 7 (1969), 870–876; reprinted by permission of the publisher and the author.

diagnosis and in known methods of intervention. While other professionals may play various useful roles, they will be ancillary to the physician, who is charged with the clinical responsibility for the welfare of the "patient" (who must be "treated" in a hospital or clinic or in the physician's private office). Even the so-called personality disturbances, and all the agonies deriving from a dehumanized and hostile environment, are diagnosed as various kinds of sicknesses or intrapersonal illnesses.

This model, which occupies the center of our clinical stage, places the identification of forces in the individual before consideration of the hostile and damaging forces in his world: it demands that we try to fix him, treat his disease (as we do other diseases), and then send him back to the continuing horrors of his world. Realistically, it causes us to treat only the small number comprising those who believe in our cures or even worse the much smaller number for whom our cures may work, thereby causing us to neglect all those people with problems we do not understand because they do not fit our model, and those people who cannot participate in, nor accept, our verbal intervention methods.

The origins of this explanation of emotional disturbance, like the origins of most human myth systems, are overdetermined and complex. Sarbin suggests that the label "illness" was first used by Teresa of Avila in the 16th century to describe emotionally disturbed people; it served as a useful metaphor to protect disturbed nuns (those who exhibited symptoms of hysteria) from the Inquisition. "If a person's conduct could be accounted for by such natural causes, it was to be regarded not as evil, but *comas enfermas*, 'as if sick' " (10, p. 448).

Werry(14), a research psychiatrist at the University of Illinois, recently called the disease model "the great operating delusion of psychiatry." Elsewhere Werry(15) says "The debate . . . between the proponents of the disease model and those who believe that emotional and behavioral difficulties belong in the moral sphere was long and acrimonious but, as you must be aware, psychiatry in the past hundred years, has achieved a substantial victory in this contested field . . ." (p. 4).

The end of moral treatment of the insane in America seems to have coincided, in the middle half of the 19th century, with the beginning of the enormous wave of foreign immigration into the United States. Most of the Yankee physicians, who had been able to extend a kind of Quaker fellowship to the insane, found themselves unable to deal with the "foreign insane paupers" who had inundated the retreats, jails, and almshouses in the latter part of the 19th century.

It was John P. Gray, superintendent of Utica State Hospital and editor of the *American Journal of Insanity*, who, in the late 19th century, became the chief advocate of the position that mental patients were really physically ill with a brain disease. Gray is often awarded the distinction of being the most influential medical spokesman for the rejection of a moral approach to insanity (with its reliance on compassion, reason, kindness, and human interaction) and advancing instead the argument that the insane were victims of some unknown brain disease.

One of the primary arguments used by contemporary psychiatry to support its basic responsibility for the treatment of mental conditions holds that there are underlying organic defects, in most cases still undiscovered, producing the disturbed behavior. Starting from this uncertain platform, psychiatry advances the conclusion that medical training, most of which has not been used since the internship, somehow provides unique qualifications to treat these sicknesses.

The gossamer web of logic is not strong enough to hold the weight of this whole proposition, and many contemporary psychiatrists have rejected this argument. In the first place, there is little substantial evidence supporting the hypothesis of an underlying organic defect in most functional mental disorders. Second, the medical training of most psychiatrists was obtained years in the past and is not especially relevant to their therapeutic activities. In other situations, where the stakes are different, most psychiatrists have refused to practice medicine in any traditional sense. (Most psychiatrists are excused from volunteer duty at community health clinics and from emergency room duty in the military service.)

Third, when a real organic cause is discovered to be the significant underlying factor in the production of disturbed behavior (as has been the case in a few genuine mental diseases), then the treatment of these conditions is removed from the psychiatric field.

As Zubin points out:

As soon as a mental disorder is traced to some organic cause, however, it ceases to belong to the psychiatric fold and is handed over to internal medicine or neurology as was the case with general paresis, pellagra with psychosis, and will probably be the case with phenylpyruvic oligophrenia. Only diseases of unknown origin tend to remain in the psychiatric domain(18, p. 2).

Barbara Wooton(16) has made a searching examination of the interaction between social and cultural forces and mental disorders. It will be clear to most thoughtful persons who examine her approach that "mental illness" is not "a disease like any other." She has spelled out certain crucial and fundamental differences between mental disorders and true diseases. She points out, quite correctly, that

. . . anti-social behavior is the precipitating factor that leads to mental treatment. But at the same time the fact of the illness is itself inferred from this behavior: indeed it is almost true to say that the illness is the behavior for which it is also the excuse. But any disease, the morbidity of which is established only by the social failure that it involves, must rank as fundamentally different from those with which the symptoms are independent of social norms(17).

In one of her examples Wooton reminds us that we diagnose a mental disease when we observe an individual disregarding the property rights of others, as for example, the adolescent who steals cars, the middle-aged suburban housewife who shoplifts, or the hippie who picks flowers from the city parks, refusing in the process to keep off the grass. Without this observable behavior we would not suspect the existence of an underlying "mental disease." So the identification of this "disease" depends on the violation of social laws which uphold the sanctity of individual or of public ownership. In a society where possessions were held in common such diseases could not exist!

The point of all this is that the social disapproval of the social consequences of behavior usually identifies the underlying "disease." In the absence of these interactions the disease would not exist.

WHAT EVIDENCE SUPPORTS
THE SICKNESS MODEL?

There is precious little evidence to support a discontinuity (sickness) model. At the center of the continuity-discontinuity argument stands the mystery condition (or conditions) of schizophrenia. There just must be a biological explanation! While the argument will not be entirely won or lost here, still the causation of schizophrenia is under constant debate, and support for a disease or defect explanation is being sought most vigorously in the blood, sweat, and tears (as well as all the other fluids) of the schizophrenic.

Recently an entire volume (some 500 pages) of the *Annals of the New York Academy of Sciences* was devoted to "Some Biological Aspects of Schizophrenic Behavior"(11). Even this elaborate production could not obscure the fact that no clear-cut phenotypical defect has yet been found which even comes close to providing a key to a possible molecular basis for this condition. All sorts of profound-sounding statements were made which, on careful examination, turn out to be meaningless. For example:

It has become quite evident that neuropathology and its allied sciences are assuming a progressively important role in the study and understanding of mental disorders. Thus far, the morphologic, histochemical, and cytobiophysical observations in brain biopsies and topectomies appeared to be of a pleomorphic character and non-specific or rather of heterogenic patterns. Therefore one must look forward to future research investigations(p. 481).

This polysyllabic nonsense says: "We haven't found anything yet, and we're still looking."

Occasionally someone finds a biological measure which does differentiate schizophrenics from controls, but as anyone knows who has followed this literature for the past 20 years, artifacts (like vitamin C deficiency or too much caffeine) have a way of confounding the significance of the differences found.

The discovery that chronic back-ward schizophrenics have smaller hearts than controls matched for age and sex would hardly prove that small hearts cause schizophrenia. Rather, a more parsimonious explanation in terms of lack of exercise would undoubtedly be suggested. But repeatedly the finding of some blood factor which differentiates backward schizophrenics from normals has been hailed as the long-sought key to the mystery of schizophrenia.

Seymour Kety(8), in an honest and straightforward review of biochemical theories of schizophrenia, refers to "a present consensus that a pathological lesion characteristic of schizophrenia or any of its subgroups remains to be demonstrated" (p. 409). He reviews the errors, the subjective biases, and the confounding effects of unsuspected or uncontrolled variables that have led to premature "discoveries." He concludes that of all the new reports of toxic materials in the blood of schizophrenics "there has been no extensive substantiation of any of them" (p. 418). He continues: "Many of the current hypotheses concerning the schizophrenia complex are original and attractive even though, up to this time, evidence directly implicating any one of them in the disease itself is hardly compelling" (p. 426).

If there is no convincing evidence that schizophrenia is an identifiable disease, there is far less scientific support for a sickness model explanation of all of the less extreme forms of human deviation, yet the American Psychiatric Association keeps issuing position statements claiming responsibility for such conditions as mental retardation, juvenile delinquency, and alcoholism. The trouble is that the sickness model demands a kind of intervention that is terribly expensive and a kind of highly trained intervener who is not widely available. Eventually, I predict, the needs of society will be better served!

If the organic approach could be demonstrated to be valid our society would be justified in demanding an enormous increase in the number of medical and paramedical professionals prepared to take their places in the battle against "mental illness." But the organic approach has not been found to be convincingly valid, and alternative models seem to hold at least as much promise for helping many more disturbed people. Further, the supply of physicians (and therefore psychiatrists) in proportion to the population has been declining for many years and probably will continue to decline(1).

Still another subtle but powerful force lending support to the sickness model of mental disorder has been the steady increase in the use of the psychotropic drugs that have become the common approach to many emotional conditions.[1] Persuasive advertisements, beamed at psychiatrists in the psychiatric journals by the drug companies, keep emphasizing the value of drug therapy. Drug therapy has been hailed by the great popular medical journals—*Time, Life, Look!*

With hundreds of thousands of daily drug users in the public hospitals, plus millions more seeking tranquility or at least relief from intense anxiety, the psychotropic drugs have become a fantastic growth industry. Understandably any threat to the sickness model is a threat to the drug salesmen. What is good for General Napoleon is good for United Chemical!

By using drugs for the poor in the state hospitals we can get by with practically no professional personnel in these tax-supported settings. (In over one-third of our state hospitals practically no psychiatric time is available, and two-thirds of our 2,000 psychiatric clinics do not have a single full-time psychiatrist on the staff[1].) Eighty percent of psychiatric practice is private office practice with a suburban upper-middle class clientele.

Jules Henry(5) says: "State hospitals today seem to exhale from their antique bricks and dark labyrinths the miasmas of misunderstanding, prejudice, callousness, and hate whose origins lie deep in our history. Who knows what happens in the pit, where their voices do not come up to us?" (p. 48).

The point of all of this argument should not be lost. Psychiatry, in insisting on its prerogatives of primary patient responsibility and control of treatment institutions and intervention efforts of all sorts, bases its argument either on rare and uncertain genetic and metabolic conditions or on those common chronic organic mental conditions which it characteristically neglects. Most of psychiatric practice is private, most of it is suburban, and most hospital psychiatry is practiced in general hospitals. None of the organic mental conditions is the central concern of current psychiatric treatment.

A great majority of the people whom psychiatrists treat are not suffering from genetic, metabolic, and arteriosclerotic conditions, or from alcoholic delirium, or from central nervous system malfunction. If psychiatrists were to devote their primary attention to these kinds of cases

---

[1]The text referred to these drugs as chemotherapy agents.

there would be little need for today's debate about models. Repeatedly, surveys show that the most common psychiatric patient in 1968 is a college-educated, white, upper-middle class, non-Catholic female between 30 and 40. She has none of the usual organic mental diseases.

Recently psychiatrist David J. Vail(13) commented on the unhappy fact that psychiatry has not been able to produce a meaningful definition of mental illness. He argues that

A recent booklet on insurance published by the American Psychiatric Association, for example, defines mental disorder essentially as those items listed in the official manual on nomenclature, in other words, a mental disorder exists when a ruling group of psychiatrists say that it is what it is. Worse yet, psychiatrists cannot agree among each other.

There are many beautiful examples of the contortions that must be performed to define mental disorder as sickness. In the recent booklet Vail refers to, the following curious statement appears: "Illness (which includes mental disorders) is any symptom or syndrome the American medical profession at the present time generally accepts as evidence of disease or disorder"(2). Doesn't that sound like Alice in Wonderland?

Not only do mental disorders include conditions which "interfere with current functioning," but also those which, while not affecting in any way current functioning "carry with them the threat of future disability" (2). In other words, with this model an individual may be diagnosed as having a mental disorder although he is functioning adequately as a member of society if, in the judgment of a psychiatrist, potential exists for future disturbance. Frankly, this is a frightening notion to those who adhere to the principle that a man is innocent until proven guilty and that no one can be convicted for the possible commission of some future criminal act.

WHAT IS THE ALTERNATIVE?

I have been arguing for the past several years that the sickness model explanation of the origins of disturbed behavior will have to be replaced with a social-developmental explanation before our society will get off its inertia and begin to do some constructive things about large-scale intervention and prevention of human misery. The intervention will emphasize the nurturance of strength rather than the search for and excision of weakness, and the prevention will take the form of social engineering to strengthen the family.

I fully expect many psychiatrists to agree with this approach because it is my experience that many thoughtful leaders in American psychiatry are saying the same thing. Don Jackson(6) pointed out that:

Each year data are collected that provide strong evidence for the fact that mental disorders, including schizophrenia, arise out of disturbed personal relationships. Each year we seem to rediscover this fact, splicing out the rest of the year with dreams of glory about the bio-chemical cause of schizophrenia, and the new happy pills.

Psychiatrist Robert Coles(4) said recently: "With respect to what can legitimately be called psychiatric disorders, I am not at all convinced that anything new will be discovered to 'cure' them. I am not even sure that we ought to call them 'diseases'." Coles goes on to ask the question that every "mental health" worker should be forced to answer:

What pills will ever dissolve the anxiety and fear that go with life itself? What will psychiatry ever know that it does not know now about the damage done by thoughtless, cruel parents to vulnerable children? What further "frontiers" do we really have to conquer, when it comes to such subjects as despair, brutality, envy?

After completing his dramatic survey of Boston's mental health resources (which exceed the resources of any city in the world and yet largely neglect those in greatest need), William Ryan(9) made a proposal so audacious, so revolutionary, so shocking in its implications that in another age he would have been tried for heresy and boiled in oil. He suggested that Boston's mental health establishment forego any further budgetary increases because their services were having no significantly beneficial effect on the public most in need of them and that the money saved be put into improved welfare services. (Dr. Ryan recently moved to Connecticut!) But Ryan is right. Casework, group work, and counseling by clergymen are reaching more of the citizens of Boston than are psychiatric facilities.

The psychoanalyst should be in the vanguard, together with the social worker and the learning theorist, in advocating the abandonment of the sickness model and arguing for its replacement with a social-developmental model. Certainly the most fundamental contribution of Freud was his discovery of the continuity between the normal and the abnormal. In discussing Darwin and Freud, Jerome Bruner pointed out that the Victorians, reeling from Darwin's discovery of a perfectly lawful continuity between man and the rest of the animal kingdom, were dealt a second and more terrifying blow by Freud's discovery of the continuity between the sane and the insane.[2] Bruner (3) speaks of the

. . . lawful continuity between man and the animal kingdom, between dreams and unreason on one side and waking rationality on the other, between madness and sanity, between consciousness and unconsciousness; between the mind of the child and the adult mind, between primitive and civilized man—each of these has been a cherished discontinuity preserved in doctrinal canons.

Freud forced the abandonment of these cherished discontinuities.

Why, in the face of this central message of Freud's life work, does the latter-day psychoanalyst continue to pay homage to the sickness model? Primarily, I think, because of the historical accident which has required the psychoanalyst in the United States to be trained first as a physician. I look forward to the day when the psychoanalysts, perhaps in continuing self-analysis, will join forces with Freud and the rest of us who believe the evidence supports a continuity model, a model which holds that it is established that the same mechanisms are operating in adaptive and maladaptive human behavior, and will help lead the scientific assault on those who seek to preserve and defend the sickness model.

WHAT WOULD BE DIFFERENT IF WE CHANGED MODELS?

I have not yet really dealt with the consequences that would follow from changing models. Very briefly, I hold that: 1) the nature of the model determines 2) the nature of the institutions we develop for intervention and prevention, which in turn dictates 3) the kind of manpower we use to deliver care. With a social-developmental model our state hospitals and public clinics would be replaced by social intervention centers, largely staffed by people at the bachelor's level—more like special education teachers and social welfare workers, potentially available in vastly greater supply than psychologists and psychiatrists. For prevention, people like ourselves would be needed as teachers, researchers, and especially as radical social activists proselytizing for changes in our society to make it more supportive, less dehumanized.

The massive deterioration of the fabric of society and its institutions results in a complex tangle of pathology. The pathology includes especially the destruction of the emotional integrity of the family. Let me

[2]I.e., that "sanity" and "insanity" are matters of degree.

emphasize here something that you already know very well. Many significant research breakthroughs have already been made. Many of the discoveries are already in. We know, for example, that the emotional climate which surrounds the infant and young child is of critical importance in determining his future—including the kind, the severity, and perhaps even the biological concomitants of his later disturbance.

Such knowledge is dangerous.. We usually shut our eyes to its implications. We go on trying to fix up damaged adults in one-to-one relationships when a more proper professional function would be to spend a considerable portion of our energies trying to fix up our society in ways that will increase the strength and stability of the family, thereby affecting positively the mental health of generations to come. It is not possible here to further elaborate upon prevention except to say that I believe, because of the nature of the human animal, it must take the form of strengthening the institution of the family.

I believe that history may judge President Johnson to have been one of the most complicated of American presidents. But his speech at Howard University's commencement will be judged among the half-dozen great landmarks in the history of our society. In it the President called for a massive attack on the central problem of our time. He said:

The family is the cornerstone of our society. More than any other force it shapes the attitudes, the hopes, the ambitions, and the values of the child. When the family collapses it is the children that are usually damaged. When it happens on a massive scale the community itself is crippled.

So, unless we work to strengthen the family, to create conditions under which most parents will stay together—all the rest: schools and playgrounds, public assistance and private concern, will never be enough to cut completely the circle of despair and deprivation(7).

Unhappily Johnson's Great Society program, which began with such hope and promise, got sidetracked by our unfortunate involvement in Viet Nam. Eventually, let us pray, we will get back to a rational concern with dealing with our important problems—people who suffer.

William Ryan(9) has put it plainly:

If the assumption is accepted that all behavior disorder and all emotional disturbance are the general province of the psychiatrist and the other mental health professionals, obviously the province remains unoccupied. At present only a beachhead has been established. Further, in view of the scarcity of mental health professionals, which will continue for many years to come, it is unlikely that the beachhead will be extended in any dramatic manner (p. 46).

Edward Stainbrook, chairman of the department of psychiatry at the University of Southern California, says:

Many of the impairments due to poor social learning and to inadequate development *don't* have to be defined as illness, and they don't have to be treated by medical doctors. . . . I think we need a new kind of institution, too . . . where people could learn, or relearn, social and occupational skills(12).

I am convinced that once society realizes that disturbed behavior reflects the results of social-developmental learning in pathological social environments (rather than intrapersonal sickness), the institutions that will be developed for intervention will be social and educational in nature.

REFERENCES

1. Albee, G.: Models, Myths, and Manpower, Ment. Hyg., 52:168–180, 1968.
2. American Psychiatric Association: APA Guidelines for Psychiatric Services Covered Under Health Insurance Plans. Washington, D.C., 1966.
3. Bruner, J.: "Freud and the Image of Man," in Nelson, B., ed.: Freud and the Twentieth Century. Cleveland and New York: World Meridan, 1957.
4. Coles, R.: The Limits of Psychiatry, The Progessive 31:32–34, 1967.
5. Henry, J.: The Human Demons, Trans-Action 3:45–48, 1966.
6. Jackson, D.: Action for Mental Illness—What Kind, Stanford Med. Bull. 20:77–80, 1962.
7. Johnson, L. B.: Remarks of the President at Howard University, June 4, 1965: "To Fulfill These Rights." Washington, D.C.: White House Press Office, 1965.
8. Kety, S.: Biochemical Theories of Schizophrenia, Int. J. Psychiat. 1:409–430, 1965.
9. Ryan, W.: Distress in the City. Cleveland: Case Western Reserve University Press, in press.
10. Sarbin, T. R.: On the Futility of the Proposition That Some People Be Labeled "Mentally Ill," J. Consult. Psychol. 5:447–453, 1967.
11. Siva Sankar, D. V., ed.: Some Biological Aspects of Schizophrenic Behavior, Ann. N. Y. Acad. Sci. 96:1–490, 1962.
12. Stainbrook, E.: One Hundred Sixty-Five Beds, Nine Thousand Patients, SK&F Psychiatric Reporter no. 32, 1967, pp. 7–9.
13. Vail, D.: editorial in the Mental Health Newsletter. Minneapolis: Minnesota Department of Public Welfare, 6:1, 1966.
14. Werry, J. S.: Psychotherapy—A Medical Procedure? Canad. Psychiat. Ass. J. 10:278–282, 1965.
15. Werry, J. S.: The Psychiatrist and Society, 1967 Velde lecture given at Bradley University, Peoria, Ill., April 26–27 (processed).
16. Wooton, B.: Social Science and Social Pathology. London: George Allen and Unwin, 1959.
17. Wooton, B.: quoted in Zubin, J.: Some Scientific Models for Psychopathology, 1967 (processed).
18. Zubin, J.: Some Scientific Models for Psychopathology, 1967 (processed).